Y2K MADE SIMPLE

A Natural Health Resource Guide

NED VANKEVICH

PARACLETE PRESS
Brewster, Massachusetts

Library of Congress Cataloging-in-Publication Data

Vankevich, Ned, 1951-
    Y2K made simple : a natural health resource guide / Ned Vankevich.
    p. cm.
Includes bibliographical references.
ISBN 1-55725-238-6 (pbk.)
    1. Survival skills—United States. 2. Year 2000 date conversion (Computer systems)—United States. I. Title.
GF86.V36 1999
613.6'9—dc21

                                                                99-26973
                                                                      CIP

10 9 8 7 6 5 4 3 2 1

© 1999 by Ned Vankevich
ISBN 1-55725-238-6

Published by Paraclete Press
Brewster, Massachusetts
www.paraclete-press.com

Printed in the United States of America.

Table of Contents

PREFACE

"This time, like all times, is a very good one
if we but know what to do with it." —Ralph Waldo Emerson

From the start, I want to make it clear that I am neither an end-of-the-world, paranoid, gun-packing isolationist, nor a survivalist fanatic. Talk about long-term emergency preparedness and survival often brings these images to mind. I am a product of urban and suburban, middle-class, "baby-boomer" American culture and therefore, for the most part, I am quite non-self-reliant. By "non-self-reliant," I mean that I have a near total dependency upon the modern technological system that creates the food, clothing, water, heating, transportation, telecommunications, and other products that I need to survive in the contemporary world.

I add the qualification "for the most part" because over the past few years I have joined the ranks of people who have begun taking an active role in determining the health and well-being of their families and themselves. For me, this process has entailed a very aggressive "natural" health approach centered around a lifestyle based upon good nutrition, preventative medicine, and the avoidance of the overwhelming amount of toxins that invade our life in the contemporary Western world—everything from bad air, impure water, harmful household chemicals, destructive emotions, and the often spiritually destructive influences of mass media and self-centered consumerism. In short, I have become what my friends call "Mr. Natural"—an urban homesteader—who seeks to maximize the physical, emotional, mental, spiritual, and environmental well-being of my world.

It was out of such concerns that I started researching the problems the Year 2000 (Y2K) computer "bug" might bring. When I first learned about the Y2K computer problem, like many people I was skeptical. What I was hearing sounded like just another version of the apocalyptic nightmares that paranoid prophets like to concoct. However, the more I read and listened to what people who know far more about computer technology than I could ever learn had to say about this issue, the more I took notice. As we will see in the first chapter, there is a good chance some of us are about to lose many of the comforts and conveniences created by our computer-dependent world.

My motive in writing this book is to help as many people as possible avoid the life-threatening problems many are predicting the Year 2000 computer "bug" might deliver. In short, I want to help empower people to deal with the Y2K issue by offering principles and products that I have found to be beneficial to our individual and collective well-being.

My fondest wish is that none of us will experience the harsh realities for which the products, plans, and procedures outlined in this manual are designed. My other hope is that if the prophets of Y2K catastrophe are correct, the type of preparation I advocate will assist you to face successfully any problem Y2K might deliver.

I want to thank a number of people for their help, wisdom, and advice in this project. At the forefront is my wife, Judi, without whose constant support, encouragement, and *joie de vivre*, I could not have gathered the information and experience this book captures. I also extend my deepest gratitude to Zuri and Alexi Skye, who graciously gave their Daddy extra "private time" to prepare and write this manual. I am also grateful to Elizabeth Kotlowski for putting me on the path to natural health, and to my student Karen Allard for taking the time to proofread my text. I also want to thank Tim Cestnick and his bride Carolyn for graciously allowing me to use their WaterStreet Group, Inc. office space while I was writing a good portion of this book. I also extend hearty thanks to my parents, Helen and Al Vankevich, my in-laws, Burt and Margaret Johnston, and to Lillian Miao and David Manuel for their encouragement and support, and to Paraclete Press for helping make this material available to a wide audience. Finally, I am indebted to a number of Year 2000 writers, commentators, and entrepreneurs dedicated to awakening the population to the significance of the Year 2000 challenge. They are too numerous to mention, but their names, books, newsletters, Web pages, and collective wisdom appear throughout this book. I hasten to add, however, that no one other than I is in any way responsible for the errors and omissions that might (inadvertently) be contained herein.

Disclaimer: The Y2K situation and emergency preparedness and survival are complex issues that require much thought, wise counsel, and planning. The author of this text makes no guarantees or warranties and assumes no liability or responsibility for errors or omissions contained in this text, or for any damages that might result from the use or misuse of the information contained and provided herein.

In addition, any information of a medical, legal, or health nature contained in this text is for educational purposes only. All readers are encouraged to consult appropriate professionals for the advice and assistance they need, especially their personal physician or licensed health care practitioner, for the diagnosing, treating, and curing of any illness or health-related problems or conditions. Neither the author, the printer, nor the publisher assumes any responsibility arising from the reader's interpretation and/or misuse of the information provided.

Note: All prices in this book are in U.S. dollars. Metric equivalents, where given, are approximate.

A Tale of Two Possibilities

Midnight, December 31, 1999

For Sam Fulton, life couldn't be better. He recently received full partnership at one of the most prestigious law firms in Boston. His daughter, Amy, just received notice of early acceptance and a full scholarship to Stanford University, and his new wife, June, was pregnant with the son Sam always wanted. On top of this, it was New Year's Eve. But not just any New Year's Eve. This was the big one, the momentous year 2-0-0-0—the dawn of a new millennium—and Sam was going to celebrate big time: A case of *Dom Perignon*—hey, millenniums only come around once every thousand years—lots of imported cheese, and his closest friends and family members gathered for the biggest bash of all time. Sam had prepared well. He had bought the champagne a year early to avoid millennial price gouging and he had cut a good deal with the owner of the local cheese specialty shop for the *Camembert, Brin D'Amour,* and *Vacherin Mont d'or*. Nothing was going to spoil this mother of all parties. And nothing did. Until the stroke of midnight, that is, when, just as he was about to kiss his wife—the lights went dark. At first Sam thought this was a prank—one of his "buds" showing off his shallow sense of humor. But this was no joke. "The whole city's gone dark!" cried Sam's daughter, Amy. When Sam looked out his harbor-front penthouse window, an eerie feeling crept down his spine. Boston had turned black.

Things couldn't have been more different for Bill Nikkel—a blue-collar warehouse employee in the suburbs of Chicago. Bill was a simple guy. For him, New Year's Eve normally meant enjoying a few brews with the guys and a little dancing with his wife, Marge. However, this New Year's was not normal. Not because it was the dawn of a new century and a new millennium, but because for months Bill had been disturbed by the news reports about an impending potential disaster. It seemed that everywhere Bill turned, people were talking about some "Y2K" computer problem. Fortunately for Bill, one of his pals was a computer geek who explained to Bill the meaning of "the Y2K computer rollover glitch." Bill's friend also warned him that the predictions about potential problems with computers worldwide was neither a hoax nor something to take lightly. What concerned Bill was his computer friend's claim that "if anything, things will be worse than most pundits predict." Bill took this warning seriously, and for the past six months he and his wife had been reading, studying the Web, asking a lot of questions, buying items, and preparing for what one analyst predicted would be the "biggest global disaster since the meteor that wiped out all the dinosaurs."

So on December 31, 1999 Bill and his family were not celebrating. Instead of drinking *Dom Perignon* and sampling exotic cheeses, Bill and his family were going through their emergency preparedness list—making sure everything was in place. Bill was grateful for his wife's support. Marge shared his concern, and she had taken the leadership role in researching and purchasing the things they decided they might need.

Bill and Marge's friends scoffed at them for skipping out on the New Year's Eve fun and for stocking up on "survival food," water, and candles, and for installing a woodstove—"just in case." "They laughed at Noah, too," Bill reminded Marge jokingly, as a way to soften their ridicule.

When the blackness struck at midnight, Bill and his family were ready. Bill took no pride in realizing he was right. In his heart, Bill prayed that the situation would not be as bad as some experts had predicted. He knew many people would be unprepared for the loss of electricity, heating, and food as the supply chain that supports our consumer society quickly unraveled. Bill's prayers were not answered in the affirmative.

Sam Fulton was one of the many caught unprepared. Sure, Sam had heard the news reports. His law firm had already made a killing and expected to make a lot more on all the lawsuits spawned by the Year 2000 computer problem. (He should have known something big was about to happen, since all his attorney buddies were bragging about the legal fee windfall Y2K would bring.) In hindsight, Sam remembered how he had teased the guy in Accounting who planned to take an extended vacation somewhere in the Caribbean, and how he had made fun of the secretary who took her family up North away from the city—also "just in case." Sam recalled too how he had taunted his golf buddy, Ted, calling him a kook for buying a cabin "out in the boondocks." Sam didn't get it. He had been so busy riding the roller coaster of personal success and had so many things going his way that he didn't take time to stop, look, and listen to what the "alarmists" were predicting was about to happen.

As his friends groped their way to their cars to go home, Sam stood in the deep, soundless blackness that surrounded him. "Ah, so what if the power goes out for a while and the local Star Market takes a few extra days to get some food," he mused. "I've got some wood for the fireplace and plenty of food left over from the party. I could use a few days off to catch up on some work." As Sam peered out at the darkest sky he had ever seen, the stars glowed in a way he had never seen before. "Maybe a little peace and quiet won't be so bad after all," he smiled. But Sam's smile didn't last long.

What Sam didn't expect was that the prophets of doom were right. Not totally right. But right enough. The damage done by date-sensitive computers was not as catastrophic as some had predicted, and the problems didn't last for years. But things did get bad—and for a while, they got very bad.

When the computers that were not prepared for the change of date at the stroke of midnight on January 1, 2000 failed, people suddenly realized how deeply dependent our modern civilization had become upon computer technology. The power outages lasted for weeks, and Sam didn't have enough food and wood to outlast the shortages. His wife, June, lost their baby and almost died from malnutrition and from pneumonia brought on by the extended period without heat and electricity. Adding to his woes, Sam's daughter, Amy, went into a deep depression from which she has yet to recover. Sam also lost 80 percent of his retirement investments when the global economy took a major long-lasting downturn and he could not communicate with his broker because the telecommunications system had crashed.

Bill, on the other hand, fared much better. No one in his family starved. Nor did anybody get sick from the cold or from lack of clean water and toilet sanitation. And Bill's children did not fall into despair. Bill knew what to expect and had prepared for it. He had heeded the doomsday prophets and was better off for it. Bill had told himself, "Sure, kooks can be irrational extremists, but sometimes they key in on things most of us 'normal' folk overlook." Bill had listened to 50 percent of what the "alarmists" had said. Sam listened to none. As you read this book, ask yourself in whose shoes you would rather be.

CHAPTER 1

Introduction: Y2K And How This Book Can Help

"In a century in which man split the atom, spliced genes,
and turned silicon into data, the tale of Y2K—how we ignored it for 40 years,
then flew into a tizzy—will not be remembered as our finest hour."
—Chris Taylor, *Time* Magazine, 18 January 1999

It's known by a number of names—the "millennium bug," the "Year 2000 Crisis," the "Year 2000 Time Bomb," "Meltdown 2000," "Cyber Armageddon," "Panic in the Year 2000," the "Ultimate Domino Effect," "the global ticking time bomb," the supreme "rollover glitch," the coming "Y2Chaos," the "Y2K Wildcard," or most simply, "Y2K." It has many interpretations—some people predict a brief time of minor disruptions in the way businesses operate, others predict a year of economic and cultural chaos and calamity, while still others are warning of the end of civilization as we know it (see Gary North's *Forum Home Page*, <http://www.garynorth.com/y2k/index.cfm>, for extremist scenarios along this line).

By now most of us know that "it" refers to the Year 2000 ("Y2K") computer problem and the way the "00" in the new century date will create disruptions in IBM-compatible personal computers (PCs), mainframe computers, and embedded microprocessing chips that have not been corrected to handle the changeover. I will not dwell on the history of the problem and why the practice of saving memory space by trimming year dates to two digits (for example, 77 for 1977) by early computer programmers will cause widespread problems when computer clocks roll over at midnight on January 1, 2000. By now most people have heard about the so-called millennium bug and the potential technological and social disruptions that might result when date-sensitive computers malfunction because of the Year 2000 number glitch. (The Appendix lists a number of books that detail the technical reasons for the Y2K problem. See also the *Electric Utilities and the Year 2000* Web site bookstore page, <http://www.euy2k.com/bookstor.htm>, which offers an extensive list of Y2K-related books.)

The Scope of the Problem

What is important to note is the magnitude of the problem that virtually our entire Western social and technological infrastructure relies in some way on date-sensitive data—including the railroads and the supertankers that deliver coal and heating oil; the "just-in-time" manufacturing and delivery system that supplies our food, appliances and clothing; and the local bank, electric utility, and phone company. Without properly running computers, the delivery of many of the everyday necessities we have come to depend upon could be disrupted. (Skeptics need only recall a recent case of technological vulnerability: Over 70% of North American pagers went out of service temporarily when a chip in a telecommunications satellite failed in May 1998. I suggest such skeptics visit the *Millennium Salons* Web site, located at <http://home.ica.net/~njarc/msalons/main.html>. This site has a number of excellent articles on the magnitude of the Y2K problem as well as concrete solutions and contingency plans for individuals and communities to consider.)

It's not just potential domestic problems that we need to think about. The global implications of Y2K are also sobering. According to the *Gartner Group* report on the "Global State of Readiness," most of the world is ill-prepared for the havoc Y2K will wreak, given that "lagging companies and governments will simply not have enough time to get their systems fixed before 2000," resulting in a "negative impact on our economy and the availability of critical resources" (<http://gartnerweb.com/pub...aboutgg/pressrel/testimony1098.html>).

Some readers might not think it matters much that a country such as Brazil or Venezuela will suffer a big hit from the Y2K problem. However, given that most Western countries depend upon so-called "developing" nations for a variety of strategic minerals, metals, oil, and other key components vital to the manufacturing industrial complex, Y2K could wreak havoc on the global economy. (In light of this, it might be wise to consult with your financial advisor for safe ways to shelter your finances from the major market "corrections" that might result. See Y2K analyst Tony Keyes's paper "The Impact of Y2K on the Global Economy," <http://www.itpolicy.gsa.gov/mks/yr2000/y2kconf/paper28fp.htm>.

Add to the above scenarios the possibility that local and regional emergency response teams could be spread extremely thin as they address a number of Y2K-related core infrastructure problems, it doesn't take a lot of common sense to realize that some preparation is in order.

My intent is not to generate panic over the problems Y2K might generate, but to awaken people to the idea that we should prepare for potential disruptions in the normal affairs of our life. I am not a Chicken Little who claims Y2K will be so catastrophic that it will take a decade for the local, regional, national, and global infrastructure to recover. Nor am I an ostrich who hides from the potentially unpleasant problems Y2K might deliver. For the purposes of this book I take for granted that Y2K is a unique phenomenon unlike an earthquake or hurricane, in that we know the precise moment when it will occur all over the world. I also assume that no one can predict just how great or how small Y2K's impact will be.

In light of this, I think it is unwise to sit by passively and hope someone will solve the problem for us—whether that someone is the government, Bill Gates, or the local public utilities. From my perspective, Y2K is too complex and too vast a potential problem for us to sit back and hope for the best. The world has never seen a phenomenon like this. What I offer is a balanced approach that admits we just don't know what will happen, but accepts that wisdom dictates we should prepare "just in case." (As a minimum, I plan to have enough food, water, heating, and lighting reserves to last at least 30 days beyond February 29, 2000—another date that could cause many computers to malfunction. I also plan to have a good supply of long-term storage grains and legumes as a buffer against the steep rise in consumer costs that Y2K might generate.)

The Power of Being Proactive

Given the short amount of time remaining before Y2K hits, the enormous amount of remedial work needing to be done, and the uncertainty of how well these repairs will work, many Y2K observers are growing increasingly pessimistic about our chances of dealing effectively with Y2K. Such an outlook often leads to procrastination and paralysis, as people become worried, confused, and overwhelmed.

Rather than giving in to apathy or anxiety, it is important that we focus actively on a simple, specific Y2K preparation program that can help us during the uncertain days ahead. This manual will help you toward this goal by offering simple, step-by-step procedures for successful Y2K preparation. It will also give you confidence to help your family, relatives, friends, co-workers, neighbors, and community members prepare for what lies ahead. Sure, some people might think you are a "kook" like Bill in the story above, but as Y2K closes in and the media play up the seriousness of this issue, these same people might be the first to panic and become paralyzed by not knowing what to do. By studying and implementing the information contained in this book, you can help ensure that Y2K brings minimal damage to the lives of those around you.

My other intent is to help you, your family, and your community empower yourselves so that you not only cope and survive but also grow and thrive through the uncertain times ahead. To do this we must take a positive, proactive approach that looks at the coming Year 2000 situation as a challenge to discover new things about ourselves and about how we can live a fuller and more fruitful life. This is what I call a "holistic," or total preparedness, orientation to Y2K. That is, if we plan and prepare properly we can use the Y2K experience as a time of growth and discovery in terms of our health, our personal relationships, and our overall well-being. In short, I want to emphasize empowerment rather than victimhood.

This journey toward empowerment has led me to see how non-self-reliant and dependent upon the larger cultural infrastructure I have become. As I anticipate that this computer-based "system" might let me down, I have begun reorienting my life toward simple skills that will help me, my family, and my community discover the benefits Y2K might offer. I encourage you also to ask what you can learn from this challenge and how you can grow and develop as a better person because of it. For some of us this might mean slowing down a bit and questioning the direction of our life. For others it might mean growing closer to our family, overcoming procrastination, or taking on more civic responsibility. The possibilities are as endless and unique as are our personalities. (See Judy Laddon and Tom Atlee's *Awakening: The Upside of Y2K* for a look the positive lifestyle changes and relationships that Y2K can generate, especially the part about how faith and spirituality can overcome any infrastructure disruptions we might face.)

Some pragmatically minded readers might wonder what value such questions have at a time like this. By asking such questions, I am trying to get you to think of emergency preparedness and survival as part of a much larger picture. The amount of effort it will take to prepare for Y2K can be overwhelming. When we put this process in a much larger framework and see that our goal is more than just "getting ready," we discover a larger purpose that can help motivate us when we get bogged down by too many details or frustrations. For some readers the value of this insight might not become apparent until they complete the action steps in the next chapter. For now, it is important to see that this book and its program involve much more than just emergency survival and preparedness. If you follow carefully the practices and principles outlined in this book, you can enter a new frontier in your personal, family, social, and spiritual life.

Where Do We Begin?

As with any program that requires a lifestyle change (and trust me, Y2K will change the way we live our lives), the first step involves commitment. You need to make a conscious choice that you want to follow through on this preparedness project. As will be seen in the next chapter, exactly what this preparation will entail will depend upon your unique situation. Each of us has different needs, expectations, budgets, desires, time constraints, health concerns, emotional issues, and a thousand other factors that will influence how we will prepare.

The sooner you commit to preparing, the better. Events are changing quickly. As the January due date approaches and the mass media harp on the implications of Y2K, a lot of people will jump on the preparedness bandwagon. This will mean both a scarcity of and higher prices for essential preparedness goods.

You must begin, as soon as possible, to decide what your individual, family, or group Preparedness Plan will be. Already many items such as some dehydrated foods and certain diesel generators are on four- to five-month back order. However, before you panic and race out to the nearest outdoors and survival shop, let me offer some advice.

How This Book Can Help

By reading this book you are already ahead of 90 percent of the population in terms of a serious understanding of Y2K preparedness. Most people will wait until the last minute (November and December 1999) when it will be too late to implement an effective Y2K Preparedness Plan. Whether you are an optimist and expect only short-term Y2K problems—less than one month, a pessimist who anticipates the need for long-term survival—a year or more, or a realist who envisions a moderate period of disruption—approximately two to four months, the important thing is that you begin now to take control over your destiny. However, unless you do your homework and implement the basic principles and action steps appropriate to your unique situation, you might waste a lot of time, money, and energy or get discouraged by the stampede of those desperately seeking to acquire skills and hoard items they think they will need to make it through the Y2K challenge. This manual is divided into twelve chapters that can spare you from these problems.

The Introduction is designed to give a brief overview of the Y2K challenge and explain why it has come about and how we can avoid falling victim to whatever it might bring. Chapter Two highlights the Basic Principles and specific Action Steps needed to organize a practical Preparedness Plan. Chapter Three offers an array of options for those who want to stock up on high-quality, shelf-stable, non-perishable "core foods." Chapter Four focuses on food preparation tools that can save you money and help maintain your health in the event that Y2K plays out as the pessimists predict. Chapter Five offers nonelectric-based ways of cooking in case the power grid fails in your area. Chapter Six highlights the way we can use herbs, supplements, and first-aid kits to help maintain our health when Y2K strikes. Chapter Seven looks at "alternative" and backup means to keep ourselves warm if the power fails during the cold days of January 2000. Chapter Eight offers suggestions for alternative lighting products to keep our lives bright during Y2K. Chapter Nine focuses on the vital issue of water and how to ensure that we have a safe and sufficient supply of this crucial necessity. Chapter Ten explores the unpleasant, but very important, issue of how to deal with human waste in the event that the embedded chips fail and we lose the capacity for our toilet and sewage systems to work. Chapter Eleven explores some of the overlooked concerns that might play a big role if Y2K becomes a protracted event. Chapter Twelve offers some concluding advice to help keep Y2K in a larger spiritual perspective.

Finally, the Appendices offer a checklist to remind us of what we need to do and to have ready for all that Y2K will toss our way, as well as a list of resources, businesses, and organizations you can contact for help and information. (The *Cassandra Project,* <http://millennia-bcs.com/examples.htm> or <http://millennia-bcs.com/nfcass.htm#top>, is one group that is dedicated to helping individuals and communities prepare for Y2K challenges as they relate to "health and safety risks" and the "interruption of basic and essential services." Their Web site offers a wide array of information and statistics dealing with potential Y2K problems and solutions. They constantly update their site, so you should place it among your "bookmarks" and consult it regularly. *The Y2K Living Journal,* <http://www.jvprofit.com/y2k/signup.htm>, is another good resource on the Web. This Web site contains lots of practical, comfort-oriented advice on how to deal with the Y2K challenge. *Big-Web Marketing, Inc.,* <http://www.coolandunusual.com/y2k/y2kstore/y5twok/orderfrm.html>, is one of many companies offering educational videos on Y2K that would be good for families and communities to view and discuss.)

Y2K TIP

This book lists numerous Web sites and e-mail addresses for quick and easy ways to find and procure what you need. Be sure to "bookmark" Web sites for faster future reference. If you do not have access to the Internet, see if you can link up with a friend or relative who does, or visit your local library.

Each chapter is designed to help you through the Y2K transition. By "transition" I mean the period between when Y2K hits and when things get back to normal. In other words, there will be the initial big hit at midnight, December 31, 1999 when the "00"-related glitches begin, followed by the period when we begin getting things back in order. How long this transition will take is anybody's guess.

Although I have kept this book short and list a bare minimum of things you should do and have on hand, some readers might feel lost amid the maze of detail. If you do get overwhelmed, slow down, take a break, come back fresh, and tackle each chapter in segments that you can absorb and act on without anxiety and panic. In addition, before you purchase anything, I strongly suggest you read this whole manual to get a sense of the scope of the Y2K challenge and how to think about it. Then go back and work on the Basic Principles and Action Steps outlined in Chapter Two before you procure the items outlined in Chapters Three through Eleven. This approach will not only help you make prudent decisions but will also generate confidence and keep you from feeling overwhelmed.

As you read through the products chapters you will also discover a way to think about Y2K that will refine your Y2K preparedness project. Therefore do not skip reading about an item even if you already have it. There might be a valuable insight, tucked in the midst of a product description, that could be beneficial to you later.

Everyone in your Y2K Preparedness Group should read this entire book (and please share it with those living near you). It is vital that families, neighbors, and communities share a common vision and work together toward common goals.

A Word About "Natural" Y2K Preparedness

Throughout this book I have done my best to emphasize products and techniques that promote health and well-being. I do this because I have found this approach has produced great benefits for me and for those around me. I also do this so that if the Y2K issue does not turn out to be as bad as some predict, you will at least have products and principles that will serve you well for the rest of your life. In other words, I have structured a program that will help you before, during, and after the Y2K challenge (unlike those people who purchase 300 pounds [135 kilograms] of wheat without the least thought of how they will use it or if they or someone in their Preparedness Group might be allergic to it).

For me, a holistic and natural approach to Y2K preparedness entails a lifestyle orientation that takes into consideration our physical, mental, emotional, spiritual, social, and environmental needs. Because of my background as a natural health-educator, I prefer products and principles that are as beneficial and health promoting as possible.

Such an approach has several guiding principles. First, I seek ways to be a responsible steward of what God has given us by minimizing waste and toxic by-products that lessen and destroy the life of those around us. Second, for me survival means more than just existing. From my perspective we were created by God to maximize our full potential as special creatures who can encounter the beauty and wonder of our world.

Based on these principles I look for products that emphasize our maximum well-being while minimizing destruction to our body and the world that sustains us. Therefore for each product I ask several important questions—does it promote health? Is it necessary? And is it community-friendly, meaning, does it do minimal damage to the environment and health of others? Some readers may disagree that every product I offer affirms these three questions. In some instances they are right. Unfortunately, many people who create products for emergency and survival preparedness are not as sensitive to health issues as they could be. In some small way I hope this book will help manufacturers see there is a market for health-friendly products. Until that time, and given the grave importance that the Y2K challenge presents, I have to be flexible in my principles. (If you find better health-benefiting and environmentally friendly products, I hope you will share them with me so that I can pass this information on to others.)

Even if you are not a "health nut" and are just reading this resource guide to find products you need, I hope you will consider some of the nutrition and health suggestions I make, given the enormous number of scientific studies that document the relationship between a healthy diet and the avoidance of health problems. This focus on health could be vital in the days ahead, especially given the March 2, 1999 announcement by the Senate Special Committee on the Year 2000 Technology Problem that "fully 90 percent of doctors haven't fixed their computers and could temporarily lose medical records" and that "sixty-four percent of all hospitals in the United States have no plans to test their Y2K updates" ("Senate Moves on Y2K Bug" <http://abcnews.go.com/sections/tech/DailyNews/y2kday990302.html>).

In Conclusion

If you search the World Wide Web you will find a lot of panic and paranoia concerning Y2K—predictions of "Doomsday," "Armageddon," social violence, and mass destruction. I am not of this camp. I feel that if we band together with a mixture of common sense, native self-reliance, and appropriate personal and community preparation we can avoid the dire scenarios some predict. (Churches and synagogues are in a good position to offer a strong community presence.)

I also submit that holistic preparedness is the best preventive medicine as we begin adjusting our lifestyle to meet the multiple challenges ahead. For some of us this will mean learning to give up junk food. For others it will mean learning a new set of skills to become less dependent upon the "system," or for slowing down and communicating with our neighbors and loved ones in ways we have never done before. In other words, Y2K can be a blessing in disguise as we face its challenges with a proactive, empowering attitude that helps ensure our mutual health, safety, and well-being.

For many people, this book and the entire Y2K enterprise will stir up a wash of emotions. This is a normal response to an event of such overwhelming and unknown potential. My intent is to instill a confident hope that you can prepare for and cope with any eventuality that Y2K presents. However, this will only happen in proportion to the amount of effort you and your Preparedness Group put into your Y2K preparedness project. My advice is simple: Be diligent as you plan, prepare, and practice Y2K preparedness.

CHAPTER **2**
Specific Action Steps and Principles for Y2K Preparedness

"Anyone who wants a guarantee that nothing's going to happen isn't going to get it." —Jon Arnold, Chief Technology Officer, Edison Electric Institute

One of the important points addressed in Chapter One is that the potential challenges associated with the Year 2000 computer glitch are real and unavoidable. In light of this fact, this Chapter will focus on some basic preparedness principles and specific action steps that will help you and your Preparedness Group gain maximum benefit from your Y2K preparations. Please don't skip the work this chapter outlines. The following principles and action steps lie at the center of a total Y2K preparedness plan. They are designed to give you the confidence, knowledge, and wisdom you will need to tackle all that Y2K sends your way. They will also save you lots of time, money, and needless stress and frustration.

These action steps are designed to get you going and to make sure you obtain the best Y2K-related resources you will need. It is important that you adapt these procedures as your situation demands. It is also important to realize that these principles and action steps are not necessarily listed in order of priority since different geographic regions and personal circumstances will make some steps more important than others. You will have to determine what order is best for you.

I encourage you to read through the whole chapter in order to get the big picture, and on your second reading detail the choices you and your Preparedness Group make. Throughout this book references will be made to writing down this or that information down so that you can refer to it later. Therefore, it is crucial to keep a Y2K Preparedness Journal for jotting down insights, discoveries, reminders, etc. Doing this will also help you crystallize your thinking, and it will act as a strong empowerment tool as you build clarity of focus and the personal confidence that you are making progress and paying attention to important details. (It will also be a good heirloom to hand down to your grandchildren after this significant cultural event has entered the history books.)

I will begin with ten general or basic principles designed to help you grasp the big picture of Y2K preparation, and then I will list specific action steps that focus on the details that will make your Y2K preparation and experience as stress-free and fruitful as possible.

Basic Principle # 1:
Sharpen Your Y2K Focus

The magnitude of the impending Y2K challenge means we might have to alter many of our normal living habits. Without being obsessive, we need to begin a new way of thinking and acting related to our specific Y2K Preparedness Plan and its mission to promote and maintain our health and well-being during the challenge ahead.

Preparing for Y2K will cost a lot of money. One sign that we are committed to accomplishing our goal is to discipline our budget by cutting down on nonessential purchases and focusing on items related directly to preparing for Y2K. Between now and New Year's Day 2000, we should consider spending the bulk of our available discretionary income on getting ready for this event. For most of us this will involve sacrifice (and a few lapses along the way). I have a basic weakness for used books and antiques. During this time of preparation, I have made a radical cutback in the number of books and antiques I buy since they will not contribute to my family's "survival." (One way I console myself is to remember that many things will be cheaper after the Y2K economic turmoil has ended. This may or may not be true, but it is a thought that helps me endure the current sacrifices.)

What I am encouraging you to do is to have a concentrated mindset that focuses narrowly on the preparedness issue at hand. Like an athlete who trains for a big event, you must begin to focus your thinking on the specific goal you want to accomplish.

Basic Principle # 2:
Accurately Assess Your Current Situation

It is important to realistically appraise your current preparedness status. If your local community were hit hard by Y2K, how long could you and your community survive? What extra resources, "just-in-case" skills, and backup items would your Preparedness Group need to thrive during the days ahead?

However, in order to know what these skills and products should be, you need to answer a number of important questions such as these: Who will be in my Preparedness Group? Will it be only my immediate family, or will it include friends, relatives, or neighbors? Knowing the answers to these questions will help determine how much food and water you should store. Other questions you should ask are these: Is someone in my Preparedness Group or neighborhood trained to handle medical emergencies? If my Y2K Preparedness Group plans to purchase a large amount of wheat and other grains, do we have a hand-operated mill to grind them or the space to store them? What will we do if the electricity fails? How will we keep warm?

(Don't assume that just because you have propane gas or oil heat you will be OK; most domestic and business heating systems need electricity to start and operate properly.) By evaluating where you stand today, you can plan better and prepare more cost-effectively for what might happen.

Basic Principle # 3:
Anticipate Potential Problems

When assessing your state of Y2K readiness it is important that you envision potential problems you might encounter. Unlike other disasters such as a hurricane, a tornado, or an earthquake, Y2K is unique in its potential for widespread simultaneous disruptions. Therefore, it is important that you envision multifactorial scenarios, that is, situations that involve a number of problems happening at the same time. For example, what will you do if a flu epidemic and a savage blizzard hit just when Y2K knocks out your electrical power and municipal water supply? How will you keep from getting pneumonia? Do you have the skills and resources to survive if Y2K disruptions last longer than anticipated? Do you have enough food and alternative heating supplies to last for three to four months?

The answer to such questions will depend upon the type of dwelling in which you live, the kind of climate your region experiences, how well your local and regional authorities are prepared, etc. People in Southern California and Florida will be less concerned about the loss of heating abilities in January and February than those in Boston, Toronto, or Denver. At the same time, people in Miami or San Diego will need more drinking water, given the likelihood of dehydration because of the warmer climate.

It is the detailed planning for potential problems that separates the emergency preparedness pros from the well-intentioned amateurs. This approach involves using your imagination to project "what if" scenarios—for example, what will we do if we can't use our toilet for a week? The more detailed you are, the more beneficial this exercise will be.

Remember, the degree to which you honestly appraise your survival skills—how well you can prepare food without a source of heat, how Mary will cope if she can't get her insulin, how you will keep warm when it's minus 20° and the furnace won't work—is the degree to which you can and will thrive through the coming Y2K challenge.

> **Y2K TIP**
>
> Given the possibility that there could be looting and rioting in some urban areas should the local infrastructure collapse during Y2K, it is important to form neighborhood support groups since a tightly bonded group of people can

protect each other better. Those living in highly fragmented communities might consider moving in with friends or relatives who live in a less crowded area, or renting a temporary "Y2K cottage" or a winterized trailer in the country—especially one that has a nonelectric form of heating, and a private well and a septic tank to help ensure water and personal comfort and hygiene needs are met.

Basic Principle # 4:

Design a Strategic Preparedness Plan Based upon Your Current Situation and Anticipated Problems

Once you have honestly evaluated your current and potential emergency and preparedness situation, the next vital step is to create a detailed, strategic plan of action. By "strategic" I mean a well thought-out plan that is based upon a careful discussion of your needs with your Preparedness Group. The action steps in the next section are designed to take you through this process.

The important point is that your strategic plan must be based upon essential needs. For example, how much drinking water will you need? The normal recommendation is two gallons a day for each adult—for drinking, cooking, personal hygiene, and washing. (You will need more if you live in a hot climate.)

A well thought-out Y2K Preparedness Plan will also determine how much food and water to stock up on, where you will store it, how you will heat your home, whether you can safely store gasoline, etc. As an advocate of good health and environmental friendliness, I prefer renewable and sustainable sources of power such as solar, wind, or a (hybrid) combination of the two. But I also have to ask if I can afford these alternatives and if they are right for my living situation—for example, what if I live on a seventh-floor apartment? I have listed a variety of books in the Appendix to help you do the type of research you need. (Reading and sharing ideas can be a highly creative and stimulating process.)

As you and your Y2K Preparedness Group work through your plan, you will discover new challenges. For example, I enjoy certified organic fruits and vegetables for juicing and for snacks and salads. What alternative will I come up with if the "just-in-time" delivery system that supplies my local health food store "crashes"? I also enjoy and need a variety of foods or I get "appetite fatigue"—an important issue that is addressed in Chapter Three. My Y2K Preparedness Plan will thus help me map out a way to obtain and store the variety of foods I prefer. However, not everyone will have the same tastes as I do. That is why it is important to have everyone—including children—have as say in what gets chosen. By asking and answering such specific questions you will be light-years ahead of the average Joe and Jane who rush out and buy a space heater without considering what type of power source they will use to run it if the public utility system goes down.

Be sure to write down the specifics of your plan. Writing helps us see things more clearly and gives us a sense of accomplishment. If writing is not your forte, then get a spouse, child, friend, relative—or hire a neighbor—to be your assistant. It is important that you see your Y2K Preparedness Plan on paper as you think things through.

Y2K TIP

For those who are beginning to feel overwhelmed—relax—and remember: You don't have to do it all yourself. This is why your Preparedness Group must be a team. Divide up what needs to be done. Someone can be responsible for learning how to use a grain mill and cook on an alternative source of heat, while others plan for and order the best foods appropriate to the taste buds and health needs of those in your group, or research the best type of backup toilet and garbage waste disposal. (Of no small consequence is the issue of how to clean dirty and used glasses, cups, plates, and utensils if you run out of biodegradable paper plates. Will you lick them clean? This might sound unappetizing, but it might be the only way to get them clean if there is a shortage of water.) By dividing up the research and skill training load, everyone will be less stressed and will feel more deeply committed to the project.

Basic Principle # 5:
Educate Yourself and Acquire What You Will Need

For many of us, Y2K preparations will mean a whole new lifestyle education. This means we will have to try out new things. It also means we will have to do some homework such as visit a hardware or camping store. I suggest you talk to people who heat their homes with a woodstove or with propane heaters. What do they like and not like about them? Make phone calls, write letters, send faxes and e-mails, check the World Wide Web to find alternative sources of power, food, and lighting suitable to your specific needs and potential challenges. (The items listed on the Internet auction site *eBay*, <http://www.ebay.com/>, under the topic "Y2K" can be very educational in helping you determine what you need.)

Having taken the time to research, discuss, and write up your specific Y2K Preparedness Plan, you need to act on it.

Principles for Wise Buying:

- Avoid panic buying. Before you buy, ask a lot of questions: "Do I really need this or that?" "Is it the best quality I can afford?" My guiding principle when purchasing is simple. Is it essential? Is it good quality? Is it healthy for my family and me? Is it friendly to the environment? These simple questions help me cut through the sales hype and focus on what will be truly beneficial for my situation.

- Get essentials first. In many areas, the rush for bulk orders of grain, freeze-dried and dehydrated foods, and power generators has reached frenzied proportions, which means you have to wait, in some cases, several months or more before you can take possession. The closer we get to the unavoidable Y2K date, the more expensive and difficult things such as flashlights, cords of wood, and sleeping bags will be to obtain. (In Chapters Eight and Nine I suggest a number of hard-to-find items such as hand-cranked flashlights and 120-hour candles to help make your purchasing experience easier.) Already there are notices such as that posted by *Fitness Industries Inc.*: "NOTE: We cannot accept any new orders at this time. All orders received on or before Oct 15, 1998 will be shipped" (<http://www.y2k-foods.com/>).

- Buy strategically. For example, instead of dairy milk my family uses *Eden Soy Milk—Extra Original,* which comes in a shelf-stable container. I know my local health food store receives shipments of this product about eleven months before the expiration date. Thus I don't want to rush out and buy a large amount that will expire in January of 2000 and thereby not have any for February and March 2000 when things could get tight. It is also important to remember that most canned foods have a shelf life of two years at the most. Check the expiration date. If you can't decipher the code, ask someone at the store to interpret it for you. Not only do canned goods spoil, but they also lose their nutritional value as they approach their expiration date—so plan accordingly.

- Buy the best quality you can afford. Remember that you get what you pay for. Quality items cost more but they often last longer, are easier to work with, and are better for you. When it comes to food I don't chintz. Good health depends upon good nutrition. And, unfortunately, good nutritional items, such as organically grown fruits and vegetables, cost more.

Basic Principle # 6:
Rehearse Your Y2K Preparedness Plan

Your research about and purchase of Y2K-related items will be more effective if you practice "real-world" run-throughs. By this I mean that you actually try living out your Y2K Preparedness Plan—cooking without electricity, using an alternative form of toilet, etc. However, remember that it is too overwhelming to try everything at once. This is why professional emergency preparedness teams practice and refine various skills over and over so they can perform them under pressure when the real thing hits. The following recommendations are also based upon many of the action steps listed below; therefore I suggest that you not conduct rehearsals until after you have gone through those steps.

First, I suggest you try going 24 hours without using any electricity. This short exercise is best performed on a weekend or a holiday with everyone in your Preparedness Group remaining at home during the entire exercise. To make this exercise more realistic, you should cut off the electricity from the main circuit breaker panel so that you will not be tempted to "forget" and use something that might not be available when Y2K strikes. This one drill will reveal vividly just how dependent we are upon high technology. It will also reveal how our Preparedness Group needs to work together as a team that encourages and supports one another. This exercise will also help you fine-tune your Y2K Preparedness Plan as it reveals the need for extra flashlights, candles, a warmer sleeping bag, a nonelectric cook stove, etc. In addition, it will reinforce the importance of simplifying your living space and organizing it in a logical and uncluttered manner. Remember to have important things in the same convenient place so that they can be located easily and operated safely.

Next, begin by going a full weekend without the use of your water, electricity, or toilets. (I can hear some of you groaning, "Man, are you crazy? I'm just a simple city person, not some SWAT team member!" I understand. However, I ask you to consider this: There is a good possibility that some people might not survive if their area is greatly disrupted by Y2K. Think about this when you need the motivation to keep preparing and practicing.) If you have the opportunity, I suggest doing this exercise during the winter months to really simulate what the Y2K January might be like (and also test how cozy your minus-10°F [minus 23°C] sleeping bag is).

Following these important tests, you might try living off your stored food supplies for a few days, that is, don't consume any fresh or frozen grocery goods such as meat, fish, fruits, and vegetables. (Given that hot food will be crucial, especially in the winter months, this exercise will be even better if you use alternative sources of cooking to make sure you have the special supplies and skills you need for nonelectric cooking.) This is a critical test to help your taste buds adapt and to determine what you are missing and still need—such as more spices, condiments, and variety. (See the issue of "appetite fatigue" in Chapter Three.)

As you record your experiences in your Y2K Preparedness Journal, make sure you answer specific questions such as these: Did you have enough power for heat and lights? How did you dispose of your human waste? Could you do this for a month? What did you use for a source of water? How did you store it and keep it pure? How did it taste? This is no small issue given that you might have to live off your stored water for a while.

As these specific questions suggest, rehearsing your Y2K Preparedness Plans can be demanding but also rewarding.

Basic Principle # 7:
Have Contingency Plans—Be Flexible

As you research and rehearse your Preparedness Plan and the products you anticipate needing for the Y2K transition, it is important that you adjust and fine-tune your program, especially in terms of having backup plans.

For many of us it will take an immense amount of patience, strength, and discipline to weather the stress and changes Y2K might deliver. If we work on being open to change and responding in a flexible and creative manner, we will go a lot further in coping with Y2K—and any other life crisis. The key to this process is not to become obsessed so rigidly with Y2K preparedness that we "flip out" and frighten those around us, or so "chilled out" that we lose a focused intensity. Using common sense, getting good counsel, and keeping a sense of perspective—remember, people in the past survived and flourished without being dependent upon computers—will go a long way to helping us maintain the balance we need to get though this time together. As a mentor of mine once said, "When things get too stressed, tell a thousand jokes." If you don't know that many, then go out and buy some joke books. Without a sense of humor, it's easy to go off the deep end.

As presented here, Y2K preparedness is a once-in-a-lifetime adventure. Keeping a larger perspective and an open, proactive, and positive attitude will make it easier on all of us.

Basic Principle # 8:
Cultivate the Practice of Cooperative Self-Sufficiency

Coping successfully with Y2K will require that we be both self-reliant and group-dependent. That is, we need to cultivate a Y2K living practice that emphasizes both individual initiative and cooperative teamwork. Most of us are too dependent on the "system," and would not know how to function if we did not have public or private transportation, could not buy the clothes we need, or could not obtain food at our local supermarket or favorite health food store. Maximum Y2K preparation means that we need to learn how to function and thrive without these conveniences. This is the fundamental principle on which all wise and effective preparedness and survival plans depend.

A number of resources are available for those in your Preparedness Group who want to learn the survival skills that many of our pioneering ancestors took for granted, such as medical self-care, cooking from scratch, sewing, mending and making clothes, and gardening and canning. Among those resources are these:

- *Backwoods Home Magazine,* <http://backwoodshome.com/>, e-mail <editor@backwoodshome.com>, has a number of back issues and articles dedicated to a host of important survival and self-reliant living skills. Their *Backwoods Home Magazine Anthology & Book Order Form,* <http://backwoodshome.com/orderabp.html>, is another great resource to consult.
- *Organic Gardening,* <http://www.enews.com/network/nnorders/>, is another magazine that offers lots of practical tips for the urban, suburban, and rural homesteader—especially back issues from the 1970s and early 1980s. The ads in this magazine are especially informative as they are a valuable resource for finding lesser-known companies that offer a variety of products that can be helpful for those of us preparing for Y2K.
- *Countryside & Small Stock Journal,* <http://www.countrysidemag.com/>, e-mail <csymag@midway.tds.net>, is another magazine dedicated to "voluntary simplicity," homesteading, and home food production. This magazine contains lots of practical, helpful, sustainable living advice and information. Their belief "that the primary reward of work should be well-being rather than money" (<http://www.countrysidemag.com/about.htm>) is an important reminder as we enter the days ahead.
- *The Online Homesteading and Small Farming Resource,* <http://www.homestead.org/>, is a valuable web site providing practical information on self-reliant living.
- See also the *Glitchproof.com* Web page, dedicated to links about homesteading, permaculture, and sustainable agriculture: <http://www.glitchproof.com/glitchproof/linabperanda.html>.

However, as we focus on self-reliance skills it is also important to realize this is not a solo adventure that we can do on our own, especially given the short amount of time left before Y2K strikes. Cooperative self-sufficiency means that we work together as members of a group or team such as our family, church group, neighborhood, or network of friends. It is important to dialogue and plan with everyone who will be in your immediate circle of support to make sure that everyone's needs will be met.

Unfortunately, not everyone, possibly including your spouse or your next-door neighbor, will take the Y2K threat seriously until it hits. This is why it's important to store more supplies than you need, given that as the Y2K transition unfolds, many of your friends, relatives, and neighbors will want to climb aboard your "ark." At the same time, if things get bad and people know (or think) you have a lot of food and water stored away, you will be a prime target for people banging at your door. It is therefore wise to use discretion about telling anyone how much you have stored away.

Basic Principle # 9:
Link Your Efforts To The Larger Community Around You

Just as effective Y2K preparation requires that we work as a team, it also means we need to link our efforts to those of our neighborhood and local community. Because of potential safety-related Y2K problems, friends and neighbors can play a vital role in protecting and helping each other. Therefore, as a guiding principle, self-reliance plus community cooperation is the most beneficial formula to help us all flourish during the uncertain days ahead.

If you feel awkward about venturing out on your own, consider joining with others to form Y2K Community Action Groups—which are already being formed in a number of areas around the country. Such groups can greatly diffuse potential civil unrest problems as people bond together and look out for one another. *Epicenter*, <http://www.theepicenter.com/>, offers the O. P. N.—*Organization of Prepared Neighborhoods* program, based upon the successful disaster plan used in London during World War Two. This packet is designed to help communities band together and formulate a comprehensive program based on the theme that the "block or community that prepares together survives together" (<http://www.theepicenter.com/bookvdo.html>). The *UTNE Reader* "Y2K Citizen's Action Guide" also offers a number of practical ways to help communities and neighborhoods prepare for specific Y2K-related problems.

It is important, too, that shelters for the homeless be prepared with extra food and water to help cut down on the type of desperation that leads to looting and other crimes. One effective way to keep neighborhoods safe and happy is to make sure everyone gets fed. *Jade Mountain Inc.*, <http://www.jademountain.com/>, carries a line of "community"-sized grain and seed grinders as well as a "village" oven that will bake hundreds of loaves of bread a day. The latter can be run on propane gas for those who live in cold climates. For a description of these and other products you can consult their home page, <http://www.jademountain.com/>, or contact them via e-mail at <info@jademountain.com>.

Several groups are providing low-cost, long-term storage bulk food at bargain prices to help feed the poor and needy. One such group is *Future Foods Inc.* (telephone 612-504-2930, fax 612-504-2943), which offers inexpensive (about 50 cents a meal), simply prepared, nutritious meals. *Future Foods Inc.* also specializes in meals for overseas missionary and humanitarian organizations. The previously mentioned Cassandra Project, <http://millennia-bcs.com/nfcass.htm#top>, is another group dedicated to helping communities prepare for Y2K disruptions.

It is also important that your neighborhood work with local police, fire, and emergency specialists and have a group protection and Preparedness Plan in place—what some are calling a "good neighbor network"—in case the "911" telecommunications system fails, or if your public assistance crews are so overtaxed that they cannot come to your rescue. It is also crucial that the local emergency assistance teams prepare for potential shortages that could cripple their capacity to serve. As with the military, it might be wise for your police, fire, and emergency rescue departments to stock up on water, *MREs* ("Meals-Ready-to-Eat"), and other forms of freeze-dried and dehydrated foods (see Chapter Three). The important thing is that we begin to think about forming a network of people who watch out for one another in terms of both our domestic situation and the wider environment within which we conduct our lives.

The issue of helping the vulnerable such as the elderly, handicapped, and infirm who live alone in your area must also not be overlooked. This could be a good outreach project for local clubs, churches and synagogues, and other groups with a large building space who might consider stockpiling food and water and having emergency generators and fuel on hand to operate as a center of refuge for those who lose their heat during the Y2K winter.

If you have elderly and infirm neighbors, you might also want to contact their nearest relatives to see if they can stay with them for the first week or two of January 2000. If this is not possible, check with your local church, synagogue, welfare and human services department, and *United Way Charities* to see if someone can help watch out for them.

Basic Principle # 10:
Decide What Is Essential and Keep It Simple

As you read through the action steps below and the numerous products listed in the following chapters, it's easy to get overwhelmed and lost amid the detail. This is why it's important to "keep it simple" by focusing on essentials. We need to plan our Y2K preparations around vital things and hold off on a lot of the extras until we have our foundational necessities in place. Doing this will help keep us from feeling too overwhelmed and out of control—two emotions that lead to gloom and apathy.

As you accumulate things for Y2K, you also need to make room for storing your preparedness items. Therefore, it is important that you "unclutter your life"— in terms of both living space and personal habits. The less disorderly we are in our thoughts and living environment, the better we will handle the stress ahead.

Another hidden blessing of Y2K is that this experience can free us from being enslaved by the unnecessary. You will be surprised at what you can live without. Therefore I recommend you consider unloading a lot of the junk that envelops our lives—including both the physical and the emotional baggage we carry. There is liberation in being—to paraphrase Mother Teresa— "unsmothered by things." You might consider having a yard sale to dump the things you have not used (or seen) for years and using the extra money to purchase preparedness items. (Those who use the World Wide Web should look up *eBay*, <http://ebay.com>, an online auction house that offers a venue for selling items in a fun and easy manner.) There is a healing and liberating power in simplifying and letting go.

If you get confused or lost in Y2K-related details, remember that maximum health and well-being depend upon a few simple principles and actions:

- A variety of good-quality, wholesome foods
- A sufficient amount of pure, clean water
- Adequate shelter—meaning not too hot and not too cold
- Fresh, clean air
- The avoidance of poisonous and toxic chemicals
- A positive, proactive mental outlook
- A spirit of sharing and helping others
- Appropriate exercise
- Safe exposure to sunshine
- Adequate rest, relaxation, and quiet time
- Meaningful work
- Fun recreation and creative expression
- Lots of laughter
- The company and enjoyment of others
- The cultivation of our relationship with God
- Humble acceptance that we aren't perfect and can't do everything

If you find yourself getting confused, discouraged, or overwhelmed by Y2K preparations, come back to these simple principles and remind yourself that animals in the wild have survived for thousands of generations without having to rely on electricity, money, or the latest entertainment or fashion fad.

Having focused on general principles, I will now list specific action steps that will help you to further develop and refine your Y2K Preparedness Plan.

Action Step # 1:
Do Something Each Day That Contributes to Your Preparedness Plan

Doing empowers. Even if it's just a thought, begin the habit of doing something every day toward accomplishing your Preparedness Plan—a phone call here, a meeting there, a purchase someplace else. Little actions such as these generate commitment and energy and give you the momentum you need.

Action Step # 2:
Get Hard Copies of All Important Records

This period of organizing and de-cluttering your life is also a good time to get all your important paperwork in order. Don't trust your records to be stored safely in computers or held on file by other people. Make hard copies (printouts or photocopies) of your passport, birth certificate, annuity funds, bank accounts, credit reports, stocks and bonds, life insurance, will, and other important documents. Many things are going to be lost, misplaced, or un-retrievable in the computer chaos that lies ahead. Having these documents secured safely in a fire- and waterproof place could come in handy later.

Action Step # 3:
Design a Healthy "Core Food" Package for Each Person In Your Preparedness Group

All emergency preparedness experts advise that you have a backup supply of food on hand. The more long-term or shelf-stable such food is, the less you have to worry about spoilage, nutritional loss, or bug infestation in your food supply. Because of the unpredictability of what Y2K might bear and the potential for a major global recession, a number of people are recommending that we stock up on large quantities of food that has been specially processed and packaged for long-term storage. Many of the companies listed in the following chapter offer "complete" packages that contain a variety of foods for breakfast, lunch, and dinner. Such complete food packages cost relatively little, are often easy to prepare, and make choosing easy.

Unfortunately, most of these packages contain bulk foods that are neither of the highest quality nor the healthiest for us since they often contain lots of sugar, refined flour products, additives, rancid oils, etc. By including such items, the manufacturers reflect a major irony of North American culture, namely that we are overfed but undernourished. This is the fundamental cause of the obesity that afflicts many people. We have plenty to eat, but much of our daily food is so nutritionally unsatisfying that our bodies are constantly craving something to eat. When we take high-quality food into our bodies, our cells are satisfied nutritionally, and we lose much of the craving (and binges) that lead to obesity.

In other words, when we satisfy the deep nutritional needs at the cellular level—through consuming "live," unprocessed, and unrefined whole foods—our body will find its own natural weight, and many of the illnesses that beset us will diminish. One of my goals in writing this book is to help people go beyond just preparing for the Y2K challenge and to look upon this event as a special time to maximize their health and well-being. In doing so, they will find another of the hidden blessings Y2K might contain: As we help each other eat better, we will acquire a healthier lifestyle.

Therefore, I suggest you design a health-promoting core food package that contains a variety of quality proteins, fats, fiber, carbohydrates, vitamins, minerals, phyto-nutrients, enzymes, etc. It is important to remember that a high-quality, health-inducing diet includes a variety of food sources, including whole grains and legumes, which contain complex carbohydrates; fresh and uncooked vegetables and fruits; fiber; and healthy oils (flax, olive, some canola). Such a diet will also include only a small amount of meat and dairy products and will avoid refined white sugar, white flour products, and transfats (margarine and hydrogenated oils). You should also plan your core food package by taking into account each person's likes, dislikes, allergies, etc.

Fortunately, many of the companies that offer bulk-quantity, long-term preparedness food, carry items that comport with a plant-based, health-inducing diet. (They also frequently let you substitute healthier *à la carte* items in their complete "package" deals.)

Y2K TIP

Many of the health-conscious people who avoid white sugar, white flour products, food additives, too much salt, rancid oils, etc., often fail to take into consideration a number of other hidden factors that influence the quality of the food they eat, such as how the food was grown—that is, whether in mineral-rich soil with sufficient sunlight and water, how it was processed—meaning, whether at the right temperature and with proper cleanliness, whether it was "refined" or altered, how the food was packaged, shipped, and stored—that is, was it stored at the right temperature, without breakage, and for how long, etc. Any one of these factors can affect taste and nutritional value as well as the length of time a food item can be stored. Be sure to ask those from whom you buy your food how it was grown, shipped, and stored. If they don't know, ask them to find out.

Action Step # 4:
Procure Essential Items First

Based on your strategic Preparedness Plan, decide what you will need, and purchase the most essential items as soon as possible. Those are the products that disappear quickly when people panic. The Y2K "early-birds" have already loaded their stockpiles, and the "mid-birds" are already well into the process. As the fall of 1999 approaches, the prices of wood, sleeping bags, candles, portable toilets, and water-related supplies will most likely skyrocket. Buying now can save you a lot of money later.

Action Step # 5:
Be Sure to Have Something For Everybody

When designing a core food program be sure to have a variety of foods that take everyone's taste buds into consideration. If one person selects all the food, often it will be what he or she likes. Don't think that just because you are starving you will eat anything set in front of you. I have read that some people during World War II starved to death because they refused to eat the same thing over and over. This problem is especially important when it comes to the elderly and young children, who may not understand what is going on during the Y2K situation. Be sure to taste-test the food(s) you might have to live with for months at a time.

If you haven't already done so, experiment with a variety of herbs and spices. They add a number of diverse taste possibilities and ways to keep your taste buds entertained—and appetite fatigue at bay. (Be sure to purchase a hand-operated herb and spice grinder.) It's also a good idea to try out your new recipes on your Preparedness Group members so that they won't rebel against them later at a time when they need good nutrition the most.

Healthy breads, muffins, cookies, pancakes, and other tasty treats may be difficult to make under the hardship circumstances imposed by Y2K, but they are worth the effort. (Keeping a record in your Y2K Preparedness Journal of the recipes and cooking times created with your alternative cooking unit, such as a solar oven or a propane stove, can save you a lot of time, frustration, and precious resources later when you are under stress.) Since this manual is written from a natural health perspective, many of my suggestions might not be appealing to the taste buds of some members of your preparedness community. This issue must be discussed during your planning and purchasing strategies. However, it's also important to remember that there might not be a lot of junk food available when Y2K hits, so now is a good time to start reconditioning our taste buds to high-quality food and at the same time lose much of the excessive body fat many of us complain about.

Action Step # 6:
Seek Out Sales

As you draft your Preparedness Plan, watch out for sales. By gradually stockpiling items on sale, you will lessen the stress on your wallet. When focusing on sale items, look for quality, not just quantity. For example, *Earth's Best* (organic) baby food has a fairly long shelf life, is nutritious, and makes a great-tasting dessert for both kids and adults. Keep an ample supply of your favorite nutritional supplements on hand. In addition to vitamins, minerals, herbs, and anti-oxidants, you might want to consider some of the "super-health builders" mentioned in Chapter Six.

Many people will overlook adequate toilet and waste-disposal backup plans. (See Chapter Ten for some innovative ideas on that subject.) If you stock up on diapers, be sure to take into consideration how big your baby might grow during the Y2K transition. If you are taking care of the incontinent elderly, you should also acquire an adequate supply of *Depends* or other adult diaper products. Even if you don't have infants and young children it might be a good idea to stock up on baby wipes for personal hygiene reasons.

Action Step # 7:
Stock up On The Little Things That Make Life Pleasant

We all have our favorites of those small items that make life enjoyable. For me, this means using a natural bristle skin brush to invigorate circulation and remove dead skin cells, natural toothpaste (*Weleda* is a good brand), dental floss, natural shampoo and conditioners (the *Aubrey* brand is health-promoting), raw almonds and cashews, herbal teas, etc. (Be aware that the word "natural" on a product isn't always what it might seem. Many marketing and advertising gurus, seeking to capture a share of the booming health product market, affix this term to products that have nothing natural about them and which in fact be very unnatural and harmful to your body. It is important to read ingredient labels closely and not pay too much attention to marketing buzzwords on a label.)

The little extras that make life pleasant will vary according to preference. The important thing is to ask each group member what treats and special foods they like and stock up on them. This is especially important for children, who will need lots of small (non-sugar-based) treasures, presents, and rewards to keep up their morale.

Action Step # 8:
Learn How to Store Your Food Properly

The shelf life, or length of time that a food item maintains its freshness and nutritional quality, is relative. The best quality freeze-dried or dehydrated food that is vacuum-sealed and nitrogen-packed in the best enamel-lined stainless steel containers for long-term storage will remain fresh and nutritious only under certain conditions. You must protect your stored food against high temperature, moisture, oxygen, light, and pests if you expect it to maintain its nutritional value and taste. Proper long-term food storage is a complicated subject, and that is why many experts recommend buying products that are packaged professionally by reputable companies.

Those interested in packing their own shelf-stable goods should consult Alan T. Hagan's "Prudent Food Storage FAQ [frequently asked questions]" Web site, <http://www.efn.org/~kathyy/foodfaq.300>. This site also has an extensive list of Y2K-related products and distributors. Hagan goes into elaborate detail on how to store grains, legumes, fats and oils, etc. The *Utah State University Extension Program* also offers an informative Web site dedicated to food storage issues and nutrition and cooking information (<http://ext.usu.edu/publica/foodpubs.htm>, e-mail <donnaf@ext.usu.edu>).

Y2K TIP

There are many vendors who supply long-term food storage equipment, including South Summit, <http://www. southsummit.com/>, which stocks five-gallon (about 19 liters) plastic containers and the easy-open-easy-close Gamma Seal lids for keeping grains and legumes. Epicenter, <http://www. theepicenter. com>, carries six-gallon (about 23 liters) plastic pails that come with a Ratchet lock lid with a built-in O-Ring Seal that makes the pails both child-proof and easy to open. Y2K Grub, <http://www.y2kgrub.com/>, and GlitchProof.com, <http://www.glitchproof.com/glitch-proof/bulfoodstork.html>sell a variety of supplies for creating your own long-term storage "super pails," including Mylar bags, oxygen absorbers, and five-gallon plastic buckets.

In short, food items should be kept in tightly sealed, waterproof, food-grade plastic, glass, or metal containers that are stored in a dry, cool, and dark place. (If you use metal containers, be sure they are enamel-lined so that metals such as aluminum won't leach into the food, or if you use plastic containers, make sure they are made from non-permeable plastic so that odors and flavors will not leach into the plastic and make them unusable for future use. *Life Sprouts,* telephone 800-241-1516, carries a line of reusable non-permeable plastic containers in pint [470 milliliters], quart [940 milliliters], and gallon [3.78 liters] sizes.)

In order to ensure prolonged shelf life and to protect against spoilage, nutritional loss, bugs, and microorganisms, many people prefer to buy professionally packaged bulk, freeze-dried, and dehydrated foods packed in either "super pails" (five-gallon [19 liters], Mylar-lined, sealed plastic containers) or enamel-coated metallic cans. Both methods have either oxygen absorber packets or nitrogen added to the container to remove over 99% of the oxygen and thereby extend shelf life. "Super pails," commonly used for bulk food items, normally hold six gallons [about 23 liters] of contents and weigh from 30 to 45 pounds (about 13.5 to 20.5 kilograms), depending on the content—for example, lentils, brown rice, soybeans, etc. Quality canneries use enamel-lined metallic cans for their dehydrated, freeze-dried foods as well as for "wet" pack food items such as corn, cabbage, soups, etc. Most cans come in two sizes, #2.5 and #10 (approximately one-quart [940 milliliters] and one-gallon [3.78 liters] sizes, respectively). The advantage of these long-term survival containers is that they store and stack easily, and if stored properly, they have a long shelf life (five to ten years on average).

Action Step # 9:
Draft a Meal Plan Based upon Your Y2K Food Storage Items

It is important that you draft a meal rotation plan based upon your food reserves. This action step offers several advantages. First, it avoids appetite fatigue by ensuring that you will not eat the same foods over and over. Second, it helps give your digestive system, liver, and pancreas a break from using the same enzymes repetitively to digest the same food. According to some nutritional experts, food rotation can help cut down on allergic reactions. A detailed meal plan will also help ensure that you have all the essential items in place, as well as the herbs, spices, condiments, and other taste enhancers you will need to make eating during Y2K an adventure and not a chore. It would also be wise to consult recipe books listed in Chapter Three and the Appendix to ensure good nutritional variety and taste. It is the little things such as these that will make life less stressful during the Y2K transition.

Action Step # 10:
Have Something Extra to Share with Others

As we stock up on food items for Y2K, it is important to think beyond the needs of our immediate Preparedness Group. As discussed earlier, a number of people will be totally unprepared for the magnitude of the impending Y2K events. In addition to the pleasure that comes from giving, and the

---

moral obligation we might feel to help others, having extra goods such as food and water to share (or sell at a fair price) will help reduce the civil stress that results inevitably when there is a shortage of such essential items. As a word of warning, I strongly suggest you not try to exploit the situation and charge (gouge) high prices for things; doing so will only create resentment and potential problems. Having extra food items will also be a good form of barter to help you obtain other items you might need or desire.

Action Step # 11:
Have Plenty of Good Water

Without enough water, we languish and die. Most of us could survive a week or more without food, but many of us would die or suffer irremediable damage to the brain and body if we had to go that long without water or liquids. (See F. Batmanghelidg's *Your Body's Many Cries for Water,* telephone 800-759-3999, for insights into why we need water and the health problems that result when we do not get enough of it.)

Fortunately, Y2K will strike in the winter when our body does not sweat as much. This is a time, too, for snow and rain—possible sources of water, but we cannot rely upon precipitation for our water. Consequently, it is important that we have a backup supply of pure water and a means to replenish it as we use it up. Even if the public water supply continues to flow, there is no guarantee that the computers that run the chlorination process will be functioning and giving us potable or safe drinking water.

We can only store so much water and, as we will see in Chapter Nine, the use of iodine and chlorination tablets is not particularly healthy, especially for children and the elderly. Therefore, I strongly urge you to get a hand-activated (pump-style) water filter or a multi-purpose water purifier that kills harmful microorganisms as well as removes harmful chemicals and heavy metals (see Chapter Nine). Such a filter will help ensure that your Preparedness Group gets an amply supply of non-health-threatening water. Be sure to practice using the filter before Y2K hits.

Action Step # 12:
Have a Backup Plan for Keeping Warm

January for most of us is not climate-friendly. Therefore, it is wise to have a safe, reliable way to heat your home in the event the power grid goes down. Chapter Seven looks at alternative ways of heating your house and keeping warm.

In addition, you should have several pairs of good-quality thermal underwear—tops, bottoms, socks, hats, and maybe face-wear—for each member of your Preparedness Group. By "good quality," I mean material that has both a high thermal capacity and a good wicking (the ability to keep you dry) capacity—sweat is an enemy of maintaining a safe and comfortable body temperature in a cold environment.

A good sleeping bag rated for your area, that is, a sleeping bag rated for comfort in temperatures of 20°F (minus 7°C), 0°F (minus 18° C), or minus 10°F (minus 23° C) is also a must. Visit your local camping goods and outdoors specialty store. The employees there will have lots of suggestions appropriate to your local climate. I advise doing this before too late in the fall of 1999, when the stampede might start. Remember, now is not the time to skimp on quality. For me it's worth spending an extra few dollars to avoid spending my nights shivering in bed.

Action Step # 13:
Have a Backup Toilet

According to some public health officials, it is the implementation of public sanitation systems and personal hygiene habits and the resulting reduction in deadly diseases, that has been a prime factor in the increased longevity of the citizens of Western countries. If the municipal water and waste disposal systems fail, you will need an alternative way to dispose of your human and nonhuman waste. In addition to stocking up on dry soap, garbage bags, toilet paper, and disinfectant solutions, you should consider a backup toilet. Chapter Ten offers some innovative and environmentally friendly solutions to these problems.

> ## Y 2 K   T I P
> There are a number of products on the market for "dry" cleansing of hands, such as Purell's Instant Hand Sanitizer and other products made by Fresh Cleanse™, <http://www.freshcleanse.com/>, that break down the cell walls of microorganisms to "safely and effectively remove bacteria, fungi, yeast, and viruses from the skin." Items such as Fresh Cleanse™ Hand Sanitizer and Towelettes can help maintain health if daily hygiene practices are disrupted. They also cut down on the use of water. At the same time it must be noted that many of us over-wash our skin with harsh soaps that remove many of the natural acids that provide a protective barrier on our skin. Wolfsong Herbs, e-mail <wolfsongherbs@mindspring.com>, carries an excellent line of gentle but effective organic and wild-crafted herbal-based antibacterial soaps, shampoo, and body washes. Each item is handcrafted in small batches to ensure quality

and potency. Dr. Bonner's liquid soaps (available at your local health food store) are another skin-healthy alternative to many of the harsh soaps that dominate the commercial marketplace. Earthshirtz, <http://www.earthshirtz.com/>, carries the natural-fiber Earth Cloth (about $3.50) that functions like paper towels for "soaking up spills, scrubbing floors, washing cars, dusting, washing dishes . . . even wiping up a sticky child," with the added benefit that it can be used over and over without waste buildup.

Action Step # 14:
Make Sure Your Medical Needs Will Be Met

Many people are concerned that access to hospitals and adequate health care could be a problem during Y2K since they are deeply dependent upon computers—everything from making appointments to the latest laser surgery. It is wise therefore to make contingency medical plans.

For some people, especially those on dialysis, respirators, etc., it is vital to consult with their physician or health care provider to make alternative arrangements for their health needs. It is also important to remember that many prescription drugs have a very short shelf life, and that doctors often will not write multiple prescriptions, so you might ask your physician what alternatives will be available in the event pharmacies are closed down. If your doctor answers, "You don't have anything to worry about," in regard to Y2K, ask her how much research she has done on the issue. In most cases it will be very little, if any, and you should press her for effective alternatives and contingency plans in case you can't get to a hospital or a pharmacy.

See Chapter Six for nonprescription herbal and nutritional alternatives you might consider, such as St. Johns Wort *(Hypericum Perforatum)*, Kava Kava *(Piper methysticum)*, or 5-HTP *(5-Hydroxy-L-tryptophan)*. Double-blind studies have shown that these over-the-counter-supplements are effective in controlling depression and anxiety.

Y2K TIP
If you have a pacemaker or some other type of electrically or microchip-operated medical device, be sure to ask your health care practitioner if it is Y2K compliant or needs to be "debugged."

Action Step # 15:
Replenish Your Herbal (and Conventional) Medicine Chest

I am an advocate of nature-based preventative medicine and therefore will make sure I acquire a variety of tinctures and medicinal teas to prevent and handle potential health problems. For people who have become dependent upon conventional medicine, this may be a radical and frightening thought. For me, not being able to do anything to help a loved one in the event of a medical emergency is the truly frightening thought. (This is why many Y2K watchers recommend that someone in your Preparedness Group obtain training in first-aid or take an emergency medical course.)

By now some readers might be feeling overwhelmed, thinking, "Not only do I have to become a food expert but a doctor too!" This concern is understandable. However, it is important to recall, as Robert Pelton, author of *The Official Medicinal Plant Survival Manual* (available from *Bruce Hopkins,* telephone 972-288-0262), reminds us, that "over 80% of the world's population (still) depends upon the use of medicinal plants for medicine, and that up until the last century most people had always depended upon self-care as the primary form of medical treatment." In citing this quotation, I am not advocating that we must take on amateur medical practice or that we must (or even can) become experts at self-diagnosis and self-cure. My suggestion is that it might be wise to investigate Pelton's insight and learn some folk-based remedies such as *Echinacea angustifolia* root for the immune system, dandelion *(Taraxacum officinale)* and milk thistle *(Silybum marianum)* for liver maintenance and repair, willow bark *(Salix alba)* and wild lettuce *(Lactuca canadensis)* for pain relief, etc. (There are a number of Web sites dedicated to herbal therapy and alternative health education, such as *Medicinal Herbs Online,* <http://www.egregore.com/herb/herbhome.htm>, and *The Natural Health and Longevity Resource Center,* <http://www.all-natural.com/>. Also see Chapter Six for more information about herbal remedies.)

> **Y2K TIP**
>
> It is important to test any new medicinal agent to make sure people in your Preparedness Group are not allergic to it. Allergies are often multi-factorial, meaning that they entail a number of co-factors. For instance, you might not be aware that you are mildly allergic to milk or wheat products, but under a stressful situation you might suffer a greater reaction and suddenly realize you have an allergy. People with allergic sensitivities should test products before they stockpile them. You also need to investigate any potential drug interactions and contraindications that may be

involved in the use of medications. Before taking any new medication, it's important to check with your qualified health care practitioner first. This is especially important for pregnant women or those who are breast-feeding.

Finally, it is important to remember that according to some natural health researchers, many health problems are the end products of a number of factors such as poor diet and improper lifestyle and thought habits. If you are chronically ill you might want to monitor your thought-stream to see how much of your thinking is consumed with fear, anxiety, anger, hatred, envy, and hurt, all of which—according to psycho-neuroimmunologists—affect your immune system and lie at the root of many chronic diseases. For example, people suffering from liver and colon cancer might consider if they are not letting go of anger, resentment, and other "toxic" emotions. Seeking the release of those damaging emotions can be healing for both our body and our soul. (Again, Y2K can be a great stimulus and challenge to change our lives in a radical way—for good.)

Action Step # 16:
Get Medical and Dental Checkups

Knowing your current health status will help you and those in your Preparedness Group anticipate any potential medical problems and determine what you will need in your contingency medicine chest. Getting a toothache and not having access to a dentist is not a pleasant prospect. Neither is having glaucoma or high blood pressure destroy your body without your knowing it. Knowing your blood pressure and cholesterol levels and other relevant physiological data can also help you fine-tune your food supply in terms of what you should and should not eat.

It also a good idea to get the name and address of nurses, doctors, and dentists living in your neighborhood, so that if something serious does develop during the Y2K transition you can contact them (and maybe barter) for their services. If your wife or a female member of your Preparedness Group is pregnant, it might be prudent to have someone in your group receive home birth training. This used to be the only way babies were born, so it is not as frightening a prospect as it seems, especially if the expectant mother eats properly and does prebirth exercises. Both our children, Zuri and Alexi-Skye, were born through natural (drug and surgery-free) childbirth. My wife and I highly recommend the Bradley Method as an effective way to prepare for husband-coached, natural childbirth (*American Academy of Husband-Coached Childbirth®*, <http://www.bradleybirth.com/>, e-mail <marjiehathaway@bradleybirth.com>). You can also contact the *LaLeche*

League International, <http://www.lalecheleague.org>, for information about breast-feeding representatives in your area who can answer questions about concerns you might have. You should also check with your local Red Cross group for advice on what to do if there are complications during or after the birth and you can't get to a doctor or hospital. It is also a good idea to locate a midwife in your area.

Y2K TIP

Those who are expecting a birth (or some other significant circumstance that will require immediate communication) and want to be sure of making contact if the telecommunications system crashes in your area, should consider purchasing citizen's band (CB) radios. See Michael Hyatt's article on CB communication during Y2K ("What kind of alternative system can I set up for two-way communication?" <http://www.y2kprep.com/askmichael/007.htm>).

While you are planning for the issue of birth, it might also be a good idea to prepare for death, especially if there are elderly or permanently infirm members of your group. What will you do if some one dies and there is no way to get to a cemetery or funeral home? Maybe you need to buy a body bag. (If this question seems strange or frightening, such a response illustrates how far removed from the natural rhythms and cycles of life our culture has become.)

Action Step # 17:
Whenever Possible Avoid Toxins

This point might also sound strange to many readers because most people do not realize the overwhelming quantity of toxins and health-destroying substances in our food, water, air, and work and home environments. The number of synthetic additives, coloring agents, artificial flavors and taste-enhancers, emulsifiers, and preservatives in food alone adds great stress to our immune and digestive systems. Unfortunately, many people (including public officials) think that just because an isolated chemical such as a pesticide or a food additive has been ruled to be safe, it really is safe. But they overlook the fact that such products have not been tested for the way they interact with other chemicals. The power of chemical combination—that is, the likelihood that toxicity increases as chemicals interact with one another—is easier to understand when we think of the complex side effects that using multiple prescription drugs often causes.

However, what is often overlooked is the influence of the numerous additives in foods and the large number of chemicals we are exposed to in our everyday life—items such as deodorizers, perfumes, shampoo, smog, cleaning compounds, etc. Many contemporary health researchers think exposure to such substances is one of the contributing factors to the overwhelming number of allergies and autoimmune diseases afflicting Western society.

Health will be a vital priority in the coming days ahead. To maintain good health, we need properly functioning immune and elimination systems (colon, liver, kidney, skin). It is therefore important that we put as little stress as possible on our immune system. One of the best ways to do this is to keep toxic antigens and invaders out of our body by avoiding contact with them. This is why I emphasize eating pure, unadulterated, and unprocessed foods, not using harmful cleaners, and purchasing only health-promoting and environmentally friendly products.

If, as many predict, the food industry is deeply affected during Y2K, a lot of people might go through junk food withdrawal, that is, the headaches, moodiness, and fatigue that come when we do not have our chocolate, coffee, cola, potato chips, and our "sugar fix." Many people might discover they are allergic to the things they crave most, such as ice cream or bread (discovering hidden food allergies is another of the beneficial ironies that Y2K might offer).

My emphasis on avoiding toxicity is also why I suggest in Chapter Seven that you look at sustainable forms of power generation. Solar and wind power are far more ecologically and personally beneficial than the noise and air pollution created by gasoline and diesel generators—the first choice among those who look for emergency heat alternatives. This suggestion might also seem radical and impractical to some, but I ask you to consider that many people, without knowing it, are very sensitive to gasoline and auto exhaust fumes. In my own experience, after I went on a full body-cleansing program—colon, liver, gall bladder, urinary tract, skin, lymphatic system, etc.—something I highly recommend you talk to your natural health care practitioner about—I discovered how automobile exhaust fumes and the "off-gassing" from paint and certain plastic products have a negative affect on my body. Without realizing it, many of us might be suffering from multiple chemical sensitivity (MCS)—a set of symptoms that often manifest themselves in a variety of ways, including chronic fatigue, auto-immune disease, multiple allergies, etc. (See the *Occupational Safety and Health Administration, Department of Labor [OSHA]* Web page, <http://www.osha-slc.gov/SLTC/multiplechemicalsensitivities/>, dedicated to MCS, and the *Fishwood Environmental Home Page* Web page, <http://members.aol.com/organ1c/EnvIll_MCS.htm>, for more information on this topic.)

I use the qualifying phrase "whenever possible" in the heading above in recognition that during emergency situations it may not always be possible to get the optimal product. Therefore, throughout this book I offer a number of items and ideas to help reduce toxic stress on the body. As we become more caring in our shopping habits and choose products that are beneficial to our personal health and environmental well-being, we will influence manufacturers to take a more proactive role in creating a healthy and happy world. Shop wisely.

Action Step # 18:
Work on Controlling Fear

Because of the numerous uncertainties associated with Y2K, a wave of fear and panic could ripple through many communities as January 1, 2000 approaches. It is important to understand that the more we lose control over a situation, the more fear gets magnified. Given that Y2K entails a broad spectrum of complex events, many people are going to feel deeply out of control as systems begin to fail and normal needs are not met. The more we prepare for these Y2K possibilities, the less panic we will experience.

Therefore it is important to determine what issues will generate the most concern for us. Living in the Northeast, after having lived in California and Virginia, my great concern is keeping my family warm if the power grid fails. Therefore, backup and alternative forms of heating will be high on my list of items as we prepare for Y2K. For others, the most important issues might be food, medical care, or personal security if civil disorder erupts.

Whatever our concern, we need to focus on maintaining emotional stability and security in our lives. Therefore, I suggest that you draw up a list of "fear killers"—those items, backup plans, and methods that will help us maintain control over the health and well-being of our loved ones and ourselves. Keep it simple. Once you have taken care of the essentials of food, water, heating, medical and personal safety concerns, dig deeper and ask each of your Preparedness Group members what they need to lighten fear and anxiety in their lives. Doing this will go a long way toward lessening the trauma many people might experience as Y2K strikes.

Another way to reduce fear is to make sure everyone in your community is prepared for what might come. This will help prevent people from panicking and turning on one another. Because we live in an age of specialization, the larger we expand our circle of contacts, the better we can cope with what will happen. As we find out who is a plumber, nurse, doctor, carpenter, electrician, firefighter, baker, auto mechanic, police officer, etc., in our neighborhood, and work out a system so that various needs and emergencies can be met by one another, we can cut down greatly on the number of unexpected events (and panic) that might arise from Y2K.

Now is also the time for communities, churches, and synagogues to begin working together to make sure the needs of the poor, infirm, elderly, and widowed will be met. Neighborhoods need to form Y2K watch groups and contact the local Red Cross or other emergency preparedness experts to learn ways to cope with the major problems that might arise. By taking the time to organize both our individual and collective lives we will go a long way toward preventing fear from causing undue stress and harm.

Action Step # 19:
Seek Out Peace

No matter how much we are prepared externally and physically for Y2K, we will not find peace unless it comes from within. For many people this will entail a return to religious roots and to a humbling awareness that we are not the masters of our fate. Many people find prayer—both individual and communal—to be helpful.

It is also important to reconcile emotionally with those with whom we have not been getting along, especially if they are in our Preparedness Group, whether they are family members, neighbors, or nearby friends. We conserve a lot of energy when we don't waste it on negative and counter-productive emotions.

Another important guiding principle is to learn to live with silence. The loss of the electrical world around us can, in some ways, be looked upon as a blessing to help recover the understanding of our need for silence, and to steer us toward the deeper things we forget when the world is abuzz around us. To reclaim this virtue can have a lasting impact on our soul.

Action Step # 20:
Find Tension- and Stress-Relievers

For many people it is hard to imagine what life would be like without radio, computer games, television, newspapers, magazines, movies, bowling, and other recreational diversions. It is important for us to find alternative ways to keep ourselves entertained and busy, to help alleviate the tension that having too much free time can generate.

If you don't have a hand-hobby, take one up. By "hand-hobby" I mean something that you can do or make that does not take a lot of mental energy— such as crafts, crocheting, drawing, wood carving, sewing, knitting, etc. The idea is to give your mind a release from everyday stress, tension, and worry— something that will mount in the days ahead. However, you must not be a perfectionist about your Y2K hobby or handcraft. You don't need the extra tension of being performance-driven. Because of the potential for power outages, it is important that such hand-hobbies not depend upon electricity.

It is also important to remember that games, craft projects, and tension relievers will be very important for the children in your Preparedness Group.

For those into alternative health therapies, now may be a good time to stock up on essential oils for aromatherapy, as well as homeopathic and *Bach Flower* remedies designed to relieve stress and tension. You might also buy feathers to give soothing and relaxing "feather massages"—a fun way to calm down children at night. The important thing is to be creative in your Y2K preparation. Cultivate a sense of mission and excitement.

Action Step # 21:
Learn to Sing, Play, and Have Fun the Old-Fashioned Way

As mentioned above, many people today do not know how to entertain themselves without the use of electronic devices. (Some theorists suspect the high incidence of ADD—attention deficit disorder—and hyperactivity are in some way connected to the rampant growth of electronic sensory stimulation that fills our environment.) Group singing, theatrical skits, and "parlor" games are also a good way to take people's minds off a stressful situation. They also help time pass more quickly, especially for children.

Playing group and family games also fosters interpersonal bonds, something sadly lacking in many of our lives. (Again, Y2K can be a blessing as we re-foster family bonds and learn new ways to live and relate without the ubiquitous electronic diversions of radio, television, and computers.) Scout out local garage sales and stock up on a variety of low-tech items such as playing cards, board games, and trivia quizzes. Battery-operated chess and checker games can also be helpful for those who prefer some quiet intellectual stimulation.

Action Step # 22:
Stock up on Good Books to Read

Just as playing games and spending fun times with others will be essential to making it through Y2K, so too will be having some quiet time for yourself. Books can be very helpful this way. Y2K might offer the opportunity to catch up on all that reading you have put off for so long.

Its important to get a variety of books—light, heavy, and humorous books, as well as mysteries, spiritual and self-help books, books of poetry, great literature, etc. Having a variety of reading materials will ensure that you have something to fit the different moods you will go through during Y2K, as well as meeting the varied interests of your Preparedness Group members.

Action Step # 23:
Prepare for Home-Schooling

If you have children, you might have to take over the their education if the serious effects of the Y2K transition last a few weeks or more in your area. If you anticipate this possibility, I suggest you get a copy of the *Charlotte Mason Companion: Personal Reflections on the Gentle Art of Learning* by Karen Andreola (available from *Amazon.com,* <http://www.amazon.com>, or your local book shop can order it). The book is based upon the learning method of nineteenth-century English educational pioneer Charlotte Mason, who weaves a seamless approach to kindling the fire of children's imaginations and helping them appreciate fine literature, music, nature, and the extraordinary wonder of life. She also offers many useful suggestions for things to do with children, such as using read-aloud books and creating their own nature study handbooks—both of which help children develop their observational and expressive skills.

Keeping children happy and occupied will be an important task, given the season when the Y2K challenge will hit. Many people have also found that *The Successful Homeschool Family Handbook: A Creative and Stress-Free Approach to Homeschooling* by Raymond and Dorothy Moore offers an "easy-to-live-with family adventure in learning" that makes learning at home enjoyable. (This book is also available from *Amazon.com,* <http://www.amazon.com>.)

Action Step # 24:
Form a Buddy System

It is important that everyone in your Preparedness Group be assigned someone they will look out for and—if possible—who will look out for them. It is especially important that young children or the elderly, handicapped, or infirm have a "Y2K buddy" to ensure maximum safety. This system can be as simple as one parent being responsible for one child, or older children looking out for younger children, or grandparents watching after grandchildren, etc. (In the event of electrical power loss it is important that children stay together so that no one gets lost, hurt, or traumatized in the dark.) Y2K might bring back the concept of the extended family as relatives decide it is best to join together and help one another through the uncertain times ahead.

Don't underestimate the maturing power of a crisis. For some people, a crisis will call forth responsibility and leadership qualities that many people do not realize they have. Looking upon this period as a time of personal growth will make the Y2K experience a lot richer.

Y2K TIP

It is also vital that you prepare your children emotionally (and spiritually) so that they will not be traumatized by what might happen. I was talking about Y2K with some young children, ages ten to thirteen, and one ten-year-old girl began to cry with fear. This was a vivid reminder that I have to tailor my message to each audience in a way that will not induce fear, or a feeling of being so overwhelmed that people become paralyzed, panicked, or apathetic.

Action Step # 25:
Practice "Just-In-Case" Games

Getting your whole Y2K Preparedness Group to understand and accept the challenges that lie ahead can be difficult. This is especially true of young children and the elderly. Making preparedness drills into a game is one way to get people moving and thinking creatively. Design "just-in-case" games that take in a wide variety of the problems you anticipate. In other words, ask your children, "Just in case there is no food at the grocery store, what will we eat?" Or, "Just in case we lose electricity during the 'Y2K time,' how will we cook our food?" Then let the children come up with solutions as you guide them to understand that they might not be able to have what they are normally used to eating.

By playing drill games and coming up with solutions, children (and the elderly) will better accept the real challenges when they occur. It will also help them, and teenagers as well, to begin to adjust psychologically to the possibility of a world without TVs, VCRs, and microwave popcorn, and make it easier to accept what might follow.

It is important not to hide from children the potential realities that lie ahead. They are much more intelligent, sensitive, and intuitive than we often give them credit for, and if they are not prepared properly, their fears will magnify under stressful circumstances.

Action Step # 26:
Learn Backyard Survival Skills

Because of the possibility of long-term infrastructure disruptions, some Y2K watchers encourage people to acquire the skills and equipment to grow their own food. Even if you live in the city or suburbs, you will be surprised at how much can be grown on a small plot of land. If you don't have any growing space, you might consider a hydroponic garden as discussed in Chapter Four, or make arrangements with people who have growing space to let you grow a garden on their land in exchange for some of the food you raise.

It doesn't take much to start a small garden—a pitchfork, a hoe, a shovel, gloves, a hose, some heirloom or non-hybrid seeds, a watering can, and some organic fertilizer. Given the toxic nature of pesticides, you should purchase an organic gardening book and start a compost heap by recycling grass clippings, leaves, etc.—be sure to turn your heap every few days. *Backyard Composting: Your Complete Guide to Recycling Yard Clippings* by John Roulac can help you along these lines. (Even if you are not into organic gardening you might have to learn this skill if the pesticide manufacturers cannot make or ship their chemicals. *Planet Natural,* <http://www.planetnatural. com/>, e-mail <ecostore@mcn.net>, offers products and information for those looking for alternatives to harsh and dangerous chemical gardening. *The Organic Gardener's Home Reference: A Plant-By-Plant Guide to Growing Fresh, Healthy Food* by Tanya Denckla—available through *Amazon.com,* <http://www.amazon.com>—offers lots of helpful garden-growing advice.) Even if things don't get too bad, you can always grow a post-Y2K spring garden in celebration of the gift of life, and eat fresh vegetables as they were meant to be. Gardening is also refreshingly therapeutic.

Even if you can't grow a garden, don't lose hope. Most people have no idea their neighborhood, backyard, or surrounding area could provide a source of life-sustaining nutrition. Many common plants we call weeds, such as dandelions, provide a storehouse of vital nutrients (that is, unless the grass and surrounding vegetation have been contaminated with pesticides and herbicides).

For some people, harvesting wild edible foods might become the only way to obtain fresh (and tasty) herbs, fruits, and vegetables during the winter and spring of the Year 2000. (I have found the green shoots of evergreen trees to be especially good tasting and nutritious.) "Wildman" Steve Brill's *Identifying and Harvesting Edible and Medicinal Plants in Wild (and Not So Wild) Places* offers loads of practical insight into plant foraging skills. In addition to showing the "gourmet" possibilities of eating nutritious wild foods, Steve conducts nature tours in New York's Central Park as proof that even urban folk can employ this technique. Many wild plants can be marinated for long-term storage, such as young fiddleheads soaked in extra-virgin olive oil. Marinating extends a plant's shelf life and can help add "fresh" green food to your long-term preparedness menu. Most wild foods books will offer easy recipes to try.

Those interested in this potentially life-saving and/or inexpensive and nutritious way to supplement their diet should consult other like-minded books such as *Cooking from the Gourmet's Garden: Edible Ornamentals, Herbs, and Flowers* by Coralie Castle and Robert Kourik, Cole: 1998; *Acorn Pancakes, Dandelion Salad and Other Wild Dishes* by Jean Craighead George, Harpercollins: 1995; or *Edible and Useful Wild Plants of the United States and Canada* by Charles Francis Saunders, Dover: 1976.

Action Step # 27:
Have Manual Backups for All Essential Items

In the event that the power grid fails during Y2K, it will be important to have items that do not require electricity to operate, such as radios, flashlights, candles, hand-operated mills for grinding flour and grains, an alternative heating source, etc. In addition, whenever possible, have duplicates of those things liable to break or malfunction. If you buy a hand-cranked battery-less flashlight (see Chapter Eight) so that you do not have to depend upon batteries, then either get a second one or have a conventional flashlight or two (and batteries) for backup. The point is that the enormous stress and unusual circumstances Y2K might generate will mean things will get misplaced and accidents (breakage) will happen.

It is better to have more candles than fewer. How many you need depends upon how many powerless winter nights you anticipate. A minimum of enough supplies for two to three months for each person in your Preparedness Group would be a wise investment. Chapters Four through Eleven list an array of nifty devices that should serve you well.

> ## Y2K TIP
>
> Many people do not realize that many household items such as their personal computer, their VCR, their fax machine, or their car might be susceptible to the millennium "bug." Consult with the manufacturer or the sales person who sold you a product to make sure Y2K-related malfunctions will be covered under the product's warranty. Getting a guarantee in writing will expedite repairs later.

Action Step # 28:
Prepare for a New Type of Economy

Some Y2K observers predict there will be a run on banks, and that many people will not receive their welfare, social security, or pension plan payments during the first days of Y2K. There is also the strong possibility that numerous small- and medium-sized businesses that have not prepared for the Y2K crisis will not be able to function or will go bankrupt, creating a shortage of numerous consumer goods. Added to these problems is the economic havoc Y2K will generate in the global markets, and its effect on international trade that could result in massive layoffs as companies lose buyers for the goods they produce. These scenarios might seem extreme, but having some non-cash items to trade and barter might come in handy. In light of these possibilities, some Y2K analysts have made the following suggestions:

T I P S for Dealing with the New Y2K Economy

- Get some silver U.S. coins—dimes, quarters, and half-dollars minted before 1965. They contain pure silver and have "melt" value tied to the price of silver, which could rise significantly during Y2K.

- Have some gold on hand. Many Y2K financial experts recommend purchasing small fractional gold coins such as one-tenth and one-quarter ounce, since the price of gold might skyrocket and a tenth of an ounce could be worth more than $100.

- Even if the Y2K fiscal nightmare does not materialize, it would still be prudent to have lots of cash in small denominations— ones, fives, tens, and twenties (or the appropriate coins and banknotes in Canada), especially if the credit card and electronic banking system fails during Y2K. Begin saving those coins and banknotes now. The fractional reserve banking system has less than ten percent cash on hand at any moment, and a bank run during the autumn of 1999 could mean you will not be able to get cash when you need it. (However, you need to be careful about storing too many valuables in your home so that you will not be the target of a robbery—see the "Self-Defense" and "Cache" sections at the end of this Chapter.)

- Have things to barter. Remember, you can't eat credit cards, paper money, gold, silver, or cash. Many people will be unprepared for Y2K and will want and need food, water, wood, lighters, etc. Many survival experts advise stocking up on extra sugar, salt, cigarettes, liquor, and ammunition for barter. I find many of these products to be destructive to good health, so I prefer items that will help rather than hinder people's well-being, such as organic grains, canned goods, olive oil, butane lighters, candles, and can openers. It is also important that you stock up on items that you like and will use later, in case you have them left over.

- It might also be wise to move your stocks and bonds, especially your retirement funds and annuities, over to government-backed and guaranteed equities, in case the financial markets take the huge hit many predict. This is especially likely given the interconnectedness of the global economy and the way that most nations are far behind the U.S. and Canada in preparing for this challenge.

Action Step # 29:
Prepare for Safety Concerns

Alarmists predict that Y2K will generate civil unrest and even result in martial law. They forecast that marauders will take to the streets, looting, stealing, and assaulting innocent citizens. Although many survival experts recommend arming ourselves with lethal weapons, I do not think such measures are practical for most people. (Guns often create their own negative synergy and influence the untrained to use them when other approaches are more viable. In addition to guns creating a child-safety concern, most people are not good shots, and stray bullets can be lethal for innocent bystanders.) I offer the following suggestions as an alternative to the harm and chaos untrained gun users could cause:

Non-Violent Ways to Deal with Social Unrest

- Issues of self-defense and ultimate survival are risky and complicated. Rather than relying on guns and aggression, it is important that neighborhoods work together to ensure that local police and civil authorities are abreast of the situation and have vigorous plans in place to prevent the looting and civil unrest that some predict will follow the collapse of the infrastructure during the times ahead.

- It is important to pray and do what we can to ensure that social anarchy will not result. The *Cassandra Project* offers good advice for individuals and communities who feel a need for protection, and suggests solutions to potential Y2K problems.

- Those in populated areas might consider moving temporarily to a less populated area. If this is not possible, it might mean stocking up on pepper spray, guard dogs, stun guns, or other nonlethal measures of active defense. If you do get a guard dog or have a pet, don't forget to stock up on pet food, especially if you have an exotic pet that eats obscure or hard-to-find items such as meal worms or special seeds. (*The Survival Center,* <http://www.zyz. com/survivalcenter/>, e-mail <sales@survivalcenter.com>, carries nitrogen-packed dog food for long-term storage.) Remember too that some self-defense items such as stun guns and pepper spray are outlawed in some communities. Check with your local law-enforcement agency for suggestions on the best legal forms of self-defense for your area.

- If you want to seriously protect your food or valuables then you might want to consider caching. Caching entails hiding a "stash" of goods such as gold or food somewhere in a place that only you know about. If you cache goods underground it is important that they be kept clean and dry. Many people use garbage bags and sturdy waterproof plastic barrels to protect what they bury in the ground. Since moisture is your chief enemy, it is important to put in some type of desiccant (water-absorbing) material to keep your things dry. It is also important to consider where you will hide your stored goods and how you will get them without being seen. I suggest you search the World Wide Web or your local library under the term "cache" for more detailed explanations of how to do this.

Final Action Step:
Develop a Smart Y2K Purchasing Plan

By now you have discovered how expensive and time-intensive Y2K preparations will be. Couple this with all the planning that you have done (or will do after going through these chapters again) and you might be feeling exhausted physically and broke financially. If this is true, then I say, congratulations. You are on the road to taking the Y2K issue with the seriousness it deserves. Unfortunately, most people will not prepare properly and might pay a far higher price than the extra fatigue and stress you will experience in your body and in your bank account.

My goal in this chapter and in the remainder of this book is to get you to consider not only what you will need to be ready for Y2K, but also what will serve you well later. In other words, the planning and purchasing I recommend becomes a form of what one Y2K pundit calls "insurance you can eat." If you make your Y2K Preparedness Plan carefully, shop wisely, and think with the long-term picture in mind, everything you purchase can and should be something you can, and will, eventually use later.

For most of us, Y2K will stretch our budgets to the maximum. Depending on how seriously we view the situation, we might have to raid our savings account or pension plan to prepare properly. But we might very well get a lot of this money back on the other end. That is, if the global economy takes a major Y2K hit, the prices of food, energy, clothing, and major appliances will skyrocket. Purchasing these items now, while prices are low, can result in savings later. Even if prices do not shoot up we can still use these items later, and the discipline we will have learned in our Y2K preparation will enable us to save a lot of money in the future.

My point is that you (and your Preparedness Group members) need to think carefully about your current and potential Y2K situation and budget accordingly. As you read through the products listed in the following chapters, think in terms of both immediate and long-term budget goals. For example, for some people, remodeling or winterizing their summer cottage into a Y2K getaway house (which you can always sell later and recoup your costs) might be the better way to go. Others might be so strapped financially that all they can do is buy extra food, sleeping bags, and candles. Whichever way you decide, you need to develop a Y2K Purchasing Plan and think through what you can afford.

Y2K will demand sacrifices from us all. Now is the time to cut back on all expenses except those related directly to Y2K affairs. We need to think, rethink, and think again about our plan, our budget, and our commitment. Do this properly and it will put you light-years ahead of those who move blindly toward a date that will be inscribed in the history books.

General Advice To Make The Rest of This Book Easier

I offer this advice to help you steer your way through the maze of products and vendors that follow in the remaining chapters:

- As you read through the products listed below, mark the page or jot notes in your Y2K Journal of the items you will want to have on hand for Y2K.

- Y2K, like any major cultural event, attracts a wide array of followers—many of whom might be considered "kooks," "flakes" and/or political and religious extremists. I suggest you look beyond these traits, given that many of these people are sincere in their effort to help others during the uncertain days ahead.

- As Y2K mania takes over, a number of companies are taking advantage of people's preparation concerns by skimping on quality or overcharging. I urge you to shop around and ask a lot of questions before you buy. Vern and Sven Kelling at *Food Storage Solutions* offer some important advice on the type of questions you should ask before purchasing items from vendors of long-term storage food, including how old the food is, whether the manufacturer of the processed food products you are buying has an on-site FDA inspector to better ensure both the quality of the food and the way it is packaged, etc. It's worth consulting their Web page, found at <http://www. permapak.net/consumer.htm>.

- Given the number of phone calls many of the companies listed below are receiving, it is often easier to contact them by e-mail or fax. Remember, very few companies offer a back-order time of six weeks or less.

- Often a brief Internet address or a telephone number for a vendor is mentioned. Consult the listing of vendors in the Appendix for a more complete list of ways to contact them.

- Look upon this process as a time of learning and discovery. Doing so will make your Y2K preparations a lot more fun.
- I often use the discussion of a product as a guide to help you understand both the benefit of a specific item and how it fits into a larger field of important considerations. Therefore, do not skip an item just because you already have it.
- I have grouped Y2K-related items according to category—Food, Water, Shelter Needs, etc. Such broad categories mean some of the items you need might be listed under an alternative heading. This is another reason to read through each section carefully.
- Before using your credit card to order something online, be sure the order line you are using offers encryption so that no one will steal or read your information. If you are not sure a line is encrypted or secure (it will normally be so stated before you send your order) be sure to e-mail or call the company you are ordering from to make sure.

CHAPTER 3

Natural Y2K Food

• •|• • • • • • • •

*"In the house of the wise are stores of choice food and oil,
but a foolish man devours all he has."* —Proverbs 21:20

In the event of a long-term emergency you can survive only as long as your essential life-supporting items last. Given the wide array of predictions and possibilities surrounding Y2K, it might be wise to have, at minimum, three months' worth of extra food, water, candles, heating supplies, and other essential preparedness supplies stored away.

This chapter will focus on specific food-related products that many Y2K watchers recommend having. However, as mentioned previously, many of the suppliers and manufacturers of survival foods are not as sensitive to health issues as they should be. Although wherever possible I include nutritional suggestions that you will not find in most preparedness manuals, I also list items that cater to conventional taste buds, meaning food items that cater to the standard North American diet (what some health experts call "SAD" for short). I do this, knowing that some members of your preparedness group are not ready to alter their diet radically.

Important General Food Considerations

Before listing the types of foods that Y2K preparedness experts recommend and the companies that sell them, a few important points need to be addressed.

A. It is important to realize that because of the swiftly growing amount of business Y2K has generated, there is a chance that quality control might not be ideal among some of the companies and vendors specializing in long-term preparedness foods. Thus, it is important that you communicate with suppliers to ensure you are getting what you order. For example, if they say their product is organic, make sure it is certified by an independent third party such as *California Certified Organic Farmers* (CCOF) or *Quality Assurance International* (QAI), who put in writing that they have investigated the grower and that no harmful and synthetic chemicals, fertilizers, pesticides, herbicides, etc., were used in the farming process. Or if the company claims their products do not contain MSG, make sure they also do not contain other flavor enhancers such as L-Glutamic acid that have been known to cause health problems in children, or monopotassium glutamate that can cause diarrhea, nausea, or abdominal cramps. A number of people report that such food additives cause side effects such as migraine headaches, hyperactivity, and allergies. Because we all are different metabolically, we need to listen carefully to our bodies to see how they react to certain foods. For more information on the potential harmful side effects caused by food additives, see sites such as *The Food Additive* Web page at <http://www.allergy. pair.com/additives/foodad.htm>.

B.   Some of the action steps in the previous chapter mention nutritional variety and quality as key principles in designing your Y2K preparedness food program. Variety and quality do more than just prevent "appetite fatigue." They also help to ensure a proper balance of the vital nutrients you and your Preparedness Group members will need to maintain health during the Y2K challenge. Most people fail to take into consideration that there are ten different types of nutrients that are critical to our health and well-being: protein, fat, carbohydrates, vitamins, minerals, fiber, enzymes, water, and assorted co-factors and phyto-nutrients—with many of the latter still being discovered. The more we eat a variety of quality-grown, minimally processed, nutrient-rich foods, the more of these valuable sources of nourishment we obtain. I stress "quality-grown," "minimally processed," and "nutrient-rich" to draw attention to the often overlooked fact that how food items are grown, shipped, processed, and packaged greatly determines their nutritional value. As mentioned in the previous chapter, most of us consume overly processed, "denatured," nutritionally challenged foods that lead to the rampant obesity and chronic diseases that afflict our culture. Because we cannot always be sure that agricultural crops are rotated properly, that mineral rich fertilizers are used, and that foods are handled, processed, packed, and stored properly, many people take supplements to ensure that they are getting the proper nutrients they need. (See the section below on "Nutritional Supplementation" for information on how best to decide what we should buy.)

C.   The issue of nutritional bio-individuality is intimately connected to the quality, and variety of the food you eat. "Nutritional bio-individuality" is a fancy term for the different ways each of us processes metabolically the food we eat. Some of us have a fast-burning metabolism and others have a slow-burning metabolism. This means that some of us do better on a high-protein/low-carbohydrate/moderate-fat diet, while others among us feel better if we consume a diet low in protein and high in carbohydrates. Although we all have the same nutritional requirements, how we obtain them, and in what quantity, will differ. This is why trying to conform to a certain diet is difficult for most people. If the type and quantity of food the diet recommends is not right for your individual needs, then your body will crave what it is not getting. Our body has numerous ways to let us know when we are not eating properly, such as excessive gas, bloating, indigestion, fatigue, crankiness, lack of mental clarity, etc. It is important therefore that you determine the best ratio of nutrients for your body and not try to fit into some pre-established, "cookie-cutter" type of diet.

D. If you are constantly craving certain foods, this often means you are not eating a properly balanced diet and your body is demanding certain nutrients. This is why "junk" food, which is filled with empty calories that do not deliver health-promoting nutrients to our cells, leads to obesity, as our body continually demands the sustenance it desires. In other words, our lack of quality food leads to the vicious and obsessive cycle of binge eating that leaves us nutritionally unsatisfied and overweight.

E. Make sure everyone's tastes and expectations are met. Now is not the time to force a narrow diet on anyone (Y2K will do that sufficiently well). Make sure everyone in your Preparedness Group has a say in the choice of food.

F. What and how much you buy for the Y2K challenge will depend upon your specific circumstances—the number of people in your Preparedness Group, their ages (the elderly and young have special needs), climate, storage space capacity, budget, special dietary needs, allergies, etc. (I recommend an allergy test before stocking up on 100 pounds [45 kilograms] of wheat or freeze-dried milk and other common allergy-aggravating foods.)

Core foods

"Core foods" are the foundation of a long-term food supply, forming the bulk of the protein and carbohydrate sources we eat. This "core" is comprised of grains such as brown rice, rolled oats, red and white wheat, and millet;

beans such as kidney, mung, lentils, garbanzo, baby lima, and adzuki; pastas (made from whole wheat) such as spaghetti and macaroni; yellow corn; and non-gluten-containing grains such as spelt, quinoa, and hulled buckwheat. Your core food supply should also include a variety of vegetables such as broccoli, cabbage, carrots, celery, mushrooms, onions, peas, potatoes, spinach, and tomatoes, as well as vegetable soup stocks and stew blends, and dried fruit such as apples, bananas, peaches, pears, raisins, prunes, etc. Soy-based meat replacements, such as *Textured Vegetable Protein (TVP®),* may offer high quality protein and can be added to casseroles, soups, rice and bean mixes, etc. In addition, your core foods should include oils such as extra-virgin cold-pressed olive and canola oils, sweeteners, and powdered eggs and dairy products (if you use them).

There are several advantages to purchasing your core food supply in large quantities (often referred to as "buying in bulk"): Buying in large quantities is cheaper and more convenient, and many companies offer complete food packages that contain a variety of foods designed to cover breakfast, lunch, and dinner for a specific length of time, such as three months or a year. Another advantage is that bulk core-food items can be purchased in special containers such as "super pails" (specially packaged Mylar-lined and deoxygenated four- to six-gallon [about 15 to 23 liters] plastic buckets) to ensure longer shelf life and nutritional value. "Super pails" are designed to keep out molds, insects, and pests that can destroy your food.

Some Important Core Food Considerations

Before purchasing a core food package you need to consider several points.

A. Don't be manipulated by fear, panic, or Y2K mania. Many people rush out and purchase large quantities of food items without considering if and how they will use them. Certain Y2K preparedness advocates have stressed stocking up on large containers (often #10 gallon-sized [just under four liters] cans, or five-gallon [just under 19 liters] "super pails," or 50-pound [about 22.5 kilograms] bags) of grains and legumes. In many cases, this is a wise and inexpensive investment to ensure that your Preparedness Group has an adequate supply of food to eat. On the other hand, learning to prepare and cook hard red winter wheat and navy beans takes a lot of effort—especially if the electrical power grid takes a hit.

B. It is also important to remember that there is currently no shortage of foods in the North American market. Do not confuse the inability of the small number of manufacturers and suppliers of long-term-storage food to handle the current booming Y2K market, with how much food is available. The current backlog that many companies specializing in long-term food storage are experiencing arises from the fact that they are a small cottage industry incapable of handling the sudden amount of business Y2K anxiety has generated. Because of this fact, many local communities and members of churches, synagogues, etc., are grouping together to purchase their own grains and prepare them for long-term storage.

C. Whenever possible, I prefer certified organic sources of fruits and vegetables because, in addition my being able to support small family farms and avoid possible contamination and toxicity from pesticides and herbicides, I am gratified by the fact that most organic farmers replenish the mineral content of their soil in a way that far surpasses the methods used by conventional and large commercial farming enterprises. This source of organic plant minerals is critical for maintaining good health. (According to some researchers, the lack of sufficient micro- and macro-minerals might be another major contributing factor to the numerous chronic diseases that afflict North Americans.) In addition, a study released in February 1999 by Consumers Union, the non-profit group that publishes *Consumer Reports*, has revealed an unacceptably high level of pesticide residue on many nonorganic fruits and vegetables, such as spinach, peaches, grapes, winter squash, apples, green beans, pears, and celery. The study also draws attention to the risks these poisons pose for children. Another study published in the medical journal *The Lancet* (1998;352:1816-1820) reported that compounds known as organochlorines that are used in agricultural pesticides may imitate the effects of estrogen in the human body and in doing so might increase the risk for breast cancer. (Toxic chemicals often gravitate toward fatty tissues.)

D. When buying large quantities of food the issue of spoilage and contamination is important. Because some insects can penetrate thin plastic as well as paper and cardboard, some emergency preparedness experts recommend using insecticides around your stored products. For me this is not a wise idea. The risks of contaminating your food or the air you breathe are too great, especially if you have children or pets, or have a chemically sensitive person in your Preparedness Group. A better alternative is to purchase your long-term food items in pest-resistant containers, meaning that they are specially built and sealed to keep insects out. If this is not possible you can mix diatomaceous earth with your dry beans and grains and spread some on and around your storage containers, to kill off pests and insects. Some health advocates also recommend mixing a few crushed bay leaves with your beans and grains. (See the Appendix for more food storage tips.)

E. Some readers might think there is "no way I'm going to need food for a year and it is a waste of money to stock up on items that I can buy at my local supermarket." This might be true. However, given, as many predict, the massive global economic implications of Y2K, the price of many items such as food could skyrocket. In addition, there is always the chance of a natural disaster such as an earthquake, a blizzard, or a hurricane, or a personal disaster such as the loss of a job, that could further complicate Y2K. Having a supply of long-term food items could thus represent a major savings for you and your family, especially given the fact that bulk food items in shelf-stable "super pails" actually cost less than the same items bought at your local health food store or supermarket (provided you buy enough to offset the shipping costs; be sure to ask vendors the cheapest way to ship their food items).

Y2K TIP

When deciding how much food to store, remember that teenagers eat at least a fourth more than adults and that a 70-year-old will not need as much food as a 40-year-old. As a general guideline, a year's supply of food for the average-sized adult male should include 200 pounds [about 91 kilograms] of grains and legumes, fifteen #10 (gallon-sized [just under four liters]) cans of dehydrated and/or freeze-dried vegetables, eight #10 cans of dehydrated and/or freeze-dried fruit, two #10 cans of dehydrated or freeze-dried eggs (if you eat them), 10 pounds (about 4½ kilograms) of sprouting seeds, 10 pounds of sweetener, 2 gallons (about 7½ liters) of oil, and 10 to 15 pounds (4½ to 7 kilograms) of spices, condiments, etc. (For more specific food storage information, see Anita Evangelista's book *How to Develop a Low-Cost Family Food-Storage System*, available from *Amazon.com*, <http://www.amazon.com>.)

Y2K TIP

If you expect to consume a large amount of beans you might want to get *Beano*, digestive enzymes, or similar products, available at your local health food store, to cut down on gas and aid in the digestion of beans. You also might consider purchasing cookbooks dedicated to creative ways to prepare (and eat) all the grains and legumes. *Amazing Grains: Creating Vegetarian Main Dishes With Whole*

Grains by Joanne Saltzman offers over 100 recipes on how to turn hearty grains such as buckwheat, millet, oats, quinoa, and teff into gourmet delights. *Magic Beans: 150 Delicious Recipes Featuring Nature's Low-Fat, Nutrient-Rich, Disease-Fighting Powerhouse* by Patti Bazel Geil offers numerous suggestions on how to turn your store-house of beans into taste-titillating delights. *James McNair's Beans & Grains* by James K. McNair focuses on how to transform both grains and legumes into elegant gastronomic fare. These books can be ordered from your local book dealer or from *Amazon.com*, <http://www.ama-zon.com>. The *Veggies Unite* home page, <http://www.veg-web.com/food/>, e-mail <veggie@vegweb.com>, offers an extensive array of over 2,700 vegan recipes for beans, *TVP®*, pasta, pizza, desserts, snacks, etc. This is a worth-while Web site to visit before Y2K hits; the site contains a number of recipes you may want to try. Be sure to keep a log in your Y2K Preparedness Journal of what you liked and of how you prepared and modified the recipes to fit your taste.

The following companies specialize in core food items prepared for long-term storage. I have placed many of the larger Y2K vendors first and listed some of the vendors with a short backlog of orders closer to the end.

Walton Feed, Inc. of Montpelier, Idaho, <http://waltonfeed.com>, e-mail <mark@waltonfeed.com>, is one of the biggest (and least expensive) suppli-ers of long-term survival food. They offer a variety of food items that come in an assortment of containers, such as bags, buckets, cans, etc. Although many of their food items cater to conventional taste buds, they do have a number of good things for the health-conscious shopper, including a line of certified organic grains and legumes such as amaranth, brown rice, buck-wheat, macaroni, millet, oats, quinoa, spelt, wheat, etc. *Walton Feed* also offers complete food packages for those who want to purchase a one-month to two-year supply of food. These packages include grains, legumes, sweet-eners, condiments, etc. They also carry non-hybrid, non-nitrogen-packed fruit and vegetable seeds for long-term storage. However, as of fall 1998, *Walton Feed* is eight to 12 months behind in back orders and might not be able to deliver orders before Y2K hits. I offer their Web site as a model for the large variety of Y2K preparedness goods available on the market. Study their site well before you buy from another company, and be sure to inquire how long it will be before you receive your goods.

Bruce Hopkins, <http://web2.airmail.net/foodstr2>, another major supplier of emergency preparedness and survival foods, has a Web site worth consulting. *Bruce Hopkins* offers a good line of certified organic grains and legumes, including non-wheat and non-gluten grain items for those who are allergic to them, such as hulled buckwheat, spelt, and quinoa. They are also a good source for certified organic brown rice (both long and the flavorful Basmati).

Captain Dave's Survival Center (Captain Dave Inc., <http://www.survival-center.com>), another major supplier of survival-related food and goods, also has a Web site worth studying. In addition to offering a large line of pasta, grains, legumes, eggs, Textured Vegetable Protein *(TVP®),* fruits, and vegetables packed in #10 cans, they carry a large shelf-stable dairy selection. *Captain Dave's Survival Center's* informative Web site also deals with all sorts of emergency preparedness issues.

SunOrganic Farm, <http://www.sunorganic.com>, e-mail <sales@ sunorganic.com>, offers a wide array of high-quality certified organically grown grains, legumes, vegetables, herbs, coffees, teas, nuts, dried fruit, oils, sweeteners, desserts, etc. in both small and bulk quantity. This is a great source for finding hard-to-get items. They also have a good article on what "organic" means and why organic foods are important (<http://www.sunorganic. com/organic.html>).

Store-Well Foods, e-mail <s-wfoods@valint.net>, offers a extensive line of organic grains, seeds, cereals, and legumes packed in "super pails" with or without nitrogen for long- and medium-long-term storage.

Safe-Trek Outfitters–Essentials Inc., <http://www.safetrek.com>, e-mail <sales@safetrek.com>, offers an extensive line of bulk and long-term-storage organic beans, grains, sprouting seeds, sweeteners and oils. They also offer one-year complete food packages (except for oil—an ingredient commonly missing in many "complete" food package programs). *Safe-Trek Outfitters–Essentials Inc.* is an exception in the bulk and long-term-storage food industry in that they focus on nutrition and use nutritional supplement experts to ensure high-quality nutrition. In addition to an extensive line of bulk-quantity long-term-storage foods such as grains, legumes, fruits, and vegetables, *Safe-Trek Outfitters–Essentials Inc.* carries vacuum-sealed 25-pound [about 11½ kilograms] bags of their *Trail Mix,* which, according to their literature, contains a complete mix of "proteins, fats, vitamins, carbohydrates, and minerals." "Trail mixes" contain a variety of nuts, seeds, and fruit and are very tasty–a nourishing treat for children as well as adults. *Safe-*

Trek Outfitters—Essentials Inc. also provides one of the shortest delivery times (currently six to eight weeks).

Purity Foods, Inc., <http://www.purityfoods.com/>, e-mail <purityfoods@vixa.voyager.net>, offers a wide range of organic and kosher bulk commodities, including grains, legumes, sprouting seeds, dried fruit, fiber, and spelt pasta.

Brain Garden (telephone 800-481-9987) carries the nutritionally dense *Pulse* that contains a mixture of "sun-dried and organically grown" nuts, seeds, fruit, and grain. *Pulse* contains a variety of protein, carbohydrates, vitamins, minerals, and essential oils—more than granola or trail mix. This sweet-tasting, nutritious mix makes a good addition to any food program.

Lumen Foods, <http://soybean.com/index2.htm>, e-mail <LumenFoods@aol.com>, has been in the alternative (vegan or animal-free) food market since 1986. They offer an extensive line of vegetarian and "healthy meat and dairy replacement products." Their vitamin- and mineral-rich *Complete Meal Systems* are a good value; they come in a normal and a special "Y2K" version. The main difference is that the Y2K versions of their products cost more because they are contained in "super pails" that undergo "CO_2 flushing, oxygen absorbers, and Mylar (or metal polyester) packaging," giving them a five-year instead of a six- to ten-month shelf life.

Lumen Foods' product line includes soy-based "meatless meats" and "meatless meals" that come in a variety of flavors, including beef and Cajun jerky, Canadian bacon, chicken fillet, pepperoni, Teriyaki beef fillet, California ham, as well as "complete meal systems" such as Chunky Chicken Stew, Sweet 'n Sour Chicken, Chicken a La King, Texas Chili, Beef Stroganoff, Italian Dinner, Hungarian Goulash, etc. *Lumen Foods' Heartline* and *Complete Meal System* food products are "virtually free of the flatugenic (gas-generating) sugars responsible for causing indigestion in most (soy) users." (Using digestive enzymes with soy and other emergency preparedness products will also aid digestion and assimilation.)

The *Lumen Foods* soy concentrate products also have a high content of isoflavones, "particularly the powerful chemopreventive, genistein," which are thought to have beneficial hormonal effects. *Lumen Foods* also makes a "Fat-Free Milk Replacement" that comes in original and carob flavor. *Lumen Foods'* products are also kosher. (Those for whom kosher is important should consult *Lumen's* note on their kosher certification, <http://soybean.com/faq101.htm>. (Consult their *Whole Earth Vegetarian Catalogue* Virtual Store Web site, <http://www.soybean.com/soybean/cat1.htm>.) Their current shipping time (about four weeks) is one of the fastest in the Y2K industry.

Lumen Foods products can be purchased in Canada from *LiteSource* (telephone 905-427-8381, fax 905-420-8421, 55 Ontario Blvd., Ajax, Ontario L1S 4S7); and *Rident Enterprises* (telephone 604-467-3340, 22015 126th Ave., Maple Ridge, British Columbia).

Note: Those readers concerned that if they stop drinking milk they might not get the calcium they need to prevent osteoporosis might want to investigate a claim made by the *Physicians' Committee for Responsible Medicine*—a non-profit medical doctors' group that advocates proper eating. The physicians base their claim on a study involving tens of thousands of nurses, conducted by the *Harvard School of Public Health*, that found that those who drank more milk are more prone to osteoporosis than those who drink less. In fact, green leafy vegetables and calcium-fortified orange juice were found to offer more usable calcium than milk (*Boston Globe*, March 3, 1999).

Desert Mountain Provisions (telephone 307-279-3595) carries an extensive line of inexpensive long-term breakfast, lunch, and dinner packages packed in #10 cans. As an example, their *Big Breakfast* Case #One, containing over 400 servings of whole eggs, soy-based bacon, and sausage and butter, costs just over $100.

Millennium Gourmet Food Reserves (telephone 800-500-9893, e-mail <food@itsnet.com>) offers a line of "gourmet" quality meat and meatless breakfast and dinner entrees.

Emergency Essentials, <http://www.beprepared.com>, e-mail <webmaster@beprepared.com>, offers an extensive line of preparedness foods, including "super pails" and #10 cans of grains, vegetables, legumes, fruits, "gourmet" soups, dairy items, etc. *Emergency Essentials* guarantees their prices are "the lowest prices in the preparedness industry" (see <http://www.beprepared.com/Support/company.html>) and is one of the few preparedness companies that will refund the difference if you find an item cheaper someplace else.

Supplies4Y2K.com, <http://www.supplies4y2k.com/catalog2.htm>, e-mail <sales@supplies4y2k.com>, offers one of the fastest shipping turnaround times for deluxe total food packages that contain fruit, vegetables, grains, soy-based protein products, beverages, dairy products, and desserts. If you mention this book they will give a $100 discount off either their Four Adult One-Year Deluxe or One Adult One-Year Deluxe long-term food packages. They also told me that their supply of foods is plentiful.

Nitro-Pak Preparedness Center, <http://www.nitro-pak.com/>, carries a diverse line of emergency and long-term preparedness products. Their dehydrated and bulk foods packing system is especially good in its sensitivity to keep plastic by-products from permeating the food. *Nitro-Pak Preparedness Center's Premier-Pak* (about $2,100) offers a one-year supply of food for one person or a three-month supply of food for a family of four. Meat lovers will like this freeze-dried pack because it offers real meat, including sirloin steak and white breast of chicken. *Nitro-Pak Preparedness Center* also offers six-gallon [about 22½ liters] buckets, Mylar liners and sealers, lid openers, vacuum sealers, and other equipment for those who want to "do-it-yourself" and pack their own long-term storage items. *Nitro-Pak Preparedness Center* also carries a vitamin and mineral supplement that has a ten-year shelf life. *Nitro-Pak* also has a number of distributors of their products, including *Y2K Survival Supply Co.*, <http://www.y2ksupplyco.com/Ultimate-Pak-II.html>.

Rocky Mountain Food Storage Products (telephone 303-368-7900) carries grains, beans, vegetables, freeze-dried meats, *TVP®*, pastas and soups by the 25-pound [about 11½ kilograms] and 50-pound [about 22½ kilograms] bag as well as a large variety of spices and other cooking aids such as olive oil, honey, yeast, etc.

The Preparedness Centers, <http://www.healthyharvest.com>, e-mail <n.russell@worldnet.att.net>, carries a varied line of bulk foods, including bags and "super pails" of grains, legumes, fruits, vegetables, pasta, *TVP®*, and cereals, as well as oxygen-free #10 cans of seeds, beans, legumes, fruits, vegetables, drink mixes, soup bases, and desserts.

The Montana Marketplace, run by *Infinet Communications, Inc.*, <http://www.webcom.com/>, e-mail <webmaster@mtmarketplace.com>, is a Web site that lists a number of companies and vendors specializing in long-term emergency preparedness foods. Some of these include companies such as *LMG Holding Company*, <http://www.webcom.com/infinet/organic_foods.html>, e-mail <og@mtmarketplace.com>, which carries certified organic grains and legumes packed in "super pails."

Y2K TIP

It is important to know what species of grain you are buying. Unfortunately, many vendors of grain do not know what type of wheat they are selling. Not all varieties of wheat are good for milling and bread baking. For example, according to a study conducted by the *Kansas State University's Department of Grain Science and Industry*, Laredo, Longhorn,

Custer, and Triumph wheat have less desirable qualities for baking and milling, that is, they are too hard for milling or have too low a protein or gluten content for baking, while Tut, Jagger, Karl 92, Ogallala and Agseco 7853 have exceptional milling, protein, and baking qualities. When you buy a "super pail" or a 50-pound [about 22½ kilograms] bag of wheat it is important to know what kind you are getting. It is also important to get wheat that is clean and free of what Leon Neher of *Paramount Farms* calls "noxious weeds, other crops, chaff, sticks, and other foreign matter" that can ruin taste or harm your grain mill. Contact Leon for more information on this important topic (e-mail <paramnt@ruraltel.net>).

Happy Hovel Storable Foods, <http://www.wwmagic.com/haphov/>, e-mail <haphov@seanet.com>, carries a substantial line of long-term-storage organic grains, beans, fruits, and vegetables as well as special cookers, and canning and food preserving equipment. They also carry complete food packages for one, three, and six months. However, you need to check their Web site and call for the availability of their products.

Lakeridge Food Storage, <http://www.shopsite.com/dehydrate/>, or <http://www.shopsite.com/lfs/>, e-mail <lfsfood@ix.netcom.com>, offers a diversified variety of long-term-storage bulk food items, including grains, legumes, fruits, vegetables, freeze-dried meats, soups, meat substitutes, desserts, *MREs*, etc. They have a good certified organic line of vegetables, beans, and grains as well as soup stocks, pancake mixes, and hard-to-find items such as apricot, blueberry, and boysenberry syrups. *Lakeridge Food Storage* also has a large inventory of emergency supplies, including items for water storage, solar battery chargers, portable ovens, etc. You can check their Web site at <http://www.reliablehost.com/lfs/page6.html> for a complete list of what they offer.

Wayne J Carroll & Associates, <http://www.y2kdehydratedfoods.com/>, e-mail <y2kfoods@2000biz.com>, offers a variety of complete food packages, such as the Y2K Skeptics Package, the Super Saver, and custom packages that allow you to pick and choose what you want. They also carry a good line of certified organic grains and legumes in "super pails."

Family Food Storage, <http://downtown-web.com/psi/famfood.htm>, e-mail <psiusa@aros.net>, carries a wide variety (over 900 products) of inexpensively priced food items, including bulk pasta, beans, grain, honey, freeze-dried meats, herbs, etc. Most of their products cater to conventional taste buds.

The American Freedom Network, <http://www.amerifree.com/>, e-mail <comments@amerifree.com>, carries a diverse line of long-term-storage complete food packages, including a good "deal" that includes nine "super pails" containing 300 pounds [136 kilograms] of light-tasting Golden 86 Wheat and 100 pounds [about 45 kilograms] of a variety of beans and legumes for under $200.

CSIN, <http://www.csin.com/>, e-mail <csin@csin.com>, carries bags and "super pails" of organic amaranth, brown rice, and quinoa at good prices. (They also offer a variety of nonfood preparedness items and equipment.)

Deer Park Emergency Preparedness Center Total Survival Center.com, <http://www.totalsurvival.com>, e-mail <sales@totalsurvival.com>, carries a full line of emergency and survival preparedness items, including clothing, grain mills, and food. Most of their food is "standard" fare, but their "family," "emergency," and "security" units are also some of the least expensive as far as complete packages of dehydrated foods go. They also currently have one of the fastest shipping times.

Food Storage On-Line, <http://users.itsnet.com/~foodnow/>, e-mail <info@foodstorageonline.com>, stocks the *Staff of Life* and *Millennial Harvest* line of long-term food storage food packages and items.

Countryside Granary, <http://www.countrysidegranary.8m.com>, e-mail <csgranary@aol.com>, has a limited-variety but readily available (as of January 1999) inventory of basic grains, legumes, dried milk, sugar, and honey.

As of January 1999 the *Yellowstone River Trading Company,* <http://www. yellowstonetrading.com/foodyrt1.html>, e-mail <info@ yellowstonetrading.com>, has "One Year Deluxe" food packages as well as a variety of canned fruits, vegetables, grains, beans, soups, and beverages available without a wait.

Y2K Prep, <http://michaelhyatt.com/food/order.htm>, e-mail <feedback@ michaelhyatt.com>, also currently has food packages available without an order delay. They offer a budget-friendly *Personalized Preparation Package for Four People* ($3,350) and a *Personalized Preparation Package for One Person* ($850). The former feeds a family of four for under $850 per person for a year's supply of food that caters to conventional tastes, with items such as soups, vegetables, fruits, dairy products, desserts, gravy mixes, and sauces, etc. Their $850 package needs to be supplemented with a variety of grains, beans, and legumes.

J&K Enterprises, <http://www.charactercounts.com/foods.htm>, e-mail <jseitz@hischaracter.com>, carries a line of quality grains and legumes available in bulk.

Y2K Food Store, <http://www.Y2KFoodStore.com/>, e-mail <nathan@y2k2000.org>, offers a fast turn-around on "Basic foods in Bulk quantities at Bargain prices."

Arizona Brand Nutritionals, Inc. (telephone 602-968-5935) offers a variety of quality bee products, including pollen, propolis, and royal jelly. Many people find bee products to be some of nature's most perfect foods, since they are high in beneficial nutrients. (Note: Some people are allergic to pollen, so you must initially take bee products in small doses to reduce the chance of allergic reaction.)

Y2K TIP

If, by the time you are reading this book, the back orders or delivery times for the companies I mention are too long, check with your local health food store or supermarket to see if they will place an order for you. You can also search the World Wide Web under headings such as bulk foods, grains, survival foods, etc. If you don't have access to the Internet, visit your local library or hire your neighbor's son or daughter to do a search. There are lots of smaller bulk grain companies that might not be as backlogged, such as *Seedtime and Harvest,* e-mail <maverick@rconnect.com>, and *Paramount Farms,* telephone 785-754-2151, e-mail <paramnt@ruraltel.net>, which carries chemical-free hard red winter wheat, corn, and jowar—a white sorghum that can be ground for tortilla-like breads or cooked as a cereal like oatmeal.

Having listed a number of places where you can purchase bulk grains and other "core foods," we must now consider ways to make them taste great.

Tips For Great Tasting Grains and Legumes

- Always rinse grains and beans before preparing them, to remove dirt and other unpleasant items.
- Soak all hard grains and beans overnight for eight to ten hours. Doing this will soften them to help make them more digestible and will save both cooking time and energy—the latter being very important during Y2K.

- Be sure to rinse soaked beans and legumes well. The water you cook them in should be clear and not milky or foamy in appearance.
- Bring grains and beans to a boil and then reduce to a slow simmer.
- Add broth, herbs, and spices according to recipe or taste.
- Keep the cooking container tightly sealed.
- Cook according to taste—usually chewy and tender. Test toward the end of the cooking time. Remember, cooking times will vary depending on the source of heat. For example, solar cookers (see below) on the average need double the amount of cooking time of conventional cookers.
- Keep a record of successes and failures. Consult these Y2K cooking notes before you begin.
- Many people find fluffing grains with a wooden spoon makes them taste better.
- Eat slowly and without stress. Chew your food well, ideally thirty chews to a mouthful. Remember, good conversation and laughter make all food taste better.
- Drinking a glass of water thirty minutes before a meal and another glass about one hour after a meal will greatly aid digestion.

(The *Whole Foods Market* Web site, <http://www.wholefoods.com/wfm/healthinfo/bulkgrains.html>, is an highly informative source of cooking guidelines on how long to soak, spice, and cook a variety of grains and beans.)

Long Shelf-Life Foods

Because we do not know how long the effects of Y2K will last, it is important to think in terms of product "shelf life," or how long a food product will last before it spoils and loses its nutritional value. In other words, a food item such as a canned good may not be spoiled but it could have lost its nutritional value. This is why many emergency preparedness experts and Y2K watchers recommend freeze-dried and dehydrated foods, which, if stored properly, maintain their shelf life and nutritional value for a long time. Freeze-dried and dehydrated foods are also easy to prepare and, depending on the manufacturer, taste close to, or better than, home cooking. Their convenience also means they are very popular, so they are often the first items to be in short supply as Y2K awareness grows.

Freeze-Dried and Dehydrated Food Products

Freeze-drying involves placing food in a vacuum chamber and removing the moisture by subjecting it rapidly to temperatures as low as minus 50°F [minus 45°C]. Dehydration works the opposite way by using heat (normally 95°F to 140°F [35°C to 60°C]) to extract the moisture. Both methods, if done properly, are effective in removing moisture and maintaining the nutritional value of food over a long period of time. Some people prefer the taste of freeze-dried foods, saying they taste and look closer to fresh food. Others prefer the taste of dehydrated foods. Many of the manufacturers and distributors of freeze-dried and dehydrated foods offer sample packs that let you try a number of their recipes before investing in large quantities. It is important to note that freeze-dried or dehydrated food requires water for it to be "rehydrated," and that once it is opened it must be treated as fresh food, that is, sealed, stored properly, and eaten as soon as possible.

Freeze-dried foods and dehydrated foods come in a variety of forms, such as complete packages, as well as *à la carte* vegetables, fruits, and desserts, to supplement a core supply of canned goods and grains and legumes (discussed below).

Vendors Offering Freeze-Dried and Dehydrated Food Products

A number of companies offer freeze-dried and dehydrated long-term-storage foods. *AlpineAire,* <http://www.Alpineairefoods.com/>, has been a pioneer in the long-term, shelf-stable food industry for over twenty years. *AlpineAire* is one of the few companies offering emergency preparedness food that is free of artificial additives, including colorizers, flavor enhancers, and preservatives. Many of the *AlpineAire* entrees are familiar foods suited to popular taste preferences. They also offer a *Gourmet Reserves* line of products that do not require cooking (just add water for a cold but satisfying meal).

Unfortunately, *AlpineAire* does not offer a line of certified organic or kosher foods—although when I talked with their food specialist, Randy White, he told me most of their products are "chemical-free." *AlpineAire* offers a variety of entrees—everything from "Vegetarian Chili" to "Leonardo Fettuccine" and "Sweet and Sour Chicken." They also have a wide variety of desserts, soups, breakfasts, seafoods, vegetables, beans, grains, and even dairy products.

Like most vendors of freeze-dried and dehydrated foods, *AlpineAire* offers both *à la carte* (individual) items or complete packages that come in one-month, three-month, six-month and one-year supplies of breakfast, lunch, and dinner. Their long-term freeze-dried and dehydrated foods are packed with state-of-the-art oxygen absorbers and come in pouches as well as #2 (approximately one quart, or 3.5 cups [just under one liter]) and #10 (approximately one gallon or 13 cups [just under four liters]) size containers. As an added health benefit, the cans *AlpineAire* uses to pack and store their products are made of heavy-gauge metal to resist rust and corrosion and are enamel-coated to prevent metal from leaching into the food. Most of the *Gourmet Reserves* items have a five- to ten-year shelf life. *AlpineAire* has many local distributors; contact them to find one in your area.

Y 2 K   T I P

Don't rush into buying a one-, three-, six- or 12-month complete food supply package that many of the Y2K preparedness supply companies offer. These packages look tempting because they offer an inexpensive way to store food and feed your family for a specified period. However, remember that you get what you pay for, and often these packages leave out vital nutrients you will need, or they are built around a very simple and limited "mono" diet (such as wheat, milk, and honey) that you will get bored with very quickly. Remember, variety and choice give you control over what you eat. If you chose a shelf-stable "complete pack" you might want one that lasts for three or four months— what many Y2Kers consider the critical time during the Year 2000 transition, January 1 to April 1, 2000.

Other suppliers of freeze-dried and dehydrated foods include *Captain Dave's Survival Center,* <http://survival-center.com>, e-mail <webmaster@survival-center.com>, and *H & W Distributors, Inc.,* <http://www.zianet.com/hwd/food.htm>, e-mail <hwd@zianet.com>, who carry the *Ready Reserve* line of dehydrated foods at a discount. *Ready Reserve* is another leader in nutritious ready-to-eat dehydrated and low-moisture food products. A number of companies, including *Buckskin Mountain Trading, LLC,* <http://www.buckskintrading.com/>, e-mail <buckskin2@aol.com>, carry *Ready Reserve* products. You can also order directly from *Ready Reserve* at <http://www.readyreservefoods.com>, e-mail <sales@readyreservefoods.com>.

Millennium III Foods, <http://www.millennium3foods.com/>, e-mail <corporate@millennium3foods.com>, carries over 90 individual freeze-dried foods that come in galvanized "evap-paks" that remove all the oxygen. You can buy each item *à la carte,* and they specialize in fast delivery time.

Noah's Pantry, <http://www.noahspantry.com/>, e-mail <mail@noahspantry.com>, offers a variety of "user-friendly" (tasty and appealing) dehydrated foods, including grains, beans, cereals, milk, butter, vegetables, Textured Vegetable Protein *(TVP®)*, soups, macaroni, fruits, etc. They also offer six-month and one-year complete packages as well as bulk discounts and a food donation program for churches.

Sam Andy®, <http://www.karinya.com/sandy.htm>, offers a variety of dehydrated food products to build a family food reserve. Their food packages range from "easy-to-use and easy-to-store" "72-hour" and "one-month" food packages, to full family units that contain enough food to last for one to two years. According to their literature, *Sam Andy®* has been in the food-storage industry for over 30 years and offers "carefully planned" food units that "provide your family with all the calories, protein, vitamins, and minerals they need" in "three tasty, well-balanced meals a day" that help prevent appetite fatigue (<http://www.karinya.com/fdunits.htm>). Many of *Sam Andy®*'s foods are geared for those people with a conventional "sweet tooth," including a large line of shelf-stable desserts and "specialty" items. *Sam Andy®* also provides hand-operated grain mills, emergency stoves, and ovens, as well as preparedness books and other survival-oriented supplies.

Y2Kfoods, <http://y2kfood.com/s39p145.htm>, e-mail <Will@y2kfood.com>, is a company that specializes in emergency preparedness foods for people with "conventional" taste buds. Their *Y2K Food Line One* items include soup bases, gravy mixes, bakery mixes, desserts, dairy products, beverages, etc. *Y2KFoods* lists shelf-stable products from a variety of manufacturers, including *AlpineAire, Ready Reserve, Y2KFOODS Food Line One, The Granary, The Vegetable Market,* and *MILSPEC®* *(MRE rations)*, etc. *Y2KFoods* also carries a small line of bulk grains and legumes in six-gallon [just under 23 liters] "super pails" and a fairly extensive line of plastic-sealed and boxed vegetables that can be stored for at least a year—longer if you repack them and remove the oxygen. *Y2KFoods* offers an especially good deal on 48-pound [just under 22 kilograms] buckets of raw, unfiltered, and unprocessed *California Honey* (at $1.00 per pound). *Y2KFoods* carries the convenient three-, six-, and 12-month *AlpineAire* "complete" food packages. In addition, *Y2KFoods* offers an extensive line of boxed, bulk dehydrated vegetables that will last up to one year before they need to be repacked in "super pails" with oxygen absorbers for longer-term storage. As of December 1998, *Y2KFoods* guarantees to ship orders within 40 days after your check clears.

Emergency Essentials, <http://www.beprepared.com/home.html>, e-mail <webmaster@beprepared.com>, is another company that carries a line of shelf-stable items that cater to conventional taste buds, such as gourmet hot chocolate. *Emergency Essentials* also specializes in the *Provident Pantry* line of dehydrated foods, which include specialty items such as Indian Bread Scone Mix, Honey White Bread Roll Mix, 9-Grain Cracked Cereal, Creamy Country Rice Soup Mix, as well as "super pails" of grains and legumes (some of which are organically grown). *Provident Pantry* also carries the convenient one-year supply of food packs. Currently they have a six- to ten-week back order, depending on the product. They also carry the *EvriDay* line of preparedness foods that meet what they call the four criteria of being "delicious, nutritious, convenient, and provident."

IPC Future Foods, <http://www.ipcfuturefoods.com/y2k.htm>, e-mail <T10319@aol.com>, is another company specializing in "affordable" dehydrated food products. *IPC Future Foods* began as a company providing food to restaurants, and according to Marcus Ladd, one of the owners, it is important to remember that "if you don't like it (the taste), don't store it." On a cost comparison basis *IPC Future Foods* products are less expensive than supermarket foods.

New Millennium Products, <http://www.newmillenniumproducts.com/>, e-mail <TPB51@aol.com>, carries over 225 varieties of freeze-dried and dehydrated "fruits, vegetables, mixes, drinks, scrumptious soups and sauces, pastas, entrees, etc." In general, *New Millennium Products* are less expensive than those from other vendors because they allow a group of people such as church members, neighbors, etc., to place individual orders, yet receive discounts based on their group-based "point system." You can contact *New Millennium Products* for information on how this unique approach works. *Millennium Products* also offers freeze-dried oatmeal and mashed potato products that parents might consider for their young ones. (However, before you stock up on large quantities, make sure your children like the taste.)

USA Marketing Associates Inc., <http://www.y2ksupplies.com>, e-mail <sales@y2ksupplies.com> or <info@y2ksupplies.com>, carries a wide variety of emergency preparedness and survival-oriented products. They also offer the *Mountain House* brand of freeze-dried foods. *Mountain House* is one of world's largest manufacturers of freeze-dried foods. Their products are expensive but some claim they taste as close to fresh food as "dried" food can get. *USA Marketing Associates Inc.* offers a variety of *Mountain House* freeze-dried stews, meats, seafood chowder, eggs, vegetables, fruits, and desserts, both *à la carte* and as complete one-year-supply packages.

Joseph's Storehouse, <http://www.josephs-storehouse.com/y2k.htm>, e-mail <brandon@josephs-storehouse.com>, is one of many distributors of the *Perma Pak* line of dehydrated foods. One of the oldest companies making and packaging dehydrated foods, *Perma Pak* conducts rigorous tests on its products to ensure that they will maintain their shelf life. You can order directly from *Perma Pak* by contacting them at *Access Perma Pak Food Storage,* <http://www.acomputing.com/food/order.html>, e-mail <access@infowest.com>.

Food Storage Solutions, <http://users.itsnet.com/~skelling/>, e-mail <permapak@iname.com>, is another authorized *Perma Pak* distributor that might have a shorter delivery time.

In addition to offering a variety of long-term survival foods, *B&A Products,* <http://www.baproducts.com/catalog.htm>, e-mail <byron@baproducts.com>, allows you to purchase "sample" packs to see if you like their products before you make a big investment. *B&A Products* will let you purchase a *Ready Reserves Foods* sample pack that contains breakfast, lunch, and dinner for two people for one day. *B&A Products* also lets you sample *AlpineAire* products in a three-day supply. This is a good way to see if the children, the elderly, the infirm, and others with distinct taste considerations will eat what you plan to purchase. (It will also allow you to experiment with ways to get them to eat, such as adding a little fruit, honey, or maple syrup to the food.) *Ready Reserves Foods* is a company that caters to more "conventional" tastes by offering instant nonfat dry milk, gelatin, sugar, salt, shortening, margarine, etc. *Ready Reserves Foods* products can also be ordered from *Captain Dave's Survival Center* as well as *Fitness Industries Inc.,* <http://www.y2k-foods.com/>, e-mail <order@2yk-foods.com>.

André-François Bourbeau, Canadian professor of Outdoor Pursuits at the University of Québec in Chicoutimi, has designed products he calls *Explo-Rations.* His family-run business can be reached at *GB Food Supply,* District Road #3, Huntsville, Ontario P0A 1K0, Canada. According to their literature, their dehydrated and freeze-dried foods contain much less sodium than many of the commercial camping food products on the market. He also designed them for the high caloric output that canoeing or kayaking in the wild demands, so you might want to inquire about the best way to use them under the less physically but more psychologically demanding stress that Y2K might produce. Canadians can also contact *Harvest Foodworks,* <http://www.harvest.on.ca/new.htm>, e-mail <thefolks@harvest.on.ca>, in Toledo, Ontario, which offers many meatless but hearty and nutritious freeze-dried and dehydrated products.

Food Reserves Inc., <http://www.osiem.org/Ospre/foodreserves.htm>, of Ivujivik, Québec, Canada, stocks *Survival Tabs,* which offer a convenient way to obtain the nutritional requirements of "vitamins, minerals, protein for strength, carbohydrates/dextrose/lactose for fast energy under desperate circumstances, and fatty acids for long endurance" (<http://www.osiem.org/Ospre/foodreserves.htm>). One bottle of these nutritional tabs offers a two-week supply of nutrients and has a ten-year shelf life. They are easily transportable in the event you have to leave your stored food items behind and at the current exchange rate are a good bargain for Americans (about $27 US).

MREs and Other Long-Term Survival Foods

Many survival-oriented people find *MREs* ("Meals-Ready-to-Eat")—the military's version of emergency and long-term preparedness food—another good long-term food item to keep on hand. Conveniently packaged in small pouches, they are, as the name implies, ready to eat without preparation. However, before running off to buy a case, you should be aware of several drawbacks.

First, fresh, "legitimate" *MREs* are hard to obtain. The dates on the pouches and boxes are hard to decipher for accuracy, and many companies sell outdated products (as much as ten years beyond their expiration dates). If they are out of date it means the *MREs* have little, if any, nutritional value. You also need to know if the *MREs* you order are civilian versions since it is against the law to sell the military ones. (Buy only from a reputable dealer.) Second, *MREs* lend themselves quickly to appetite fatigue. Government studies show that 21 days is the maximum time span most people can tolerate them. Third, *MREs* require a special heating unit called a *"Flameless" Ration Heater* to cook them. (Most places that sell *MREs* carry *Ration Heaters,* or you can contact *Rivard International Corporation,* <http://www.rivard-usa.com/>, e-mail <help@rivard-usa.com>, for more information.) Fourth, *MREs* are poorer in nutritional quality compared to other forms of "emergency" food. *MREs* tend to be high in fat, salt, and sugar (to give quick energy in a highly stressful situation such as a war) and might contain MSG. It is important to remember that high-calorie foods can help you through a short-term emergency—one to two weeks—but without the right balance of protein, fats, and carbohydrates, and the vital addition of vitamins, minerals, co-factors, phyto-chemicals, enzymes, and fiber occurring in a more naturally balanced diet, your health will deteriorate rapidly.

Given that *MREs* are designed to be carried in the field, you might recommend that your local authorities and municipality purchase some for their police, fire, and emergency teams in case of a local infrastructure collapse that disrupts the local food supply. You can purchase *MREs* from a variety of places such as *Bruce Hopkins,* <http://web2.airmail.net/foodstr2>; *Major Surplus,* <http://www.MajorSurplusNSurvival.com>; and *The Wornick Company* (telephone 210-687-9401). *Epicenter,* <http://www.theepicenter.com>, offers *Full Meal MREs* by the case as well as vegetarian *MREs* and *MRE* heaters.

A&B Products, <http://www.baproducts.com/catalog.htm>, e-mail <byron@baproducts.com>, and *Epicenter* also offer a new alternative *MRE* product called *HeaterMeals,* which are entrees that have a long shelf life and require no refrigeration. Unlike *MREs, HeaterMeals* are self-heating, meaning that they come in a little "oven" that has a self-contained or built-in heating element that cooks the food in about 15 minutes. They come in boxes of 12 with entrees ranging from chili with beans, to grilled turkey and mashed potatoes, to green pepper steak with rice. Although they are a bit pricey (about $6.50 a meal), they save on heating fuel and can come in handy for short-term use. They have a two- to three-year shelf life.

Epicenter also carries a line of vegetarian shelf-stable "heat and serve" *Tamarind Tree* Indian dinners by the case—you can also find them at local health food stores. These "exotic" dinners are quickly cooked in boiling water—something you could do over a large (50- or 120-hour) emergency candle. Be forewarned—most of these entrees are "spicy hot." You can dilute their hot sauces (and make them able to feed more people) by mixing in ingredients such as brown rice, lentils, or beans from your "core" food stock.

Other Important Food Items

In addition to grains, legumes, pasta, and dehydrated and freeze-dried fruits and vegetables, there are a number of other important foods that need to be considered as you plan a complete nutritional package to ensure that you and your Preparedness Group eat well during the Y2K transition.

Meat Matters

For many people the issue of meat, or lack thereof, could be an important consideration during the Y2K transition. Unless you have a solar- or propane-powered freezer (see *Jade Mountain Inc.,* <http://www.jademountain. com/>, e-mail <info@jademountain.com>) or some alternative source of electrical power, the anticipated Y2K-related local power outages or supply-chain disruptions might force some meat eaters to look for substitutes.

For many health-conscious readers, this will not be a problem since they tend to be light meat-eaters anyway. However, for some families this might cause stress—especially those with young children who are used to fast food. However, it is important to note that a large number of healthy and happy children have been raised on a vegetarian diet. Indeed, many healthy children have been raised as "vegans," that is, those who do not eat any animal-based product such as meat, dairy, or eggs. For those who would like more information on how to help your family adjust to a meatless way of eating, you can check the vegetarian book section at your local health food store or consult Web pages such as *Feeding Vegan Kids* by Reed Mangels, Ph.D., R.D., <http://www. natural-connection.com/resource/file_exchange/feeding_vegan_kids.html>. You should also consult the findings of the *China Project*—a study conducted by Cornell and Oxford Universities, which found the peasant populations of China, who eat little meat and no dairy products, to be much more healthy and disease-free than the more affluent North Americans and Europeans who consume large amounts of meat, harmful fats, and dairy products. (See the *China–Cornell–Oxford Project* Web page <http://www.human.cornell.edu/dns/chinaproject/chinaproject.html>, e-mail <lc26@cornell.edu>.)

Luckily there are a variety of meat substitutes on the market. One such popular substitute is "meat-flavored" Textured Vegetable Protein (*TVP®*)—made from soybean products. *TVP®* comes in a variety of flavors—bacon, sausage, pepperoni, chicken, beef, Sloppy Joe, barbecue, taco, and seafood—and although it does not contain any real meat products, the taste of good-quality *TVP®* has been known to fool some hard-core meat eaters. Because of its high protein content and familiar tastes, *TVP®* has become an important addition to many emergency and long-term-storage food programs. It can easily be added to beans and rice products for a hearty (and tasty) meal.

However, it is important to point out that not all *TVP®* products are of good quality and that not everything labeled *TVP* is authentic. As the Frequently Asked Questions (FAQ) section of *Lumen Foods'* Web site, <http://soybean.com/faq101.htm>, notes, the term *TVP®* is a registered trademark of *Archer Daniels Midland Co. (ADM)* and refers only to products made from "textured soy flour." The term has been generalized incorrectly to include any and all textured, soy-based products. However, the site says, "today's better soy-based meat replacers use (soy) concentrates and not raw flours," and thus those products should not be classified as *TVP*. I elaborate on this distinction because many people think of *TVP®* as an unappetizing, rubbery, tasteless substance, when in fact many of the high-quality soy-based meat substitutes are quite appetizing.

Many of the vendors of freeze-dried and dehydrated foods mentioned above offer great tasting soy-based products. Two examples of such vendors are *Lumen Foods*, <http://soybean.com/index2.htm>, e-mail <LumenFoods@aol.com>, and *Euresia Co.* <http://www.euresia.com>, e-mail <Info@euresia.com>. *Euresia Co.* is meticulous about the quality of their soy products, using only certified-organic, nongenetically altered soybeans. They also pride themselves on offering easy-to-digest soy products. *Harvest Direct,* <http://www.harvestdirect.com/>, e-mail <maryellen@harvestdirect.com>, is another company that offers an extensive line of specialized soy-based meat and seafood alternative products. Their *Harvest Direct Protean*™ ground beef, chili, barbecue mix, and taco substitutes require only that you add water and heat the product. They also offer an extensive array of ethnic entrees, vegetarian jerkies, gourmet soy nuts and soymilk, and dairy alternatives. As with most products mentioned in this manual, I suggest you try soy-based meat substitutes before you buy them in bulk.

Y 2 K   T I P

Those who want fresh meat and eggs and who have yard space might consider breeding and raising chickens. These could also be a strong barter item with your "carnivorous" neighbors and friends. If you can't raise your own livestock, *Major Surplus,* <http://www.MajorSurplusNSurvival.com>, offers a one-year *Deluxe* food supply that includes "real" meats. If you purchase freeze-dried real meats remember they need to be consumed as quickly as "fresh" meats once the container is open.

Other Meatless, High-Protein Alternatives

There are a number of other alternative products for the "carnivores" in your group who feel they need lots of hearty "protein" to be satisfied, such as canned chicken, tuna, ham, salmon, and other common supermarket items. However, beans and legumes are an inexpensive and nutritious form of protein.

Beans and Legumes

Few foods contain as much quality protein as is found in beans and legumes such as soybeans, kidney beans, black beans, and lentils. Beans and legumes add nourishing bulk to soups, and if you prepare them with the right herbs, spices, sauces, and condiments, they can be not only palatable but even of gourmet tastiness. There are several ways to purchase beans and legumes. Purchasing them in the above-mentioned "super pails" or 25-pound (11.33 kilograms) and 50-pound (22.66 kilograms) bags from the above mentioned bulk-food companies offers both the convenience and the price advantage of buying in bulk. Beans and legumes can also be purchased at your local health food store. Keep an eye out for sales. You can also check to see if there is a food co-op in your area.

Y 2 K   T I P

When purchasing heavy items such as bulk foods, I recommend that you encourage friends, relatives, churches, synagogues, and communities to buy together. This will enable you both to get large volume discounts on the products and to save on shipping costs. Always ask your vendor about the least expensive way to ship heavy items. Some companies have a "hundredweight" shipping price that is much cheaper than conventional parcel shipping rates.

Protein Bars and Powder

So-called "protein" or "health food" bars available at most vitamin and supplement stores can also be another good source of protein. Although many of these products contain large amounts of sugar (be sure to read the label carefully), some of the newer generation of these "energy" bars are worth considering as a special treat or emergency backup meal replacement, especially since the ones of higher quality taste good, offer decent nutrition, take up little space, and have a fairly long shelf life.

The *Breakthru* bar, created by *Glenn Foods* (telephone 800-211-9796), is a "100% vegetarian and dairy-free" meal replacement bar that contains "organic" ingredients. This bar covers a number of nutritional basics and even includes EFAs and FOS (fructooligosaccharide, an aid to the growth of intestinal microflora—see Chapter Six) for building healthy intestinal flora. These bars are kosher and do not contain hydrogenated oils.

Hi-Country Snack Foods Inc., <http://www.hicountry.com>, e-mail <mt@hicountry.com>, makes the high energy and endurance *TREKBARR,* which contains natural ingredients such as rolled oats, figs, and oat bran that release a high level of slowly absorbed complex and simple carbohydrates that, according to their literature, provide "energy flow without energy depleting, high sugar dropouts."

A&B Products carries a line of vegetarian and kosher Emergency Food Bars that are approved by the U.S. Coast Guard and the Canadian Department of Transportation. They come in packets of nine bars (about $10.95).

A number of companies geared toward the weightlifting crowd make "hi protein" bars. Though most of these bars contain lots of sugar (to help give athletes a quick energy boost and to cover the taste of the some of bitter ingredients such as *CLA)*, some such as the *Pure Protein Bar* made by *Worldwide Sport Nutritional Supplements* (telephone 800-854-5019) offer a good protein-to-fat and carbohydrate ratio. Given that they have a one-year shelf life, often taste good, and contain a mixture of vitamins and minerals, you might consider buying a few boxes in a variety of flavors to break up any monotonous eating routine you might fall into during Y2K.

Though they take more preparation time—mixing, stirring, and cleaning up—high quality "designer" protein powders can be beneficial. As with the protein bars, this is not the optimal form of nutrition as is true of whole, fresh, unprocessed foods, but they can be a convenient way to ensure adequate nutrition. *Naturade Products Inc.,* <http://www.naturade.com/>, e-mail <mzreik@naturade.com>, carries a line of high-quality, health-friendly, "all natural" protein formulas. You can find their products at health food stores or order from the company directly.

Prolab Nutrition, <http://www.prolabnutrition.com>, makes *100% Pure Whey Protein* that, unlike many of the "designer" protein powders, contains very few additives and synthetic ingredients.

Bio-X The Ultimate Engineered Food (available from *Bio-Tech USA* <http:/www.mloproducts.com>) is another "high protein" mix that does contain aspartame, phenylalanine, artificial colorings, or artificial flavors.

Essential Dietary Fats and Oils

The issue of nutritional oils is critical—especially given the dietary and lifestyle changes Y2K might bring. Many emergency preparedness experts recognize that oil storage is difficult because once separated from their natural protective casing, nutritional oils spoil quickly. It is important to note that rancid oils not only taste bad but also foster free-radical damage in the body. Free-radical damage results when molecules that lose an electron, become unstable and begin to roam, like a scavenger, for an extra electron, and in doing so, destroy other atoms they come in contact with. The current understanding is that such free-radical damage results in a number of problems in the human body, including accelerated aging, heart disease, cancer, autoimmune disease, etc.

To avoid free-radical damage, it is important, whenever possible, to buy dietary oil that is unrefined, "cold pressed" (made without heat or chemicals), and packaged in dark bottles that have had the oxygen removed to cut down on rancidity. It is also important to remember always to store your bottles of oil—extra-virgin olive and canola are generally more healthy than most of the others—in a cool, dark place. Light and heat hasten rancidity and spoilage.

For the potentially uncontrolled and unfamiliar alternative sources of heat you might have to use for cooking during Y2K, you might want to try *Spectrum Naturals Super Canola* oil (e-mail <spectrumnaturals@ netdex.com>). This oil is a special version of regular canola oil that holds up well under heat. You also might consider purchasing a high quality vacuum sealer to keep oils from going rancid. (See the section on Vacuum Sealers in Chapter Four.)

Y2K TIP

Although jarred nut butters are popular, it is important to realize that all commercially processed nut and seed butters, including peanut, almond, cashew, sunflower seed, flax, and tahini butters, go rancid after 72 hours. Rancid oils are very destructive to the body, producing much free radical damage. Remember too that the oils in flour go rancid quickly, and ideally we should grind our flour fresh as we need it. Therefore, I plan to stock up on various nuts, seeds, and wheat berries and grind my own fresh nut butters, oil, and flour. See the product list in Chapter Four, or ask your health food store to order a hand-operated nut and seed grinder. If you've never tasted fresh nut butters, you are in for a treat. If the prospect of grinding your own nut butters sounds like too much work, remember if the infrastructure does collapse and we cannot go to work and lose access to electricity-based entertainment such as movies, television, home computers, etc., we will need productive things to occupy our time.

Essential Fatty Oils

While on the subject of oils it is important to point out that our bodies also need EFAs (Essential Fatty Acids). EFAs (also called Omega-3 and Omega-6 fatty acids) are vital to a number of bodily processes, including healthy skin, blood clotting, and the proper functioning of our muscles, glandular and immune systems, and the myelin sheath that encases our nerve tissue.

Many health researchers believe it is the lack of EFAs in our modern diet that has contributed to the vast number of degenerative diseases that afflict our population, including heart disease, cancer, arthritis, strokes, allergies, psoriasis and eczema, high blood pressure, etc. (See Udo Erasmus's *Fats That Heal, Fats That Kill: The Complete Guide to Fats, Oils, Cholesterol and Human Health,* available at your local health food store or from *Amazon.com,* <http://www.amazon.com>.) For example, researchers have found that some people, including those who are deficient in certain nutrients such as vitamins A, C, E, B2, B6, pantothenic acid, B12, biotin, and minerals such as calcium; the elderly; and those who suffer from MS, diabetes, asthma, cystic fibrosis, and alcoholism, might lack an enzyme in the body that converts omega fatty acids such as the linoleic acid found in flax and other seed oils to prostaglandins (see the *Go Symmetry* Web page, <http://www.go-symmetry.com/flax-seed.htm>, for more information about this important topic). In light of this, those suffering from degenerative diseases might want to consider stocking up on both a quality food-form based multiple vitamin and mineral supplement (such as *Rainbow Light*) as well as bottles or capsules of EFAs.

EFAs can be purchased at any health food store. Be sure to consult with your health food store counselor or health practitioner to make sure the EFA-rich oils you purchase have a proper mix of Omega-3, Omega-6 and Gamma-Linolenic Acid (GLA). GLA helps the body convert Omega-3 and Omega-6 EFAs into prostaglandins and thus is beneficial for those suffering from degenerative diseases. Primrose Oil and Borage Oil are also a good source of EFAs. EFAs also come in capsule form available at your local health food store or through the Internet from companies such as *Puritan's Pride,* <http://puritan.com/>, e-mail <info@puritan.com>, which offer an extensive line of capsulated EFAs. *Puritan's* "Nutritional Oils" Web page gives a good summary of the various types of beneficial oils available from their home page, <http://puritan.com>, click on "online catalog," then click on "Nutritional Oils".

Y2K TIP

Because most of the dietary sources of EFAs—including fish, fresh green leafy vegetables, certain nuts, and seeds might be hard to obtain during the Y2K times ahead, it might be wise to stock up on EFAs. However, if you do stock up on bottles, remember that they need to be refrigerated in airtight, light-proof bottles—something that might not be that easy to do during Y2K. One simple solution for this potential challenge is to stock up on certified organic whole flax seeds (remember that the shell of whole flax seeds forms a natural barrier to keep oxygen and light out, and that hulled and ground seeds go rancid quickly since exposure to air oxidizes the oil inside) and sprinkle them on hot cereal, soups, rice, etc. Flax seeds are tasty and chewy, and they have a mild, nutty flavor. You can also grind the flax seeds in a coffee bean grinder and spread them over hot cereal, salads, or hot meals.

Of Sugar, Sweeteners, and the "Sweet Tooth"

Children (and many adults) are notoriously attracted—some say addicted—to sweets. And that is no secret. Except for the fruit and vegetable sections at most supermarkets, there are few food items in conventional supermarkets that do not contain some kind of processed or added sugar product. If you investigate closely you will see that sugar is disguised under a number of ingredient names, including fructose, corn syrup, cornstarch, sucrose, malto-dextrin, dextrose, lactose, and maltose, as well as dulcitol, xylitol, and mannitol—all of which contribute to the astronomically high amount of sugar consumption in our culture.

Technically, we cannot live without sugar, if by "sugar" we mean the complex and simple carbohydrates that get broken down into glucose by enzymes in our body. Glucose plays a vital role in our body's energy production and metabolism. Unfortunately, most of the sugar consumed in the average North American diet is of the calorie-laden simple kind that quickly enters our bloodstream, causing our blood sugar level to rise quickly. This rise in turn causes our pancreas to dump insulin into our blood, quickly counteracting the sugar and lowering our blood sugar level, causing us to feel tired or to experience the "sugar blues." This process makes us crave more sugar to offset the uncomfortable feeling of having a low blood sugar level. This sugar/insulin swing in metabolism causes stress on many of our bodily, hormonal, and emotional functions. It is also one of the reasons sugar makes us fat. (Technically, it is not sugar itself that makes us fat, but the insulin that stimulates the conversion of digested food into fat.)

The refined white sugar, corn syrup, and the host of other simple sugars many manufacturers add to food seem addicting because of the way they affect our emotions. As we prepare for Y2K, it is important to focus on quality sugars and sweeteners that will both sustain energy and contribute to good health. Such sugars contain complex carbohydrates that get stored in the liver as glycogen, an energy reserve that gets broken down more slowly, and thus enter the blood at a more appropriate, less mood-altering rate. Examples of these more beneficial whole, natural-form complex sugars and sweeteners include brown rice syrup, date sugar, maple syrup, blackstrap molasses, honey, and barley malt sugar.

Other sweeteners include "sucanat," which is sugar cane juice in an unrefined and crystalline form. Sucanat contains all of the naturally occurring vitamins, minerals, fiber and enzymes contained in the sugarcane plant. Barley malt, like sucanat, can be added to a variety of food items, including breads, beans, rice, tofu, etc. Some people are also advocating *Ki-Sweet*, the all-natural "no calorie" sweetener made from kiwis that does not induce insulin production, as a health-maintaining, broad-use sweetener. *Ki-Sweet* (telephone 888-688-6354), a network-marketing product, can found on a number of Internet sites, such as <http://feelfine.com/KSfat.html> or <http://www.citywideguide.com/freecar/whatsnew/sweety.htm>. Except for *Ki-Sweet,* all of the above-mentioned natural sweeteners can be purchased at your local full-service health food store.

Pure, raw, cane sugar in its "natural," unrefined form contains vitamins, minerals, enzymes and fiber, all of which make it better for us than the denatured overly-refined "white" sugars—which have been melted, clarified, and "bleached" to remove all non-sucrose by-products—used in many of the food items at supermarkets. Using natural whole-form sugar to sweeten some of the potentially bland foods we might consume during Y2K will be more beneficial for our health.

Y2K TIP

If you have not cooked with the more health-benefiting sweeteners listed above, it would be wise to experiment with them since some of them will react differently than conventional white sugar. For example, date sugar can be substituted for overly processed brown sugar, but it needs to be cooked at a lower temperature so that it does not "brown" too much. Remember to log your culinary experiments in your Y2K Journal.

Dehydrated Fruit

Dehydrated fruit is another health-benefiting way to satisfy our sweet tooth. Purchasing a good quality dehydrator and preparing your own dehydrated fruits and vegetables from certified organic produce gives you control over what you are putting into your body. (Unfortunately, because refined sugar is so overwhelming, it takes a while for some people—especially children—to recover the taste for natural sweets such as fruit.)

Dried fruits such as pineapple, mango, papaya, banana, apricots, apple, raisins, and dates make both a good snack and good "sweeteners" to add variety to your core-food package. This is especially important since most children do not find beans or dehydrated broccoli too appetizing.

Get the children involved in making dehydrated fruits and vegetables. This will help them understand how food is prepared and make them more open to try new taste sensations. It will also give you quality bonding time when you can gently share what Y2K is all about.

Liquid Sweeteners

If you are going to make bread, muffins, or pancakes, organic black strap molasses, honey, and maple syrup can go a long way toward making them taste like gourmet meals—especially if they are cooked on a Y2K "alternative" stove and get a little undercooked or burned. You can also add these "whole-form" sweeteners to your core foods to help children and the elderly eat regularly. (If you are concerned about "corrupting" their taste buds, you can always do a gradual "dial down," or weaning, after the Y2K transition has passed, by slowly adding less and less sweetener.)

Baby and Children Concerns

Unfortunately, most children in North America crave the wrong foods. Both mass marketing and the lack of proper nutritional knowledge and education by parents have led to the over-consumption of nutritionally empty "junk" foods. Y2K might force some children to change this habit. However, such changes cannot be done at the last moment. Children will be under a lot of stress during Y2K, and during such times the psychological comfort of certain foods will be important.

This is why we can't wait until Y2K hits to feed children foods that are not familiar to them. Loss of appetite could have serious consequences. It is important to experiment now and discover what they will and won't like among the foods you will have on hand.

Fortunately there are some good-tasting, healthy-alternative, shelf-stable foods available for young ones. For those with infants and young children, you might stock up on *Earth's Best Baby Foods,* <http://www.earthsbest.com/>, a line of certified organic baby foods available in many health food stores and conventional supermarkets. *Earth's Best Baby Foods* have an 18-month to two-year shelf life. Their unsweetened fruits and vegetables can serve as a nutritious ready-made snack for young ones. (I also know adults who enjoy them.)

Boxed cereals are another "semi" shelf-stable ready-to-eat snack for children. By "semi," I mean they have about a nine-month shelf life. Experiment with health food store brands to find cereals made with organically certified grains and without added sugar and coloring agents—ingredients that some parents swear make their children hyperactive and inattentive. An easy way to stock up is to purchase an extra box or two every time you shop—especially during the fall of 1999, so that the food will last at least five or six months into the Year 2000. Just be sure to rotate the boxes as you consume their contents.

The important thing is that you look for health-promoting foods that your children like. *Annie's Homegrown,* <http://www.annies.com>, e-mail <bernie@annies.com>, *Organically Grown Whole Wheat Shells and Cheddar* dinner is an example of a nutritious, tasty substitute for the more popular national brand that has lots of artificial colors, flavorings, etc.

> ## Y2K TIP
> Our third child will be six months old when Y2K strikes. This is a vivid reminder that pregnant women and families with infants, toddlers, and young children must make special preparations such as anticipating how big our infants will grow as we stock up on diapers, socks, shoes, cold weather clothes, etc.

Other Important Staples

The following list of supplementary items is not inclusive, but is meant to stimulate your thinking as you plan for and procure items that are inexpensive, shelf-stable, healthy, and easy to prepare.

Lesser-Known Grains

Many people prefer hard red winter wheat berries because, according to the literature of *Paramount Farms* (telephone 785-754-2151), they are "low in fat but high in complex carbohydrates, vegetable protein, B vitamins and trace minerals," and because they are versatile, meaning that they can be "cooked whole for side or main dishes, cracked for cereals and breads, sprouted for salads and sandwiches, or ground for whole wheat flour." In addition to a variety of common core food staples such as brown rice, oats, and red and white wheat berries, I suggest you try nonwheat (nongluten) "grains" such as spelt, buckwheat, teff, quinoa, and amaranth. If you are not familiar with these nutritious and different-tasting wheat alternatives, you should visit your local health food store and try them out and explore recipes that enhance their flavor. (For example, the grain amaranth has a tasty, nutty flavor and offers a healthy balance of protein, high fiber, and minerals. It also contains a high amount of two amino acids—lysine and methionine—that most grains lack, and is high in iron and phosphorus.

Those who are allergic to wheat should try White Milo (Jowar) berries, which are used for bread and cereal by African and South Asian cultures, or try *Kamut®*. *Kamut®* is a form of wheat that has a rich, buttery flavor, with 20 to 40 percent more protein than most kinds of wheat, has a higher profile of amino acids, lipids, vitamins and minerals, and is more easily digestible than other types of wheat. In addition to *Kamut®*'s nutritional superiority over regular wheat, research studies reveal that those with wheat allergies can better tolerate it. *Kamut®* can be used in a variety of recipes, including bread, pasta, and pancakes.

Condiments

Having a variety of condiments, herbs, spices, and sauces on hand will make Y2K eating a lot more pleasant. In addition to natural sea salt, cayenne and black pepper, paprika, exotic mustards, chutneys, tamari, honey, jellies and jams, soup stocks, relish, vinegar oils, miso, garlic, carob, dried fruit, and other personal favorites, you might consider *Bragg's Liquid Aminos* (available at your local health food store) as a delicious salt and soy sauce substitute (try it on brown rice!). *Bragg's Liquid Aminos* has a two-year shelf life and is made from "chemical-free" soybeans aged in distilled water. *Bragg* also makes an organic raw *Apple Cider Vinegar* that can be combined with the *Bragg's Liquid Aminos* and olive oil to make a tasty, fresh salad dressing. (The Bragg Web site, <http://www.bragg.com>, offers a variety of health-related information.) (Canadians can contact *Sprout Master,* <http://www.absolute-health.on.ca/>, e-mail <sproutm@webgate.net>, the "largest distributor of quality sprouting supplies in Canada," for information on local dealers who carry *Bragg's Liquid Aminos,* and a host of other organic foods, supplements, and health care items, including many mentioned in this book.)

For those who prefer regular salt, *Brain Garden* (telephone 800-481-9987) makes *Solsaltz,* which according to their literature, is a natural salt that is "vacuum panned" to remove the "heart-stressing, artery-clogging, microscopic sand" that normal table salt contains.

Canned Goods Ideas

Canned food items can add variety to your core food program—especially soups and fruits such as pineapple and peaches (without added sugar), which can make a variety of foods taste better. (However, be aware that tests have shown canned tuna to have high mercury levels. Canned salmon might be a healthier substitute, especially since it contains EFAs.)

To be safe, it is better to use a canned product at least several months before its due date in order to assure adequate nutritional value. Unfortunately, the expiration date codes on many canned goods are not always easy to decipher. Ask your local retailer how to interpret them. It is also critical to have a supply of manually operated can openers and to date canned goods clearly so you can rotate them before they lose their nutritional value.

When using wet canned foods, the issue of bacteria contamination and toxicity is an important consideration. Canned foods are susceptible to harboring and breeding bacteria, especially if not done with the right equipment. Home canning should be done with a pressurized unit that sustains the right temperature for the right amount of time to kill the lethal *clostridium botulinum* (botulism) spore. Boiling food will not kill these lethal bacteria. If you discover that a can is bulging or the contents smell bad when you open it— throw the food away. Don't risk food poisoning (or death). Do research on proper canning techniques and get advice from those who have been canning for a while. (The *Food Canning Forum* offers good advice [<http://www.home-Canning.com/Bulletin/bernardin/0400.html>].)

For many people, metal contamination is an important concern when using canned goods. Unless canned goods are packaged in special ways, there is the risk that metals such as aluminum can leach into the food, especially from acid-based items such as tomato sauce. Some companies such as *Health Valley* (telephone 800-423-4846) are aware of this problem and use a "poly-enamel food-safe coating" to prevent metal leakage into the food—the same as the #2 and #10 cans that the freeze-dried and dehydrated food companies offer. (It always a good idea to ask companies how they manufacture their goods.)

Some examples of quality canned goods include *Health Valley*'s line of fat-free *Soups in a Cup* that include hot cereal, chili, spicy black bean, corn chowder, lentil, pasta *Italiano*, creamy potato, and garden split pea. Though only some of the products in this line are certified organic, all of them are free of preservatives, additives, coloring, and artificial and synthetic flavor enhancers, and they have a shelf life of 13 months. *Eden Foods Inc.* offers a line of canned beans and legumes called *Eden Organic*—including kidney, adzuki, and black beans. (The latter comes mixed with ginger and lemon but I found it still needed some seasoning to keep from being bland.)

Milk Concerns

Given the complex methods used in producing milk, there is a good chance dairy products will be scarce at the beginning of Y2K. Therefore, if you drink milk, it might be wise to stock up on shelf-stable milk substitutes. If you are not already using a nutritious milk and dairy alternative, you might want to try the soymilk products made by *Eden Foods Inc.*, <http://www.healthyreferral.com/sponsors/eden/>. Soymilk can be used as a substitute in any food mix or recipe that calls for traditional cow's milk. (If you haven't tried it you might be pleasantly surprised.) *Eden Soy Extra* also has added B12 for vegans and vegetarians as well as calcium, beta-carotene, and Vitamins D and E. *Eden Foods' Eden Soy Extra—Original* has a higher protein content than the *Vanilla* variety and has a good carbohydrate-to-protein ratio for those concerned about their glycemic (blood sugar) index. (Along this line, rice milks and rice cakes are too high in simple carbohydrates and cause a sudden rise in the blood sugar.) *Eden Soy* milks come packaged in shelf-stable containers with an expiration date stamped on the top and have an 11-month shelf life. Summer and fall 1999 would be a good time to begin stocking up on cases of this product.

Juices

Juice can help members of your Preparedness Group drink fluids when the taste of the water you have stored away might not appeal to them. Many of the companies specializing in long-term storage foods also sell fruit juices in a pouch or a long-term storage container, or you can purchase fruit juices at your local health food store or supermarket. However, many juice products, especially those at conventional supermarkets, can be deceptive. If you plan to stock up on juices, don't be fooled by the "no added sugar" claim on the labels. Many of the popular juices (not the "drinks" that disclose their added sugars such as fructose and sucrose) found at conventional supermarkets are labeled "unsweetened" or "all natural," but in fact they are loaded with extra sugar. Companies get away with this because instead of directly adding "sugar" they run the juice through a special process that doubles and triples the "natural" sugar content in juice so that you end up with an unnaturally super-sweetened juice.

Therefore I recommend stocking up on unprocessed juices such as glass gallon jugs of "pure" apple cider during the fall of 1999. Warm apple cider with organic cinnamon sticks will be a great "winter warmer" and a tasty treat during the Y2K winter. (This can also make a fun family event for children as they warm up the cider by candlelight—an effective cooking method addressed in Chapter Nine.)

I also plan to have a good supply of "dry" juices such as carrot, beet, barley, Kamut®, etc. (I prefer freshly extracted juice, but the possibility of Y2K electrical and water problems means I might need a healthy alternative.) In essence, dry juices are freeze-dried and/or dehydrated fruits and vegetables that come in a finely powdered form which, when mixed with water, becomes a highly nutritious drink. Because of the special processing involved, dry juices maintain the maximum nutritional value of the original vegetables from which they are made. Such "dry" juices might be the one of the few sources of "live," enzyme-rich foods during Y2K. Dry juices are available through a variety of network marketing companies as well as from your local health food store. *Green Kamut® Corporation,* <http://www.

galaxymall.com/retail/phyto/>, is a non-network marketing company that offers an excellent line of nutritionally rich, certified-organic "dried" juices, such as Kamut®, barley, carrot, and beet. You can contact them directly for bulk quantity wholesale discounts or purchase their products in health food stores. (Friends, relatives, and neighbors might want to consider combining orders to take advantage of large order discounts.)

Sea vegetables

If you live near the coast, sea vegetables (what some call seaweed) such as bladderwrack, dulce, kelp, alaria, and laver (similar to Japanese nori and wakame) can be dried out and used for food. Sea vegetables form a nearly endless supply of one of the most nutritionally rich food sources on the planet for those fortunate to live near unpolluted ocean waters. They add great flavor to soups and hot noodle broths. You can contact *Maine Coast Sea Vegetables,* <http://www.seaveg.com/Intro.html>, e-mail <info@seaveg.com>, for a wide selection of certified organic phytonutrients from the sea sold by the ounce (28.33 grams) or the pound (450 grams). *Maine Coast Sea Vegetables* practices environmentally sensitive and responsible, sustainable harvesting practices. Their Web site also offers a good bibliography and research directory of available articles and abstracts on the nutritional value of sea vegetables, as well as a variety of mouth-watering recipes.

Mendocino Sea Vegetables, <http://www.seaweed.net/>, e-mail <info@seaweed.net>, is another company specializing in "wild crafted" North American sea vegetables, which they sell by the ounce (28.33 grams) or the pound (450 grams). This site also contains recipes and information on how to order the *Sea Vegetable Gourmet Cook Book* and the *WildCrafter's Guide* by Eleanor and John Lewallen (Mendocino Sea Vegetable Company, 1996)—books that reveal the health-giving properties contained in sea vegetables—the food the Japanese consider fit for "kings and gods."

Those in Canada (and the U.S.) can contact *Roland's Sea Vegetables* (telephone 506-662-3468) for a good selection of nutrient-dense sea vegetation. Roland is a delight to talk to and has recipes and information on a variety of sea vegetables available.

> ## Y2K TIP
> A number of Churches of Latter Day Saints (Mormons) operate a "Welfare Cannery" and allow nonmembers to rent their dry pack cannery equipment to store food items in #10 cans, as well as in nitrogen-packed and vacuum-sealed bags. (They will show you how to do this.) They also might have preparedness food items for purchase.

Concluding "Core food" Comments

As you prepare for the uncertainties that Y2K might bring, it is important that you design a food program that maximizes variety to ensure that you get adequate and well balanced nutrition. If you are going to purchase three-month, six-month, or one-year "complete" food packages, be sure to examine closely the quantity and quality of the calories they contain. Because of the extra stress and added manual labor many of us might undergo during the Y2K transition, the average adult will need a minimum of 2000 calories found in "quality" foods each day. By "quality" I mean foods that contain naturally occurring vitamins, minerals, proteins, carbohydrates, fiber, fats and oils, enzymes, co-factors, and other phyto-nutrients. In contrast, the denatured "empty" calories found in most of the overly processed and refined food items found in conventional supermarkets do not serve our bodies well.

In essence, the better the quality of food we eat, the better our health will be. This principle is especially true for those who have compromised or vulnerable health conditions such as the elderly, the chronically ill, pregnant women, and young children. It is important that we stock up on quality oils, grains, legumes, seeds, nuts, fruits, and vegetables to ensure we will get proper nutrition. The old Hippocratic adage, "Let Food Be Thy Medicine," will become important in the days ahead.

Once you have purchased your preparedness food products, it is equally important to understand how to cook and prepare them. This topic is taken up in the next chapter.

CHAPTER 4

Y2K Food Tools

• • | • • • • • • • •

"Our children . . . should enter adulthood with a basic knowledge
of how to store food over winter without the cooperation
of a nuclear power plant a hundred miles away. Every animal
in the forest is taught this skill; we owe our children no less." —Jerry Minnich

As you stock up on core food supplies you must be sure you can prepare them properly. In other words, all the core food supplies in the world will not matter much if you can't make meals that people will eat. The following list of equipment and food-related items is designed to make your Y2K food supply more nutritious and enjoyable.

Grain Mills

The ability to make your own whole-grain flour and from it make bread, muffins, pancakes, and other hearty and nourishing baked goods, makes you less dependent upon the vulnerable food supply chain. Grinding your own flour also ensures your family that you are not eating rancid flour—something you cannot always be sure of when you buy commercially made items, even those bought in a health food store. Unfortunately, much store-bought flour is rancid, meaning that the oils it contains have been exposed to oxygen during the milling process and have spoiled. (It takes about seventy-two hours for flour to go rancid.) As mentioned in the last chapter, rancid oils are a prime suspect in the cause of premature aging, heart disease, and cancer. Therefore, whenever possible, it is wise to use freshly ground flour. (Visit the *Village Bakery on the Web* home page, <http://countrylife.net/bread/>, for information, tips, and recipes on home bread making. *Cris Enterprises* also has a Web page, <http://www.grainmills.com/milling.htm>, that contains practical information on milling and baking your own flour and bread products.)

> ## Y2K TIP
> Grinding and baking your own baked goods not only helps prevent appetite fatigue, but allows people with common food allergies such as wheat and corn to experiment with a wider range of grains and legumes. Surprisingly, flour can be made from a variety of food items, including sweet

potatoes, yams, potatoes, pinto beans, navy beans, kidney beans, lentils, rice, and sorghum. It is also worth noting that many people with "untreatable" chronic diseases and emotional problems have been helped once they discover, and stop eating, foods to which they are allergic. Those with food allergies and other related digestive and autoimmune problems should consult the *Special Foods Home Page,* <http://www.specialfoods.com>, e-mail <kslimak@ix. netcom.com>—a site dedicated to supplying products and information for those with food sensitivities. They should also read books such as *Your Child's Food Allergies: Detecting and Treating Hyperactivity, Congestion, Irritability and Other Symptoms Caused by Common Food Allergies* by Jane McNicol (John Wiley & Sons, 1992), *The Elimination Diet Cookbook: A 28-Day Plan for Detecting Allergies* by Jill Carter (Element, 1997), or *Allergy Cooking With Ease: The No Wheat, Milk, Eggs, Corn, Soy, Yeast, Sugar, Grain, and Gluten Cookbook* by Nicolette M. Dumke (Starburst Element, 1992). All are available from *Amazon.com,* <http://www.amazon.com>.

Grain Mills To Consider

When choosing a mill, be sure it can grind both oily and non-oily grains, nuts, seeds, legumes, etc. Oily items include soybeans and nutritious nuts and seeds such as almonds, sesame, sunflower, and flax seeds. Remember EFAs— Essential Fatty Acids—are critical for the body, and having the ability to grind organic flax seeds will mean having a fresh supply of these vital oils. (My family makes a great-tasting mixture of finely ground, organically grown flax seeds, almonds, and sunflower seeds that we sprinkle on top of our salads or hot cereals.) Non-oily grains include wheat, rye, oats, spelt, etc.

You might also want to consider purchasing a mill that allows you to add a grain "flaker" that will let you make fresh cereal from small, dry, whole grains such as oats, spelt, or wheat. Fresh cereals can add a nutritious and satisfying variety to your breakfast menu. (You can also add flaked grains to snacks, soups, and myriad other foods to help prevent appetite fatigue.)

Fortunately there are a number of vendors offering a wide variety of grain mills in terms of price and quality. As with most items in this book, I suggest you purchase the best quality unit you can afford. It is also important to get a hand-operated mill that is easy to work so that you will use it after Y2K is over. For a good brief overview of the pros and cons of grain mills and grinders see the *Walton Feed* Web page, "Which Grinder is Best for You?" <http://waltonfeed.com/grinder.html>.

Jade Mountain Inc., <http://www.jademountain.com/>, e-mail <info@jademountain.com>, and *Lehman's Non-Electric,* <http://www. lehmans.com>, carry a variety of hand-operated grain mills. *Lehman's* makes their own mill, which comes with a stone burr for grinding fine flour for bread and other baked goods, and cast iron burrs for grinding oily seeds and nuts. They also carry what they consider the "Rolls Royce" of hand-operated grain mills, namely the Danish-made *Diamant* (about $540) and the *Country Living* mill (about $350). Both machines use a "force feeding worm auger" that can grind both oily and non-oily items with the same burr. However, the *Diamant,* which is made of cast iron and weighs about 60 pounds (27 kilograms), as compared to the 21-pound (9.5 kilograms), aluminum-bodied *Country Living* mill, allows you to purchase an extra-fine burr that will grind all grains (including corn) to "dust-like" flour, and an extra-coarse burr for cracking grain for livestock feed and breakfast cereal. *Lehman's* also carries a powerful hand-driven, high-speed mill that will grind anything, including hard roots; it can be used to make large quantities of flour. (Churches, synagogues, and neighborhood groups might consider purchasing a unit such as this one.)

Christian Family Resources (telephone 719-962-3228) carries an extensive line of grain mills. Their catalog ($3) gives a good description of the strengths and weaknesses of various kinds of mills. Two of their favorites are the *Country Living Grain Mill* (about $375) and the *Family Grain Mill* (about $120). Both are high-quality, versatile mills with the *Country Living* being able to grind finer flour more quickly and easily. The *Country Living Grain Mill* has two important options, the "Power Bar" (about $26), which enables even children to grind the toughest grains into powder-fine flour suitable for baking; and the "Nut and Large Bean Auger" (about $30) for making nut butters and grinding larger beans such as limas and great northerns. (Exercise buffs should note that the *Country Living Hand Mill* can be driven by an exercise bicycle.) Companies offering some of the best prices for the *Country Living Hand Mill* include *Homestead Products,* <http://elaine. teleport.com/~dany/mill/>, e-mail <dany@teleport.com>; and *Home-Health Resource,* <http://www.homehealthresource.net>, e-mail <hhr@piggott.net>, whose Web page says they "will match any price on the 'Net on this item." As of March 1999 the *Country Living Mill* has an eight- to ten-week back order.

For its price, the *Family Grain Mill* (also available from *Cris Enterprises,* <http://www.grainmills.com/auth_retail.html>, e-mail <sales@cris-enterprises. com>) is one of the best mills to consider. The *Family Grain Mill* has a "Flaker Mill" option (about $140, or $190 for both the "flaker" and the grain mill).

Many people also like the simple, German-made *Jupiter Deluxe* (under $130) hand-operated grain mill available from *Magic Mill–Linda's Home Products* (telephone 801-943-8860) and *On-line Health Products*, <http://www.dhi.com/>. The *Jupiter Deluxe* weighs about four pounds and will grind flour as fine as an electric mill. It has stainless steel milling burrs that will grind rice, beans, wheat, and lentils, but not field corn or maize. The *Jupiter Deluxe* has a simple adjustment that allows you to grind as finely or coarsely as you need. This unit will also grind seeds, spices, and even coffee.

The sturdy and economical *Back to Basics Grain Mill* (about $65) is available from a number of vendors who sell bulk grains and legumes (such as *Bruce Hopkins, Captain Dave's Survival Shop,* and *Walton Feed*) as well as from *The Living and Raw Foods Marketplace*, <http://www.living-foods.com/marketplace/>, e-mail <help@discountjuicers.com>.

Y2K TIP

Before consuming large amounts of wheat, it is important to give your body time to adjust to this particular food item. Many people develop allergies to wheat and wheat-related products, or experience intestinal distress (gas, bloating, etc.), because they do not give their body time to adapt to wheat. Some people find that sprouting wheat grain for a few days before using it in cereal, bread, pasta, etc., helps prevent wheat-related digestive problems.

If you plan on making lots of bread, muffins, and other staples that need mixing, you can order a hand-operated dough mixer from *Back to Basics*, <http://www.backtobasicsproducts.com/>. Making fresh-baked bread can be a fun-filled adventure for both children and adults as we experience the simple joys that get overlooked in the normal course of our busy lives.

Dehydrators

A good food dehydrator is another valuable tool to save money and gain control over the quality of the food you will eat during Y2K. This handy item allows you to prepare an unlimited variety of nutritious food items—everything from dried pineapples, peaches, and tomatoes, to spicing herbs and turkey jerky—for long-term food storage. By slowly and evenly blowing dry, heated air across fresh fruits and vegetables, food dehydrators preserve and often enhance the taste of these vital foodstuffs. It is far less expensive to dehydrate food yourself than to purchase it commercially. Another advantage of dehydrating your own food is that you can grow or buy organic food sources that are free from pesticides, added sugar, preservatives, coloring agents, and other toxic substances. (It is easier to be kosher this way, too.)

When buying a food dehydrator, there are several important features to consider. Most important, you should buy a quality dehydrator that removes all the moisture. If your food items are not dried properly they will spoil quickly. It is also vital that you obtain a unit that gives you control over the temperature at which the food is being dehydrated so that you will not overheat the items and destroy valuable enzymes and nutrients. If you are serious about food dehydration and good nutrition, you should invest in a high-quality unit that offers these important options.

In general, there are two different types of dehydrators—those with a horizontal airflow, and those with a vertical airflow. Most people prefer the horizontal airflow systems that have the heating unit and fan located on the side of the dehydrator to circulate air evenly across the top of each tray. The advantage of horizontal drying is that, unlike the vertical units that blow heat from top to bottom, horizontal units move the dry air across each tray individually. This means that you can dry different types of fruits and vegetables at the same time without the food flavors and juices mixing with one another, a problem that often occurs with a vertical drying unit.

Top-of-the-line dehydrators allow control over both the time and temperature of dehydration. This is important, because some fruits and vegetables need a specific amount of heat for a certain length of time to reach their maximum dehydration potential. Having a unit with a temperature control from 85°F (30°C) to 160°F (71°C) will enable you to dehydrate both plants and meats (however, temperatures over 115°F [46°C] can begin to destroy the vital enzymes that help ensure proper digestion and assimilation of nutrients found in plants). Having a timer means that you don't have to baby-sit the unit or get up in the middle of the night to prevent scorching. If you already have a dehydrator and it does not have a timer, or you cannot afford the extra cost, you can purchase a timer at a hardware store and hook it to your unit.

Y2K TIP

Some people plan to use an electric dehydrator during the summer and fall of 1999 to dehydrate fresh fruits and vegetables and store them in airtight, vacuum-sealed glass jars so that they will have a supply of tasty and nutritious "live" foods during the winter and spring of 2000. In addition, they also plan to have a backup, nonelectric dehydrator on hand for the spring and summer crops during that year.

It is important to purchase a unit that has a number of trays so that you can cut down on your dehydration labor time. (However, it is important to remember that different foods require different drying times, and that you must follow drying times closely to ensure maximum flavor and nutritional value.) Make sure, too, that your unit comes with different kinds of trays, such as mesh trays that prevent food items from sticking to the tray, as well as metal trays designed to make fruit "leather"—tasty, candy-like, pure fruit "roll-ups" that children (and adults) will enjoy. (Linda at *Magic Mill* suggests this natural way to keep fruits such as apples, bananas, and peaches from turning an unpleasant brown color: Dip them in pineapple juice before you dehydrate them, or add 500 milligrams of vitamin C as you cut them up in a blender.)

Dehydrators To Consider

Many people consider the *Excalibur* (base price about $120) to be one of the top dehydrating systems. The unit comes in four-, five-, and nine-tray sizes and has a heating unit that generates a temperature-controlled, even, horizontal flow of air across each tray so that you don't have to rotate the trays every few hours. The *Excalibur's* thermostatically controlled heat ranges from 85°F (30°C) to 145°F (63°C). It can be purchased from *Perfect Health*, <http://www.juicing.com/a1.shtml>, e-mail <perhlt@juicing.com>, or from *Jade Mountain Inc.*, <http://www.jademountain.com/>, e-mail <info@jademountain.com>. *Perfect Health* also offers the book *Preserve it Naturally* by Excalibur Products (about $20), on the art of food dehydration, that will stimulate your gastronomic imagination.

The *GardenMaster* by *NESCO American Harvest* also ranks as one of the top dehydrators on the market. This nifty unit allows you to stack as many as 30 trays and still maintain an evenly pressurized, horizontal airflow and an exceptionally broad range of adjustable drying temperatures, for example, 90°F to 165°F (32°C to 74°C). This easy-to-clean unit also comes with a number of handy accessories such as leather and mesh sheets for making a variety of tasty treats. The *GardenMaster* can be purchased from a variety of places, including Mary Bell's *The Dry Store*, <http://services.polaristel.net/~drystore>, e-mail <marytbell@aol.com>.

Air Preserve II (about $200) is another recommended dehydrator. The special patented, quiet design allows each tray to be dried individually so that you can dehydrate a variety of fruits and vegetables at the same time. The *Air Preserve II* also offers a large drying capacity (up to 30 trays) as well as a versatile thermostat control (from 95°F [35°C] to 160°F [71°C]). You can also purchase a number of helpful accessories such as special detachable fruit leather sheets, *Clean-A-Screen* mesh screens for easy clean-up of sticky, dried-on fruits and vegetables, a *Yogurt Factory* that allows you to make fresh and natural yogurt, and a special unit that helps you make "jerky." It also comes with a free "How to Dry Foods" video. The *Air Preserve II* can be purchased from *Magic Mill–Linda's Home Products* (telephone 801-943-8860) and from *On-Line Health Products*. Both places also offer the *Magic Air II*, a rectangular dehydration unit that is primarily designed to dry various forms of jerky at a preset (nonadjustable) 140°F (60°C).

For those on a limited budget, a less expensive (and less versatile) non-temperature-adjustable convection air dehydrator unit, the *Deni Food Dehydrator* (item number K165776), can be purchased from *Ronco* (telephone 800-971-8877). Another inexpensive unit can be purchased online from the Internet video shopping channel *iQVC*, <http://www.iqvc.com/>, or by telephone (888-345-5788). A solar-operated dehydrator can be purchased from *Jade Mountain Inc.*

For those who expect to be without electricity for a long time or who prefer to cultivate "off-the grid" living skills, *Life Sprouts* (telephone 800-241-1516) carries the *Hanging Pantry* natural air convection dehydrator. This unit can be hung either indoors or out to dry fruits and vegetables. *Family Food Storage* also carries the *Food PANtrie* (about $50), a nonelectric food dehydrator and seed sprouter that enables you to "preserve foods the way Mother Nature meant it to be done." Since air rather than heat is used to dry herbs, fruits, and vegetables, this unit protects all naturally occurring enzymes.

Those readers interested in learning some of the finer points of food dehydrating and thereby save a lot of time and money, can consult books such as the *Complete Dehydrator Cookbook* by Mary Bell, *The Dehydrator Cookbook* by Joanna White, or *Dehydrator Delights* by Noreen Jo Thomas. These can be ordered from your local book dealer or from *Amazon.com*, <http://www.amazon.com>.

Vital Seeds and Sprouting

For some people, sprouted seeds might form the only "fresh," "live" foods they consume during the winter months of the Y2K transition. Sprouting has several important advantages. First, it helps break down the seedcase to both release a seed's nutrients and make it easier for digestion. Second, fresh sprouts are an exceptionally potent source of vitamins and minerals. Third, sprouting can be done year-round, is highly economical—about 50 cents for a pound of fresh "greens"—and it doesn't take a green thumb or a lot of experience or expensive equipment and fertilizer to grow sprouts.

I strongly recommend that you purchase a good seed sprouter and practice this vital survival craft. Equipment to sprout seeds can be as simple as a sprouting jar purchased from your local health food store, or as elaborate as a unit with multiple trays such as the *Sprout House* and *Flax Sprout Bag* offered by *The Sprout House*, <http://www.sprouthouse.com/>, e-mail <info@SproutHouse.com>, and the *Sprout Master*, offered by *Life Sprouts* (telephone 800-241-1516 or 435-245-3891) and *On-Line Health Products*, <http://www.dhi.com/>, e-mail <zaccardi@juno.com>, which allows you to sprout several different types of seeds at one time. (See the *Sprout House* Web page, <http://www.sprouthouse.com/benefits.html>, for a chart showing the optimal growing environment for different types of sprouts, as well as a list of books to broaden your sprouting skills and gourmet tastes.)

The advantage of a good quality sprouter is that it is designed to keep your sprouts from getting sour. Too much moisture for too long a period begins to destroy the sweet taste that sprouts should have. Most of these sprouting units are inexpensive (under $15).

Ten Sprouting Commandments

To ensure successful sprouting remember these guidelines:

1. Thou shall not let your seeds pre-soak in water too long. Although each seed has its own requirement, if in doubt, soak for about 12 hours and see how well they sprout and taste.
2. Thou shall not let your sprouting seeds sit in water—unless you want them to taste sour and moldy. Remember to wet and drain, not soak and drown your sprouting seeds. You want your sprouts to be young, fresh, sweet, and tender.
3. Remember to use pure, non-chlorinated water. Chlorine can harm or kill your sprouts.
4. Remember to nurture your growing seeds at the right temperature (between 50°F [10°C] and 80°F [27°C]). Too much heat, and your seeds will die; too little warmth, and they will not grow.
5. Thou shall not sprout for too long. Four days is the maximum time you should incubate your sprouts. Remember, you want a sprouting seed, not a growing plant.
6. Thou shall not let your seeds or sprouts dry out. Remember to water (and drain) them when you awaken, two or three times during the day, and again before you retire for the night. Brown sprouts mean dry (lifeless) sprouts.
7. Remember to buy fresh, vital seeds. Old seeds will neither sprout well nor taste good.
8. Remember to buy organic seeds. Chemically treated seeds will not deliver the health-promoting benefits your body needs. (Contrary to what promotional literature might say, common sense and logic

leads us to see that herbicides, insecticides, and pesticides bring death, not life. Why risk the health and well-being of your family and loved ones by ingesting chemicals that have death as part of their name?)

9. Remember, a small quantity of seeds goes a long way. Sprout sparingly and often, so that you have a continuous supply of fresh, sweet, tender sprouts.

10. Remember to persevere. If you soak your seeds too long and they die, or you don't water the seeds enough and they dry out, don't get discouraged. Good growing habits, like anything worthwhile in life, take practice.

(These tips were inspired by ideas contained in *How to Grow and Serve Sprouts* by Bruford Scott Reynolds, Orangeville, Utah: Reynolds Enterprise, 1972.)

Seeds and Sprouters To Consider

It is important that you purchase food-grade sprouting seeds that are specially harvested for food sprouting, rather than garden-grade seeds for growing. Reputable vendors who specialize in sprouting seeds also test for mold and make sure the seed batch you get does not contain overly mature and hard seeds that will not sprout well.

Note: Recently, some newspaper articles have told of some people contracting *e-coli* poisoning from alfalfa sprouts that were contaminated from farm animal dung or products. Given that the *e-coli* bacteria cannot survive in a non-moist environment such as a dry seed, this contamination most likely came from poor processing practices during the sprouting process. Be sure to keep all animal products away from your seeds, sprouting water, and sprouting equipment. As an added precaution, you can spray your seeds with food-grade hydrogen peroxide to kill off any potential offenders.

You can buy sprouting seeds at most full-service health food stores, or you can buy them in bulk quantities from places such as *Life Sprouts* (telephone 800-241-1516 or 435-245-3891), *The Sprout House* (<http://www.sprouthouse.com/>), and *On-Line Health Products,* (<http://www.dhi.com/>, e-mail <zaccardi@juno.com>). These vendors carry a varied line of certified organic and "chemical-free" individual and multiple seed mixes, including alfalfa, mung beans, cabbage, clover, spicy garlic, chives, radishes, mild lentils, buckwheat, sunflower, fenugreek, adzuki, and triticale. Each of these seeds and beans has a different nutritional value and flavor. Sprouts are versatile. Experiment placing them in breads, soups, salads, sandwiches, salad dressings, or casseroles, or mix them with rice, beans, and legumes. You can even put them in cookies.

Life Sprouts offers a one-year supply of sprouting seeds for approximately $139.50. They come in a food-grade plastic six-gallon (23 liters) bucket container (about 50 pounds [23 kilograms]). *Life Sprouts* also carries quart-sized (about 10 ounces) [just under a liter, or about 288 grams] containers of seeds that come in special plastic bottles that do not leach or give off-gassings—which might be an issue for those who are chemically sensitive.

Ready Reserve, <http://www.readyreservefoods.com>, e-mail <sales@readyreservefoods.com>, carries a sprout and sprouting kit combination (under $35) that contains six cans of sprouting seeds and a dual tray sprouter for easy soaking and drying. This system can be purchased from *B&A Products,* <http://www.baproducts.com/catalog.htm>, e-mail <byron@baproducts.com>.

Y 2 K   T I P

According to some experts, the nitrogen used in long-term storage containers to extend shelf life, kills the vital germ inside seeds and renders them useless for sprouting. Seeds both for growing and sprouting need to be aerated periodically or they will smother and die. About every year (or two at the most), seeds must be oxygenated by moving them from one container to another. (This is another good reason to label your stored items well, so that you can rotate them properly.)

Captain Dave's Survival Center, <http://survival-center.com/>, e-mail <webmaster@survival-center.com>, offers sprouting kits, trays, and accessories. *Perfect Health,* <http://www.juicing.com>, e-mail <perhlt@juicing.com>, also offers a nonelectric combination *Food Dehydrator and Sprouter* (about $60) for those who want to save money and get two important health-enhancing tools in one.

By spraying *Liquid Kelp Fertilizer* on your sprouting beans or adding a few drops to the soaking water you can add a rich array of organic minerals to your sprouts. You can also purchase *Liquid Kelp Fertilizer* from some of the sprout vendors mentioned above, such as *The Sprout House,* <http://www.sprouthouse.com/>, e-mail <info@SproutHouse.com>.

The Sprout House also carries a *Manual Wheatgrass Juicer* (about $79). Wheatgrass (sprouted wheat) is a potent juice that is both nutritionally dense and helps "cleanse" the body of toxins. A little goes a long way and can help maintain health during the Y2K transition.

I suggest you keep a record of your sprouting adventures in your Y2K Preparedness Journal. Place seed-rinsing reminders around the house until your sprouting skills become second habit.

Sprouting is also a great hobby or chore for little ones. Young children love to see things grow. (However, don't let them become too diligent and over-water. Be sure to explain the "Ten Sprouting Commandments" and show them how to water the seeds properly.)

It is also wise to consult books dedicated to the art of sprouting. "Sproutman" Steve Meyerowitz has authored two helpful books, *Sprouts: The Miracle Food,* and *The Kitchen Garden Cookbook.* Both are available from the *Sprout House,* your local bookshop, or from *Amazon.com,* <http://www.amazon.com>.

Vacuum Sealers

Vacuum sealers are another handy emergency preparedness and long-term storage tool. They come in two general types—electric and hand-operated units. Vacuum sealers are designed to remove all oxygen (or nearly all—the less expensive the unit the less oxygen it removes) from an airtight container. Vacuum sealers not only keep food items from spoiling and going rancid, but they also help to keep bugs out. According to some vacuum sealer advocates, the lack of oxygen prevents bugs, insects, and related pests from smelling the food inside a container and thus keeps them from being attracted to the food items inside.

Vacuum sealers can be used on jars, cans, and plastic bags. They can also be used to help preserve home-dehydrated foods longer by sealing them in airtight containers. (One long-term food storage advocate recommends using wide-mouth half-gallon [1.9 liters] jars for dehydrated foods instead of the plastic bags that many people use because the sharp edges of some fruits and vegetables can subtly puncture plastic, leading to decreased shelf life and freshness.)

Vacuum sealers are especially good at keeping fresh oils from going rancid. One professional food sealer recommends using jars with a "regular" (not wide-mouth) lid jar for preserving oil.

On-line Health, <http://www.dhi.com/>, e-mail <zaccardi@juno.com>, carries the *Magic Vac Food Saver* (about $250), a versatile, "commercial quality," vacuum food packing sealer. This unit comes with a variety of options and accessories that can vacuum seal almost any type of jar, bottle, can, or plastic container. Food storage jars (such as *Ball, Keer,* etc.) can be purchased at your local grocery store or food canning supply shop. (Good vacuum sealers allow you to reuse the lids of canning jars over and over. You simply use a knife, a screwdriver, or a coin to pop the seal open; reseal the jar once you are done.)

ASONTV.COM, telephone 800-368-3763, <http://www.asontv.com/>, offers the *FoodSaver Deluxe* for $200. This unit comes with lots of user-friendly options such as automatic "hands-free" operation and an LED light that lets you know when the sealing is done.

If the more "commercial" type units are out of your budget range, *The Sportsman's Guide*, <http://www.sportsmansguide.com/>, carries reconditioned *FoodSaver* vacuum sealers for under $100. Or you might consider purchasing a *Pump 'n' Seal* food freshness preserver. This hand-operated gadget creates a vacuum seal in jars, cans, and zip-locking bags so that you can safely store your dehydrated food. The *Pump 'n' Seal* can be purchased from a number of places, including *ASONTV.COM* and *Epicenter*, <http://www.theepicenter.com>, e-mail <bjnelson@TheEpicenter.com>. This unit comes with a self-explanatory video. You should also purchase extra *tab-check* seals. Although the *Pump 'n' Seal* cannot compare in its sealing ability with commercial-quality units, it does not need electricity to operate, and hence could prove very useful in the event of a Y2K-induced power outage, especially for keeping oils fresh.

Family Gardening

For those who think Y2K will be truly bad and who have access to land, growing your own food could prove prudent.

In recent years, much attention has been focused on using "non-hybrid" or "heirloom" seeds. As modern society has developed, people have lost the art of seed saving and have become dependent upon seed companies to supply seeds. In order to ensure continued sales, major seed manufacturers have bred plants that produce seeds that no longer have a perennial ability. They have also produced "hybrid" strains of seeds that have been bred to meet the requirements of mass food production. Jeffrey T. Maehr succinctly states the seriousness of this overdependence on these types of seeds: "Most of the world's staple crops are a 'monocultural genetic stock.' That is, the genetic base for these seeds has become very limited through selective breeding for specific advantages. In this process, much of the natural genetic protection, inherent in the variety that was once used, is lost. This makes the entire country-wide crop susceptible to drought or disease and insect infestation" (<http://www.true-health.com/garden.htm>). (See his Web site for a brief but vigorous defense of non-hybrid seeds.)

In short, hybridization has resulted in plants, fruits, and vegetables that cannot reproduce and which have lost much of their taste and nutritional value, such as the cardboard-tasting tomatoes at the local supermarket. In contrast, non-hybrid or heirloom seeds maintain the ability to produce year after year and retain their rich taste and nutritional value.

Many Y2Kers recommend stocking up on heirloom seeds for both personal gardens and for bartering if things truly get bad. A number of companies
specialize in heirloom quality seeds. Geri Guidetti's *The Ark Institute,*
<http://www.arkinstitute.com/>, e-mail <arkinst@concentric.net>, offers a
Survival Seed Package that includes over ten pounds (4.5 kilograms) of
assorted non-hybrid seeds. This package (about $159) includes enough seeds
to grow over 50 different fruits, vegetables, and legumes and can feed a family of four for one to two years. This offer also includes Geri's book *Build
Your Own Ark! How to Prepare for Self-Reliance in Uncertain Times...Book
I: Food Self-Sufficiency.* (See Geri's articles focused on protecting and preserving our natural heritage of seed stock at <http://www.arkinstitute.com>.)

Y2K Grub, <http://www.y2kgrub.com/>, also offers an extensive line of
heirloom seed packages as does *Seeds Blum,* <http://www.seedsblum.com/>,
e-mail <webmaster@seedsblum.com>. The *Seeds Blum* Web site also offers
non-hybrid seed kits, plus lots of practical information about garden growing, and is one of the best sources for books dedicated to organic and high-
yield gardening.

Morning Dew Farms, <http://ascc.artsci.wustl.edu/~jjharlan/mdf.html>,
e-mail <jjharlan@artsci.wustl.edu>, another company dedicated to "backyard biodiversity," offers a variety of culinary herbs, flowers, and heirloom
vegetables.

Back To Eden, <http://www.farmboys.com/seeds/>, e-mail <seeds@
tlchub.com>, offers inexpensive *Back To Eden Survival Seed Kits* for those
who want to plant a garden as a way to provide a renewable food source for
their family. The advantage of these kits is that they are put together according
to the climate zone where you live—an important factor to consider before
you race out and buy a lot of seeds that might not grow well in your area. All

of their kits contain at least 55 different kinds of seeds to ensure a wide variety of freshly grown food items.

You can also order organic seed stock from *Seeds of Change*, <http://seedsofchange.com/catalog/index_cat.html>, e-mail <gardener@ seedsofchange.com>, which offers an extensive line of certified organic seeds (and soup stocks). Contact them for their highly educational catalog.

An Old-Fashioned Storage Alternative

Those interested in an old-time, "off-grid" storage system to ensure a supply of "fresh" fruits and vegetables during the Y2K winter should look up *Walton Feed's* "Root Cellar" home page, <http://www.lis.ab.ca/Walton/old/cellars.html>, which highlights how our ancestors kept fruits, vegetables, dairy products, and meat, cool and fresh, year 'round. This Web site offers loads of detailed information on construction methods, temperature concerns, air circulation, optimum storage conditions for different products, etc. It even includes a diagram on how to make an "underground storage area" for those who have a limited amount of space (<http://www.lis.ab.ca/Walton/old/cellar2.html>) as well as construction blueprints for an "Old Time Dugout Root Cellar" (<http://www.lis.ab.ca/Walton/old/cellar1.html>). This site also includes "The Granddaddy Of All Underground Areas" (<http://www.lis.ab.ca/Walton/old/cellar3.html>), which utilizes "culverts" to create a "livable" storage space. Culverts are strong, lightweight, galvanized, corrugated steel pipes that are used to drain water. They come in a variety of diameters and are rustproof. The site's pictures show how one innovative chap used a 50-foot-long (15 meters) culvert, eight feet (two and one-half meters) in diameter, to create an underground home and storage center. Those who think Y2K might be profoundly disruptive to the infrastructure in their area might want to look up this site and contact companies that specialize in culvert construction, such as *Thompson Culvert Company,* telephone 800-325-2150, <http://www.thompsonculvert.com/menu.html>, e-mail <tcc-sales@ thompsonculvert.com>. In Canada you can contact *FSI Culvert Inc.*, telephone 403-489-7733, fax 403-489-1821, <http://www.fsiculvert.com/>, e-mail <admin@fsiculvert.com>.

You can also consult survival expert Ted Wright's contemporary version of the old root cellars, which he calls a "Pallet Root Cellar." Ted's diagrams and directions can be found at *Epicenter's* Emergency Preparedness "Tip o'da Week" site located at <http://theepicenter.com/tipoweek.html>.

Hydroponic Growing

Hydroponic growing gives everyone with a small amount of indoor space the ability to grow fresh food items at relatively little expense and without the tedious drudgery that "dirt" gardening demands. In essence, hydroponic growing entails the cultivation of herbs, fruits, and vegetables in tubs of water and a nutrient solution—without the need for fertilizers and pesticides. The amazing thing about this process is that a 200-square-foot (18.5 square meters) hydroponics area can yield the same amount of crops as a 5000-square-foot (465 square meters) traditional earth garden, with a minimal use of resources, time, and energy.

Those interested in hydroponic growing can contact companies such as *Big-Web Marketing, Inc.*, <http://www.coolandunusual.com/y2k/y2kstore/y5twok/orderfrm.html>, that offer inexpensive hydroponics starter kits. *Big-Web Marketing, Inc.* has two kits—one for growing your own medicinal herbs and the other for setting up a small hydroponics greenhouse to grow your own fruits and vegetables (about $139 each).

Ed Sherman offers a basic introductory text on hydroponic growing— *How to Build a Bigger and Better Hydroponic Garden for Under 20 Dollars.* For a more advanced treatment of the subject, Howard M. Resh's *Hydroponic Food Production: A Definitive Guidebook of Soilless Food-Growing Methods* offers a plethora of techniques for both the commercial and serious home hydroponic grower. Raymond Bridwell's book *Hydroponic Gardening: The "Magic" of Modern Hydroponics for the Home Gardener* is a hydroponics "bestseller" that shows how to automate hydroponic growing so that you don't have to spend much time tending your year-round crops. You can order these books from your local book dealer or from *Amazon.com,* <http://www.amazon.com>.

Having looked at some important Y2K health-related food preparation tools, I will now explore an important part of any winter food preparedness plan, that is, how to cook and heat meals if the power fails.

CHAPTER 5

Backup Cooking Systems and Supplies

• •|• • • • • • • • •

"We know there will be some nasty surprises.
But we have to walk a tightrope between provoking panic
and keeping people from going to sleep at the wheel."
—William Curtis, Director, The Pentagon's Year 2000 Compliance Office

The advantage of some freeze-dried and dehydrated foods such as *AlpineAire's Gourmet Reserves,* outlined above, is that they do not need to be cooked. Just add water and you have an instant meal. However, most of us, aside from the fact that we like our food hot during the winter months, will have many food products that need to be cooked if they are to be eaten or properly digested.

Many experts are predicting there will be periodic "brownouts," where only a small amount of electricity is delivered, or complete "blackouts," where all power is lost during the early days of Y2K. This means that many of the major appliances such as microwave ovens, electric and even gas stoves (many of which have an electric starter) might not work when we need them. Therefore it would be wise to have backup cooking alternatives on hand. My hope is that you will consider purchasing and using cooking (and heating) alternatives that are both economically efficient and environmentally sound so that you can both save money and our precious natural resources at the same time.

The following list of off-grid (nonelectric) cooking devices can serve you well in the days ahead.

Cook stoves

Wood-burning cook stoves can provide both heat for cooking and warmth for your living space. (This presupposes that you will have a large enough supply of dry, "seasoned" hard wood. Stock up early. The price of wood will most likely skyrocket before Y2K hits. If you don't have time to let your wood "mature," you might have to buy the more expensive "kiln" dried hard wood—however, this might not be a bad investment if the price of electricity, heating oil, or gas jumps dramatically during Y2K. You will also need a secure place to store your wood so that it will not be stolen.)

The variety of woodstoves available today is almost overwhelming. It will take some research and consultation to determine what type of stove will be right for your needs. *Lehman's Non-Electric* <http://www.lehmans.com> is a company dedicated to establishing and maintaining a home life free from dependency upon electricity. (Their catalog is an education in the number of nonelectrical products available.) They offer an extensive line of woodstoves for both heating and cooking. The important thing to consider, whether you are purchasing a stove for backup cooking or as a way to cut down on your heating bill, is that you get a unit that is heat efficient and does not emit smoke or toxins. You will be safer if you choose a unit that goes well beyond the Canadian and American governments' environmental minimum standards for wood-burning stoves. (Unfortunately, most of the more romantic and "old-fashioned" looking models do not attain this minimum standard.)

You should also consider purchasing a unit that has a thermostat control so that you can adjust the temperature for both heating and cooking. This will save on your wallet and on the number of items you burn. You also want a unit that generates both convection (circulating), and radiant heat, so that your larger living space will be heated comfortably as you cook on your stove. Be sure to have your stove installed professionally to make sure fumes and smoke are vented properly and that the unit does not consume too much of the ambient room oxygen. You should also install both a fire/smoke detector and a carbon monoxide alarm nearby.

Lehman's Non-Electric also carries a line of cook stoves that burn both wood and coal, making them versatile if there is a shortage of or a price increase on either fuel. The *Enterprise* models (made in Canada) are simple but sturdy cook stoves that generate even-burning (no hot spots or cold spots), precise cooking control, and a warming oven for drying herbs, keeping food warm, or getting bread to rise. *Lehman's* also offers very inexpensive Amish-made wood- and coal-burning cook stoves (some beginning as low as $200). *Lehman's* even offers a portable (22-pound [10 kilograms]) woodstove that you can take with you to a friend's or relative's place. Most of these less expensive stoves are neither airtight nor fuel efficient, and therefore should not be considered for long-term use. *Lehman's* also offers a cook stove water heater that can connect to your household plumbing and generate gravity-fed hot water for baths or showers.

Pilgrim's Products (telephone 785-966-2900) offers a line of inexpensive "emergency" woodstoves. For under $500 you can get a unit that has also has a water tank for hot water and a bake oven accessory. *Riley Stove Company* (whose products are available through local woodstove dealers) also specializes in small emergency backup and hunter's cabin stoves.

Those who plan on doing a lot of woodstove cooking should consider

---

purchasing books such as *Woodstove Cookery: At Home on the Range* by Jane Cooper and Sherry Streeter, which offers lots of advice on the art of cooking on a woodstove. (Though some of the recipes might not be the healthiest for you, the woodstove cooking principles and woodstove care that the book advocates are worth reading.) *How to Live Without Electricity— And Like It* by Anita Evangelista (Loompanics Unlimited, 1997) is a good reference book geared to helping families live comfortably without the use of electricity. (Both are available from *Lehman's Non-Electric* and *Amazon.Com*, <http://www.amazon.com>.)

Portable Cook Stoves

Many people like the safety and convenience of butane stoves. *The Preparedness Centers,* <http://www.healthyharvest.com>, e-mail <n.russell@worldnet.att.net>, carries the *Portable Butane Burner* (about $60), a miniature stove with a single burner that uses butane fuel canisters. A case of 24 cans (about $60) will last about two months at the rate of three 30-minute cooking periods a day.

IPC *Future Foods,* <http://www.ipcfuturefoods.com/y2k.htm>, e-mail <T10319@aol.com>, and *New Millennium Products,* <http://www.newmillenniumproducts.com/>, e-mail <TPB51@aol.com>, carry the *Burton Mr. Max Portable Burner* (about $60), which is safe to burn indoors. The *Burton Mr. Max Portable Burner* also has the optional *Stove Top Grill* that makes cooking a lot easier and healthier by allowing grease to drain from your foods. Each *Burton* butane gas canister will supply cooking heat for up to eight to 12 hours. (Butane stoves can also be found in ethnic food shops and restaurant supply houses.)

The *Optimus No. 11 Explorer Multi-Fuel* (about $100) is a rugged and handy cooking unit that is said to burn a variety of fuels, including kerosene, white gas, diesel fuel, methyl alcohol, Coleman fuel, and even good quality canola or rapeseed oil. It is available from *Homestead Products* <http://elaine.teleport.com/~dany/mill/>, e-mail <dany@teleport.com>.

You also might want to consider other cooking alternatives such as a cook stove using natural gas, propane, or kerosene. However, beware that some of these systems give off toxic fumes that should not be inhaled. The *Brown* line of ranges (offered by *Lehman's,* <http://www.lehmans.com>, *Jade Mountain Inc.,* <http://www.jademountain.com/>, e-mail <info@jademountain.com>, and other retailers) runs on natural gas or propane and has the convenience of non-electricity-dependent, instant-on burners. (Most conventional gas ranges use electric starters and will not operate if there is an electricity failure.)

Lehman's also offers inexpensive ($90 to $170) portable propane gas cookers that you can transport to your cottage or Y2K get-away home, as well as Amish-made *Perfection* brand kerosene cook stoves. *Major Surplus,* <http://www.MajorSurplusNSurvival.com>, e-mail <info@ MajorSurplusNSurvival. com>, carries a variety of alternative and rugged large-capacity cooking stoves, such as the *Campchef Bulk Propane Stove* (about $185). This durable unit, which can be hooked up to ordinary 20-pound [nine kilograms] propane tanks, would be good for neighborhoods, churches and synagogues, and other groups who want to provide hot food for the poor, elderly, and others during a Y2K blackout. *Major Surplus* also offers heavy-duty single- and double-burner portable, cast-iron, "suitcase designed" stoves that fold up easily and can be taken almost anywhere.

Jade Mountain Inc., <http://www.jademountain.com/>, e-mail <info@ jademountain.com>, is a company dedicated to helping people live "off-grid" and to finding the "appropriate technology"—simple, responsible, and grass-roots solutions—to fit your specific goals and needs. They carry an extensive line of novel cooking sources such as the innovative *Sierra Zip Stove,* which is said to use wood, pinecones, twigs, bark, charcoal, or any solid fuel, and which can quickly produce an intense heat output (up to 18,000 BTUs per hour). The *Sierra Zip Stove* is extremely lightweight (less than a pound [453 grams]). *Jade Mountain Inc.* also carries the heftier *Eagle Stove* which, like the *Sierra Zip Stove,* does not require gas or propane. Both units work like a blacksmith's stove and use small, battery-operated fans to blow air to create an intense source of heat. The *Eagle Stove* produces about 35,000 BTUs per hour and provides a contained fire that can boil a gallon (3.78 liters) of water in a very short time.

Coleman, <http://www.colemanoutdoor.com/>, makes a variety of single- and multiple-burner camp stoves, available at most local camping gear stores. If you plan on doing a lot of cooking it might be wise to get a unit with several burners so that you can cook more than one thing at a time. Be sure to have proper ventilation, since multiple units consume a lot of oxygen, and smoke from grilling foods can be very unhealthy.

Y2K TIP

Cooking indoors on "portable" stoves that run on propane, kerosene, butane, or gas can be dangerous. Any naked flame that is not connected to some type of chimney or air-intake system will steal oxygen from your living space. It is the lack of oxygen that causes a stove or heating unit not to burn fuel properly, resulting in excessive carbon monoxide production. It is this carbon monoxide (which you cannot see or smell)—not the lack of oxygen—that kills people in close quarters such as small rooms, tents, trailers, etc. (See the Explore "Gear Talk" archive, <http://www.explore-mag.com/gearearc/stove.html>, for important safety information about cook stoves.) It is therefore a wise idea to acquire extra battery-operated carbon monoxide and smoke detectors. You might also consider installing an outdoor vent to one of the rooms in your house or building a fireproof outdoor shelter for cooking. Check with your local hardware shop employees for helpful ideas. (They are an invaluable source of free information and practical advice.)

For short-term use, that is, a few days or a week, both *Cascade Designs*, <http://www.cascadedesigns.com/cascade.htm>, and *Campmor*, <http://www.campmor.com/>, e-mail <webmaster@campmor.com>, offer a variety of *Traveling Light* small portable ovens that also double as frying pans. These versatile, fuel-efficient units sit on top of your personal camp stove and allow you to control the temperature of the foods you cook. This feature allows for a wide variety of culinary opportunities.

The Survival Center, <http://www.zyz.com/survivalcenter/>, e-mail <sales@survivalcenter.com>, carries the *Outback Oven* (about $72), which has a temperature-controlled *Teflon* pan and a convection dome that fits atop any single-burner adjustable stove, allowing you to bake a number of tasty items, including pizza, cake, bread, etc. These portable ovens are especially good for rehydrating and heating freeze-dried foods.

If you need an outdoor grill, the *Red Devil Grill* (telephone 800-220-9955) comes with a special temperature-controlled oven hood that lets you bake bread and other hard-to-make-on-a-grill items. The *Alpaca Kerosene Cook Stove* is a reliable standby for outdoor cooking; it has an 8500 BTU output and its 9/10-gallon (3.4 liters) tank lasts up to sixteen hours. You can purchase it from a number of outdoor specialty shops or places such as *Bruce Hopkins* or *Walton Feed.*

Y2K TIP

When buying cook stoves, always consider your cooking requirements. Remember that a stove with multiple burners is more kitchen-friendly, and inquire if the distributor/retailer sells special cookware designed specifically for the unit. If they do, this is often a good investment since such cookware is usually designed for perfect fit, and heat and fuel efficiency.

Gelled Fuels and Mini-Stoves

Some readers might want to explore cooking units that use renewable energy resources, such as wood pellet stoves. These units burn special wood pellets so efficiently that they generate very low particulate emissions and ash. They also require very little cleanup and have the added advantage of your not having to stock and chop wood. Check your local woodstove shop for more information, or contact *Rich's* (telephone 800-354-3633).

Embassy Imports (toll-free number 877-y2kfuel [925-3835]) offers the innovative *Ecofuel. Ecofuel* is made from the glyco family of alcohol, which means it is broken down into carbon dioxide and water when it burns. This makes *Ecofuel* a safer form of heating and cooking fuel. *Ecofuel* comes in nine-ounce (265 milliliters) nonflammable cans, which also means it is safe to ship. Each nine-ounce can will burn eight hours when used as a warmer or four hours when used as a source of cooking fuel. *Ecofuel* will not leak and will self-extinguish if it falls over. A case of 24 cans costs about $60. (As this book was going to press the makers of *Ecofuel* were also in the process of offering a special flat-folding cooking stove for the *Ecofuel* cans, and a hurricane-style lamp that burns for 100 hours.)

Alco-Brite, <http://www.alco-brite.com/>, e-mail <alcoinfo@alco-brite.com>, makes a gelled ethanol fuel made from renewable resource agricultural biofuels. According to their Web page, one 16-ounce (470 milliliters) can produces approximately 10,000 BTUs of clean, dependable heat and burns for up to four hours, depending on the oxygen supply, altitude, and damper setting (<http://www.alco-brite.com/frmain02.htm>). Depending upon altitude and oxygen supply, one can of fuel will last for four to five hours.

Alco-Brite also makes a "Snap-on-Stove" with a damper control kit (about $12) that allows each can of their fuel to generate up to 2,500 BTUs of heat, enough to cook food, boil water, warm a room, etc. This is enough heat to create a 60°F to 65°F (15.5°C to 18°C) temperature in an average-sized room.

B & A Products, <http://www.baproducts.com/catalog.htm>, e-mail <byron@baproducts.com>, and *The Survival Center,* <http://www.zyz.com/survivalcenter/>, e-mail <sales@survivalcenter.com>, are among many vendors carrying *Alco-Brite's* products. Contact *Alco-Brite* for other distributors in your area.

Insight Discounts, <http://www.insightdiscounts.com/y2k.htm>, e-mail <sales@insightdiscounts.com>, carries the inexpensive *Heat It* (under $2 each) six-hour fire canisters that can be used to boil water or cook food.

Solar Cookers, Ovens, and Other Cooking Supplies

Fortunately, there are other more environmentally and personally safer means of cooking than the fossil fuel units described above. Solar ovens and cookers, which rely on the heat of the sun, are an inexpensive, simple, non-polluting, and portable way to prepare food. They come in three types, "Box," "Panel," and "Parabolic" cookers, names that indicate their dominant type of design. These units can reach temperatures of 400°F to 600°F (204°C to 316°C). Solar cookers can also be used to heat and boil liquids. *Jade Mountain Inc.*, <http://www.jademountain.com/>, carries a full line of solar cookers and sun ovens. *Real Goods,* <http://www.realgoods.com>, e-mail <techs@realgoods.com>, also offers several excellent units. Generally, solar ovens range in price from $250 to the affordable $11.29 units offered by the non-profit group *Solar Cookers International,* who provide solar ovens and cookers to developing nations. *Sun Ovens International* (telephone 800-408-7019) produces the *Global Sun Oven* and the *Village Sun Oven* that are in use in over 126 countries. The latter is, as the name implies, large enough to cook for a small-sized village.

Canadians can contact Craig Shearer at *Solar Freedom International* (telephone 306-652-1442) for information on where to purchase a solar cooker in your area. You can also contact the *Solar Cooking Archive,* <http://www.accessone.com/~sbcn/Default.htm>, an organization dedicated to helping developing nations use solar cooking, for a variety of information on the art of solar cooking.

If you are interested in this method of cooking you should consult Beth and Dan Halacy's *Cooking with the Sun*, a book full of practical, how-to solar cooking ideas, plans, recipes, etc., or Harriet Kofalk and Warren Jefferson's *Solar Cooking: A Primer/Cookbook* (available from *Real Goods,* <http://www.realgoods.com>, e-mail <techs@realgoods.com>, *Amazon.com,* or your local book dealer).

Y2K TIP

Magic Mill–Linda's Home Products (telephone 801-943-8860) carries the *Zojirushi Automatic Bread Maker* (under $200). The advantage of this taste-friendly tool is that it only uses 600 watts of energy and has a "rapid" setting that does not use power when the bread is rising. It is thus ideally suited for use with limited sources of power such as solar panels, or a gas or diesel generator.

Masonry Ovens

Neighborhoods and small communities might want to look into communal baking ovens as an inexpensive way to provide large-scale cooking. Bread and pizza never taste better than when prepared in old-style masonry bake ovens. Years ago, this was a popular way for villagers to both socialize and make sure everyone had something to eat. (The book *Bread Ovens of Quebec* by Lise Boily chronicles this old tradition that might need to be revived in some areas, if Y2K proves as bad as pessimists predict.) Masonry bake ovens can be designed for domestic or commercial use. Some domestic bake oven units are dual purpose, meaning that they allow you to both heat your house and cook at the same time. If large-scale bake ovens are properly constructed, the cost of fuel to heat them is about two cents a loaf. And they need not be expensive. Small domestic units can be built for under $500. Those interested in more information about masonry bake ovens for home or community can contact *The Brick Oven Page,* <http://mha-net.org/msb/html/bakeov.htm>, or Alan Scott, <http://www.nbn.com/~ovncraft/>, e-mail <ovencrft@nbn.com>, a master oven crafter who both consults and offers detailed building specs and plans for communities, businesses, and organizations interested in large-scale stone and brick baking ovens.

Dutch Ovens

Depending on the type of backup cooking system you employ, you might want to invest in a *Dutch Oven*—those sturdy kettles designed to cook food evenly over outdoor fires. *Dutch Ovens* are especially good for cooking large amounts of food—something to consider if families, friends, churches, synagogues, and neighbors band together to make life safer and more enjoyable during Y2K. *Dutch Ovens* are usually made of cast iron or aluminum. Though iron pots are heavier and harder to clean, many people prefer the taste of food cooked in them. Iron is also less susceptible to cooking temperature changes and does not pose the risk of aluminum getting into food. *Lehman's,* <http://www.lehmans.com>, carries an extensive line of cast-iron *Dutch Ovens,* skillets, griddles, and accessories. If you plan on cooking over a live fire and handling hot pots and pans it would be wise to buy fireproof gloves, a shovel, and a pair of "hot pot" pliers. These items can be found at a local fire and safety supply house or at a hardware store.

Some *Dutch Oven* and Other Iron Cookware Pointers

- Take the time to treat your iron cookware properly. A little preventative oiling will pay off big-time later.
- Remember to never let a cast-iron kettle, pot, skillet, griddle, or pan sit in water. (They don't say they "rust" for nothing.)

- Don't use soap to clean iron pots—it will seep into the pores of the metal and flavor your next meal.
- Don't heat iron too quickly or it will crack.
- Don't pour cold water onto hot iron—unless you want to buy a new pot.
- Use wood rather than metal instruments to scrape and clean your iron cookware. This will prevent iron flakes and filings from entering your food.
- For more tips and cooking recipes see Mike Audleman's *Dutch Oven Cooking* ©1990, which can be found at <http://shoga.wwa.com/~oakes/dutchoven.html>, or consult *Lehman's Non-Electric,* which carries the *Dutch Oven Cookbook* by Michauds Kohlers and a video by Diane Thomas on the art of cooking over an open flame.

Specialty Stoves

American Freedom Network, <http://www.amerifree.com/>, e-mail <comments@amerifree.com>, and *Safe-Trek Outfitters—Essentials Inc.,* <http://www.safetrek.com>, e-mail <sales@safetrek.com>, among other vendors, sell the *Volcano Cook stove* (about $200 for the special stove and *Dutch Oven).* The innovative draft system in this unit, described as being of 18–20 gauge cold-rolled steel, means that 12 charcoal briquettes will generate enough heat for 12 hours of cooking, and, according to the manufacturer, 25 pounds (11.3 kilograms) of briquettes will cook two meals a day for two weeks in a 12-inch (six-quart) [305 millimeters (5.6 liters)] Dutch oven for up to 12 people. You can also contact the manufacturer directly *(Volcano,* telephone 801-566-5496) for the best prices and a number of handy accessories for this valuable unit.

Preparedness Centers, <http://www.healthyharvest.com>, e-mail <n.russell@worldnet.att.net>, stocks the *Pyramid Cooking System* (about $80), which uses an inverted design to reflect heat to the cooking surface, thus requiring fewer charcoal briquettes. For example, nine briquettes can cook a meal for six people. Its patented "Super Heat Grate" can generate temperatures from 350°F to 1100°F (176°C to 593°C). The stove unit also comes with an oven, a roaster, and an optional smoker (about $70), and the entire system folds down flat for easy storage and portability.

On a smaller scale you can experiment with "thermal cooking"—the use of a Thermos bottle to cook soft grains such as millet, amaranth, oats, rye, rice, and quinoa. Thermal cooking helps preserve nutrients that are lost through the heat-induced oxidization process of conventional cooking methods. In thermal cooking, you add your grains to hot—not boiling—water (about 160°F

[71°C]) in a Thermos bottle and let them cook for about six to seven hours. The vacuumed-sealed heat will cook the grains gently so that you end up with a rich-tasting, nutritious meal. This cooking approach saves energy since you have to heat water for only a short time. Thermal cooking also saves clean-up time and water since the grains will not stick to a Thermos as they do to the bottom of a pan. *Perfect Health,* <http://www. juicing.com>, offers a giant-sized *Thermos Cooker* (about $200) with a large opening, that holds about five quarts (4.75 liters) of grain and water.

Perfect Health also offers *Low Temperature Waterless Cookware,* employing a dual-wall chamber that allows water in a special internal cavity to be heated and turned into steam, which then heats up a second chamber and cooks the food. The unique thing about this process is that food is never cooked over 220°F (104°C) and therefore preserves more of the nutrient value often lost during high-temperature cooking.

Although the ideal is to "let food be thy medicine," sometimes we need some added assistance. The next chapter focuses on remedies, herbs, and supplements that can help us maintain maximum health during Y2K.

CHAPTER **6**
Of Medicines, Herbs, and Supplements

• •|• • • • • • • • •

"The Lord hath created medicines out of the earth;
and he that is wise will not abhor them." —Ecclesiasticus 38:4

Disclaimer: The following information is for educational purposes only and is not meant to help you diagnose health problems or prescribe cures or remedies. The information and products presented are designed to help you maintain and promote good health and should not be used without consulting your health care practitioner or personal physician. Although the Food and Drug Administration (FDA) classifies herbs, vitamins, and other nutritional supplements as foods and not drugs, many of these items might have medicinal or therapeutic value and therefore should be taken only under the guidance of a health care professional—especially if you are pregnant. No guarantees are given for any product listed, and the author, publisher, and distributors assume no liability or responsibility for how readers use this information without a physician's approval. It is important to bear in mind that you should never substitute or discontinue any prescribed drugs or medications without the approval of your physician or health care professional.

For some people the notion that the body can heal itself might seem strange. After all, we have been brought up to believe that only doctors and their hospital equipment and medicine can cure our health problems. However, history teaches otherwise. For thousands of years people have relied on plant-based medicine to help heal and cure health problems. Of late, there has been a revival of interest in the Western World of what is known as herbal or "green" medicine. This increased awareness has led to the scientific validation of many of the herbal remedies that common folk have used for centuries to heal their ailments.

I do not mean to imply that modern medicine has not produced its own miracle cures—emergency surgery, trauma medicines, and powerful antibiotics have saved many lives. Unfortunately, much of modern biomedicine is "hi-tech" and dependent upon computers, and thus is vulnerable to the crippling factors that Y2K might deliver. In addition, many people have begun to question the notion that we should treat only symptoms and not address the root cause of chronic diseases and health problems. Many of these same people also distrust the harsh side effects that many modern pharmaceutical drugs generate. Issues such as these have led millions of people to explore the benefits of more natural approaches to health and healing. The recent interest in herbal medicine lies at the center of this new approach to health care.

My emphasis here is on preventative medicine and self-care as a way of gaining control over factors that might harm our health in the days ahead. In this chapter, I will present products and protocols many people have found to be beneficial. I will begin with a look at dietary- and plant-based remedies first. In the remainder of this chapter, I will list a number of products and items that can be beneficial for minor medical emergencies and problems during the uncertain days ahead. However, those desiring a more in-depth exploration of this topic should consult books such as *The Complete Illustrated Holistic Herbal: A Safe and Practical Guide to Making and Using Herbal Remedies* by David Hoffmann (Element, 1996).

Herbs, Spices, and Teas

Many people take the purchasing of herbs, spices, and teas too lightly. Herbs are subtle and powerful nutritional agents of health and healing. Numerous studies have vindicated their capacity to assist the body in its ability to heal itself. The *Boston Globe* carried an article (Wednesday, November 11, 1998) on the *Second International Scientific Symposium on Tea and Human Health,* which found that not only do herbal teas contain "flavonoids" that promote health and prevent disease, but they are increasingly playing an "adjunctive role in the treatment of disease," including cancer, liver, and heart disease prevention.

However, if we are to gain maximum benefit from herbs they must be of good quality. By "quality" I mean plants that have strong potency, or the vital active constituents that enable them to promote health. The quality (and safety) of an herb varies immensely depending upon the kind of herb it is and how and where the plant was grown, processed, packaged, stored, and shipped. Sadly, there are far too many poor-quality herbs that have lost their potency because of poor growing, shipping, and storage practices.

It is always wise to check with your local herbalist or health food store herb specialist to ensure the quality of the herbs, teas, and spices that you buy. I always prefer either third-party certified organic herbs, spices, and teas, or those that have been ethically "wild-crafted"—meaning picked in the wild in such a way that ensures the plant will be neither over-harvested nor gathered in areas that expose the herbs to harmful chemicals and pollutants. Such extra effort helps to better ensure that I get products that are pure, fresh, and potent.

Types of Herbal Assists

The universe of herbs and herbal remedies is large. People often ask what is the best type of herb product to buy. Should I get a tincture or liquid extract (meaning that the herb has been soaked in alcohol, water, or glycerin to extract its medicinal or health-giving properties), a capsule (which contains the herb in a dry, powdered form), or a standardized extract (meaning that that the specific active constituents, ingredients, or medical properties have been isolated)? Or should I buy herbs in their whole-plant form and use them as an infusion (where the softer tissues of leaves, petals, and flowers are brewed as a tea), or a decoction (where the tougher parts of the plant such as roots, bark, stems, and tubers are soaked and boiled for a while to remove their active ingredients)? Or should I eat the herb fresh or consume it dried, as we do with common spices such as oregano, parsley, etc., that we add to our food?

In essence, there is no easy answer to these questions since the type of herb and its preparation will depend upon circumstances unique to your situation, namely your present health condition, your needs and personal preferences, etc. It is wise to consult with a qualified herbal practitioner or health food store specialist to find what will be best for you. (Some people prefer standardized herbal products, in which the active constituent is isolated in its purest form to help achieve a faster, more direct effect. Personally, I prefer working with the whole plant, which often contains a synergistic blend of active ingredients that work best together as "nature" intended.)

Y2K TIP

A number of companies on the World Wide Web offer herbs in "bulk." *Home-Health Resource,* <http://www.homehealthresource.net/catalog.html>, e-mail <hhr@piggott.net>, carries an extensive line of certified organic and wild-crafted bulk herbs. *Earthen,* <http://well-being.com/earthen-scents/>, e-mail <DrFrog@frognet.net>, is a company with a strong line of bulk herbs that you can purchase in one-ounce (28 grams) increments. *The Internet Business Directory,* <http://www.okdirect.com/Biz/5/5499A.html>, is good source for finding local vendors of herbs, vitamins, supplements, and numerous other products.

First-Aid Kits And Herbal Medicine Chests

Having a good first-aid kit and a well-supplied medicine chest is imperative for the days ahead. Many preparedness experts recommend that we acquire a combination of "standard" first-aid products and "alternative" items. By "standard," I mean the "conventional" products that can be bought at a local pharmacy, and by "alternative," I mean natural and herbal products.

When buying a first-aid kit and assembling an herbal medicine chest, be sure their contents will cover a variety of circumstances and common problems such as cuts, bleeding, scrapes, burns, rashes, bruises, sprains, headaches, insect bites and stings, colds, flu, sore throats, respiratory conditions, upset stomach, mouth problems, muscle aches, diarrhea, constipation, infection, etc.

Many people prefer to customize first-aid kits to fit their unique needs. If you decide to make and pack your own first-aid kit, consult with your health care practitioner and local pharmacist for things to include, such as a variety of sterile bandages and Band-Aids, butterfly closures, sterile gauze pads, trauma dressings with ties, splints, surgical tape, scissors, tweezers, cotton swab tips, antiseptic wipes, eye wash, reusable hot and cold packs, latex exam gloves, eye cups, Ace® bandages, alcohol swabs, EMT shears, extractors, space blankets, hydrogen peroxide, a small flashlight, etc. You should also get a good first-aid handbook (I found an inexpensive one at a used book store).

Y2K TIP

Even if you purchase a ready-made first-aid kit, you might want to add supplies appropriate to your own personal needs such as those suggested by *Xtreme Needs,* including dust masks, energy bars, toilet paper, antibacterial soap, wool blankets, Handy Wipes, duct tape, tooth brush and tooth paste, medications, glasses/contacts (and solution), Leatherman® tools, garbage bags/plastic bags, family photos, etc. (<http://www.xtreme-needs.com/survival/masterpack. html>). Designing and making your own first-aid kit and medicine chest will be a good learning experience that will draw attention to many items that might be overlooked or not considered. Many in the Y2K preparedness community are recommending *Where There Is No Doctor: A Village Health Care Handbook* by David Werner, Carol Thuman, and Jane Maxwell (Hesperian Foundation, 1992), available from *Amazon.com,* <http://www.amazon.com>, or your local bookstore.

First-Aid Kits

Captain Dave's Survival Center, <http://survival-center.com/>, offers several types of first-aid kits, including a large family-sized kit and a smaller personal kit, as well as a special unit called *First-Aid Supplies in a Can,* which is especially packaged for long-term storage. *Epicenter,* <http://www.theepicenter.

com>, also carries several kits—though they are not as complete as *Captain Dave's*. *Outdoor Kids' Source,* <http://www.kidssource.com/>, e-mail <oks@mt-mansfield.com>, carries a line of first-aid kits designed for families with children. (They also carry a number of other outdoor gear products for young people.) *Rescue Northwest* <http://www.rescuenorthwest.com/> offers a wide variety of *Adventure Medical* first-aid and "professional" medical kits (priced from $5.50 to $350). *Safe-Trek Outfitters—Essentials Inc.,* <http://www.safetrek.com>, also carries an extensive line of *Adventure Medical* first-aid kits.

Those with medical experience and training might want to contact *Xtreme Needs,* <http://www.xtreme-needs.com/survival/>, e-mail <xtreme@ rmci.net>, for the *Expedition Kit 465* by *Adventure Medical*—a professional-quality first-aid kit that includes instruments for serious wounds, traumas, toothaches, etc. *Xtreme Needs* also supplies the *Sawyer Extractor Pump* (about $18) for removing poison and venom from an insect bite or a snakebite. Those living in areas where venomous bites are a problem might want to consider purchasing one of these valuable health-maintaining tools. *Xtreme Needs* also carries the *"Master Pack" 72 Hour Survival Kit*. This unit is pricey (about $535), but it includes many vital items that you might need in an emergency—including a water purifier, a *Sawyer Extractor Pump,* a *Beygen Wind-Up* AM/FM/Shortwave radio, a *Beygen Self-Powered* lantern, MREs, *Nuwick* 120-hour candles, a professional-quality first-aid kit, an *On Duty Multi Purpose Emergency Tool* that "Shuts off Gas, Shuts off Water, Pries open Doors, Digs thru Debris," emergency blankets, a tent, etc. This kit is designed both for a quick "bug out" in the event of an imminent emergency, or for a complete emergency preparedness system to get you through the critical first 72 hours of a disaster.

USA Marketing Associates Inc., <http://www.y2ksupplies.com/>, also carries a variety of serious medical and first-aid kits, including the *Mountain Medic* (about $360), which includes "paramedic"-quality equipment and supplies.

Herbal Medicine Chest

For those inclined toward "natural" and "alternative" medicine, botanical-based medicines often offer health-promoting analogues, or safe substitutes for many over-the-counter and prescription drugs dispensed by physicians and pharmacists. However, it is important to note that natural approaches to health and healing involve more than just taking a pill or an herb to alleviate this or that symptom. Natural medicine seeks to address the cause of illness rather than just relieving pains or symptoms. Pain is our body's cry for help. We will encounter true health only if we nourish and assist our body in deep-level healing—that is, addressing the physical, structural, emotional, spiritual, relational, and lifestyle problems that created a particular disease.

> ## Y2K TIP
> Part of the allure of natural medicine is its inherent simplicity. As Dr. F. Batmanghelidg, M.D., reminds us in his book *Your Body's Many Cries for Water,* something as simple as drinking water (at least two quarts a day) can alleviate both the symptoms and the cause of many chronic diseases such as dyspepsia, back pain, arthritis, etc. See his intriguing book filled with numerous case studies that highlight the way chronic dehydration at the cellular level underlies many degenerative and chronic diseases. His book is also an important reminder of why we should have plenty of pure drinking water on hand.

With this caveat in mind, I will highlight some herbal and nutritional remedies for many of the health challenges we might face during Y2K. Exactly what herbal products you obtain will depend upon the needs of your Preparedness Group. For my family, my herbal medicine chest will include a variety of extracts and tinctures, plant-based salves, ointments, and antiseptics, as well as herbal "spices" to season and enliven the large amount of beans, rice, and legumes I anticipate us eating, and herbal teas to help keep us warm at night.

It is important, however, to point out that just because something is "natural" does not mean it is always safe. Herbs can cause allergic reactions in some people, and certain herbs can cause harmful and lethal reactions when mixed with some prescription drugs. The FDA publishes a *Supplements Associated with Illnesses and Injuries* Web site, <http://www.fda.gov/fdac/features/1998/dietchrt.html>, that lists the possible health hazards of herbs and nutritional supplements it considers unsafe. For example, a recent article in the *Boston Globe,* <http://www.boston.com/globe/>, "Herbal Hazards" (November 26, 1998: C1–5), stated that because ginkgo *(Ginkgo biloba),* ginger *(Zingiber officinale),* and feverfew *(Tanateum parsenium)* thin the blood, they might cause excessive bleeding if taken with aspirin or the prescription drug *Coumadin.* Therefore, always consult with your physician or health care practitioner before taking herbs along with prescription drugs. At the same time, it must also be noted that millions of people take herbs every day with few or no complications.

Specific Botanicals

The following examples offer a brief overview of some of the more popular and effective botanical remedies people have used for centuries to promote health.

Australian Tea Tree oil is an example of a safe and effective traditional natural remedy. Australian Tea Tree oil is obtained from the leaves of the *Melaleuca alternifolia* tree and is growing in popularity as a general natural first-aid product. The oil in this herb has been found to contain a number of valuable antiseptic, bactericidal, and fungicidal (fungus-killing) properties. Used by the Australian Army and Navy during World War II as a "cure-all," Tea Tree oil can help a number of health-related problems, including insect bites and stings, skin infections, wounds, yeast infections, chronic cystitis, itchy scalp, and acne. The "Tea Tree Oil Information Site," <http://www.teatree.co.uk/>, offers a wealth of information about Tea Tree oil, including a helpful Web page entitled, "What's your Problem: A Guide to the Health Benefits of Tea Tree Oil," <http://www.teatree.co.uk/ailments.htm>. Tea Tree oil also makes a good, natural household disinfectant that can be purchased at any local health food store. *B&A Products*, <http://www.baproducts.com/catalog.htm>, offers several books dedicated to the dosages and use of Tea Tree oil. (Some people find Oil of Cajeput *[Melaleuca cajeputi* or *Melaleuca minor-leucadendron]*—an aromatic oil derived from the same plant as Tea Tree oil—to be even more effective than Tea Tree oil. Oil of Cajeput is available from *Pure Herbs*, <http://herbnook.com/pureherb.htm>.)

Rosemary *(Rosmarinus officinalis)* tincture is another effective natural "antibiotic" that can be used internally or topically (on the skin). Arnica *(Arnica montana)* is an herb that many find helpful for sprains, sore muscles, bruises, or other physical traumas to the body. However, it must never be applied to broken skin. Comfrey *(Symphytum officinale)* is another good herb to have around. Comfrey is also known as "knit-bone" and in times past was used to heal broken bones. Comfrey contains allantoin, a healing compound that when used as a poultice—soaking a cloth in comfrey tea and applying the cloth to the injured part of the body—can promote the healing of external wounds, sores, and bruises.

The gelatinous liquid in the Aloe vera leaf *(Aloe Barbadensis)* contains antibacterial, anesthetic, and tissue restorative properties, and is helpful for burns, insect bites, and skin rashes. I prefer using the fresh plant. Simply break off a leaf and apply the cooling gel directly to a burn or rash. (Having an Aloe vera plant could come in handy during Y2K—especially if we will be cooking with unfamiliar stoves and alternative sources of heat.)

Cayenne pepper *(Capsicum annuum)* is another good general "cure-all" to have on hand. The powder can be used externally on the body to stop bleeding. Be careful not to get the powder in your eye (it will sting, but not harm your eye). Cayenne pepper can also be combined with peppermint *(Mentha piperita)* oil to make a liniment that soothes bruises, sprains, and sore muscles.

Many migraine sufferers find the herb feverfew *(Tanacetum parthenium)* to be effective in helping to relieve migraine headaches without the side effects that accompany conventional pharmaceutical drugs. White willow bark *(Salix alba)* contains the active ingredient found in aspirin. For some people white willow works just as effectively as aspirin without its unhealthy side effects, such as the aspirin-induced Reye's Syndrome in children.

People the world over have used ginger *(Zingiber officinale)* as an excellent herb for nausea and stomach-related issues. Hawthorne Berries *(Crataegus laevigata)* have been shown in a number of scientific studies to aid heart-related problems, and Butcher's Broom *(Ruscus aculeatus)* aids those suffering from circulatory problems as well as maintaining and assisting vessel and capillary function. Common garlic *(Allium sativum)* is a potent, broad-spectrum antimicrobial that acts against certain viruses, fungi, and bacteria, as well as containing active ingredients that inhibit platelet aggregation and help reduce the risk of blood clots in heart attacks and strokes.

Many people have found the fruit of the South Pacific Noni plant *(Morinda citrifolia)*—available as a capsule or liquid juice—to help a wide spectrum of health conditions, including cancer, heart disease, auto-immune problems, etc. (While writing this book, I found four ounces [120 milliliters] a day of Noni juice boosted my energy reserve and enabled me to require less sleep.)

Many people find wild cherry bark *(Prunus serotina)* to be soothing for sore throats, and elder *(Sambucus nigra)*, yarrow *(Achillea millefolium)*, lobelia *(Lobelia inflata)*, and peppermint to be good for chest congestion and respiratory conditions. An infusion or tea of peppermint leaf *(Metha piperita)*, orange peel *(Citrus sinensis)*, rose hip *(Rosa canina)*, and yarrow *(Achillea millefolium)* can help you sweat and "drive out a cold" from your body. Many people have also found the old-fashioned remedies of garlic *(Allium sativum)* or mullein leaf *(Verbascum thapsis)* in olive oil to assist the body in healing ear infections. This, coupled with ear candling—the use of waxed cones to draw foreign material from the ear—has helped victims of ear infection. Ear candles are available at your local health food store. (Many people have found earaches to cease once they have stopped eating dairy products.)

Herbs that are commonly called "bowel cleansers" are highly effective in unblocking constipation. Such herbal formulas often include senna leaf *(Cassia angustifolia)*, cascara sagrada bark *(Rhamnus purshiana)*, psyllium *(Plantago psyllium)*, and fennel *(Foeniculum vulgare)*. Fennel is also a good remedy for bloating and gas. Such bowel cleansers normally come in a capsule or tea form, with the tea usually having a milder effect.

Bentonite clay or charcoal tablets are great for controlling diarrhea and for detoxification in the event of accidental poisoning. Slippery elm bark *(Ulmus rubra)* and fennel are also soothing to the stomach. Many people find fennel, anise seed *(Pimpinella anisum)* and peppermint to be effective "digestive aids."

The silymarin in Milk Thistle *(Silybum marianum)* has been shown to aid damaged livers.

Most health food stores carry a variety of herbal salves and ointments for skin rashes and related problems. Effective formulas often include comfrey *(Symhytum officinale)*, olive oil, calendula *(Calendula officinalis)*, bees' wax, plantain *(Plantago major)*, St. John's Wort *(Hypericum perforatum)*, and mullein leaf *(Verbascum thapsus)*, among other herbs.

When thinking of first-aid we must not forget about our emotional needs. Many people find teas and tinctures of Kava Kava *(Piper methysticum)*, and the relaxing nervines scullcap *(Scuterllaria lateriflora)*, St. John's Wort *(Hypericum perforatum)*, valerian *(Valeriana officinalis)*, and hops *(Humulus lupulus)*, to aid emotional distress and to be beneficial for calming nerves. A number of herbs also aid in helping to fall asleep, including hops *(Humulus lupulus)*, passion flower *(Passiflora incarnata)*, chamomile *(Matricaria recutita)*, scullcap *(Scuterllaria lateriflora)*, and valerian *(Valeriana officinalis)*. Many people also find the homeopathic flower-based *Bach Rescue Remedies*—especially *Rescue Remedy*—to be helpful in calming jagged nerves and lessening emotional trauma.

Given that the number of beneficial and medicinal herbs is almost endless, I suggest you consult your local natural health practitioner to help find safe herbal substitutes for the therapeutic needs of those in your group.

Ready-Made Herbal Kits

A number of vendors sell ready-made herbal first-aid kits, including *REI,* <http://www.rei.com/>, which carries the *Adventure Medical Herbal Medical Kit* that combines both conventional and herbal remedies. *Real Goods,* <http://www.realgoods.com>, and *Elixa,* <http://www.elixa.com/nutrient/travel. htm>, e-mail <psafier@elixa.com>, also offer basic herbal first-aid kits.

> **Y2K TIP**
>
> There are many companies offering high-quality herbal tinctures and extracts, such as the *American Botanical Pharmacy* (telephone 310-453-1987). Dr. Richard Schulze, their master herbalist and formulator, has devised a number of exceptionally potent, natural (certified organic and wild-crafted) herbal formulas based on his years of clinical practice. Among his many excellent formulas, Dr. Schulze's "plague" remedy and *Deep Tissue Repair* are something to consider having on hand for any potential threats to the immune system and potential muscle aches and pains you might encounter. *Pure Herbs* products, <http://herbnook.com/pureherb.htm>, e-mail <glyndak@yahoo.com>, created by master formulator Eugene C. Watkins, offer another potent line of herbal tinctures and extracts. In Canada *Sayfer Botanicals,* <http://www.herbmeds.com/>, e-mail <wizard@herbmeds. com>, manufactures exceptionally effective herbal formulas for a variety of conditions. *Gia Herbs* products, offering some of the more potent formulas, are available at many local health food stores.

Sayfer Botanicals, <http://www.herbmeds.com/>, e-mail <wizard@ herbmeds.com>, offers what they consider the "ultimate" herbal first-aid kit, capable of helping over one hundred common ailments and conditions. (They also offer innovative and simple-to-use equipment to make your own herbal remedies.)

Western Botanicals, <http://www.westernbotanical.com/>, also offers one of the most extensive full-system *Herbal First-Aid Kits,* designed to treat a multitude of common ailments by natural means, as well as herbal kits designed to make it easy for you to make your own herbal formulas.

Herbs First, <http://www.herbsfirst.com/pricelist.html>, e-mail <herbs@ herbsfirst.com>, which sells products based on Dr. John Christopher's formulas, is another company dedicated to effective and high-quality herbal remedies. Dr. Christopher was one of this century's most influential American natural healers and herbalists; his products have helped millions of people. (His products can also be obtained from *Dr. Christopher Enterprises,* <http://www.drchristopher.com/>.)

Those interested in first-rate, practical books on herbal "first-aid" and remedies can contact *Herbs First* to order *Dr. Mom* by Sandra K. Livingston Ellis, or *Bruce Hopkins,* <http://web2.airmail.net/foodstr2>, to order *Herbs to the Rescue: An Herbal First-Aid Handbook* by Kurt King. Former students of Dr. Christopher, both authors have written manuals that cover a wide array of emergency and medical problems and the way herbs can treat them.

For those who like homeopathic remedies *Brian Golden* (telephone 303-440-4893) offers an *Emergency Homeopathic Remedy Kit* that contains formulas for 50 remedies in both 30 cc. and 200 cc. dilution (about $130 and $150). The kit also contains a guide for using the formulas.

Y2K TIP

In addition to keeping a section in your Y2K Preparedness Journal about your new culinary adventures, I suggest you keep a Y2K herbal log of your herbal and first-aid supplies— what you have in stock, what they are used for, and how to use them. It would also be wise to have someone in your Preparedness Group take a course in herbal first-aid. *Dr. Christopher Enterprises,* <http://www.drchristopher.com/>, among others, offers an excellent course.

Immune System Activators

As good as all the herbs listed above are in promoting health, none of them can cure people. Herbs and other nutritional aids support the body, but it takes a fully functional immune system to bring about a cure. The issue of a healthy and empowered immune system becomes even more important during the uncertain days ahead. At any given moment, our bodies are under attack from a host of health-enemies, including allergens, bacteria, viruses, parasites, fungi, molds, and other microbes and antigens. If our immune system is not functioning properly, we lose this battle and ill health results.

The issue of epidemics induced by potential water and sewage disposal disruptions is also something to consider. (Many researchers claim that attention to personal hygiene and public sanitation, more than any other factor, has contributed to the diminishing of the plagues and killer diseases that once afflicted the Western world.) If epidemics do occur we will need to support our immune system. This is especially true for the immune system-compromised such as the elderly, the infirm, those suffering from asthma, heart disease, diabetes, cancer, etc.; those on immunosuppressive medications; or those with lupus, AIDS, multiple sclerosis, etc.

Y2K TIP

In case of a cholera outbreak, you may want to keep on hand some oral rehydration salts (ORS) packets or the natural cell salts contained in non-sugar-added sports drinks such as *Recharge*. Taken with water, rehydration salts help replenish the body with the minerals and electrolytes the body needs during or after a bout of intense vomiting and diarrhea. These salts and sports drinks are available at your local pharmacy or health food store. You might see a push for flu shots in the days ahead, especially for those most vulnerable to potentially deadly forms of influenza. However, it must be remembered that flu shots are the *Center for Disease Control*'s (<http://www.cdc.gov/>) best guess at the three main strains of flu that will appear. In some years they have been correct in their guess, and in other years, they have missed entirely. Therefore flu shots offer no guarantee that you will be protected. Flu shots should not be given to those who are allergic to eggs, since many of the viral cultures are grown in egg solutions.

In light of these potential scenarios, it is important to consider having some immuno-modulators on hand in your medicine chest. By immuno-modulators, I mean those nature-based nutritional supplements that stimulate and potentiate the immune system to function at optimum capacity. Such supplements help offer support against the new emerging strains of bacteria and viruses that are increasingly resistant to pharmaceutical-grade antibiotic and antiviral medications.

Most health food stores carry a wide array of herbal supplements designed to support and stimulate the immune system. Common examples include teas and tinctures of *Echinacea angustifolia* and *Echinacea purpurea,* Golden seal root *(Hydrastis canadensis), Astragalus membranaceus,* and Oregon Grape root *(Mahonia aquafolium)*— a good antibacterial and immunity-enhancing substitute for the popular but expensive and endangered golden seal root.

However, it is important to point out that there is a difference between stimulation and potentiation. Herbs such as *Echinacea angustifolia* stimulate or stir the immune system into action, while nutritional supplements such as *Beta-1, 3-D glucan* potentiate, or cause, the immune system to function at full capacity. Both are important to ensure that our immune system is fully active and ready to combat any problems that might arise during Y2K. Given its relative obscurity and documented ability to potentiate the immune system, *Beta 1, 3-D glucan* needs to be addressed in detail.

Beta 1, 3-D glucan, discovered by medical researchers, is made from the cell walls of a type of yeast called *Saccharomyces cerevisiae,* or baker's yeast. (Although *Beta-1, 3-D glucan* is derived from a yeast, it, ironically, may actually help those who are sensitive to yeast or suffering from *candida albacans.*) Researchers have discovered that the *Beta-1, 3-D glucan* is an immunomodulator that "selectively enhances the microbicidal activities of neutrophils and macrophages, without stimulating proinflammatory cytokine production" (see A.O. Tzianabos and R.L. Cisneros, Annual New York Academy of Sciences, 25 October 1996). In short, what this means is that *Beta-1, 3-D glucan* is a nonspecific immune system enhancer. "Nonspecific" means that it activates the cells within the immune system such as macrophages (the tiny "PAC-man"-like cells that gobble up antigens) to kill a variety of microbial invaders. *Beta-1, 3-D glucan* has proven to be highly effective in clinical trials to potentiate or crank up the immune system to function at full capacity. Unlike *Echinacea, Beta-1, 3-D glucan* does not put stress on the immune system and can be used continuously without needing to give the body a respite, as *Echinacea* requires. *Beta-1, 3-D glucan* is also a strong antioxidant with free-radical scavenging capabilities. A supplement such as *Beta-1, 3-D glucan* could be very important when we are cold, under stress, not eating properly, and living under less than sanitary conditions.

Transfer Factors are another relatively new immune system enhancer that you might consider. *Transfer Factors* offer what is called a specific cell-mediated immune response by "transferring" the immunity from one mammal to another. To simplify what this means, it can be said that when an animal such as a cow is infected with an antigen, its immune system creates an antibody to kill off the specific invader. This process involves the T-cells (produced by the thymus gland) learning to discern who the invader is and signaling to the NKs, or natural killer cells, to destroy the invading microbe or antigen. Researchers have discovered a way to transfer the learned cell response of a cow or other mammal's immune system to human beings. This might sound strange or unnatural, but this is the same procedure that takes place when a human mother's first milk, known as colostrum, helps build up the immune system of her newborn. *Transfer Factors* are non-toxic and have been found to be highly effective against a variety of antigens. *Transfer Factors* are antigen- or condition-specific, so you must inquire as to what each *Transfer Factors* product will do. You can contact *Lois Garish* (telephone 978-465-

3614) for more information on both *Beta-1, 3-D glucan* and a *Transfer Factors* product that is effective against 20 antigens, including *e-coli*, herpes, and chicken pox.

Important Nutritional Supplements

Our immune system cannot function well unless we supply our body with the vital nutrients it needs to build and maintain proper health. Millions of people take some form of dietary and nutritional supplement each day. Skeptics may claim that we can get all the nutrients we need from the food we eat. In theory they are right. But in practice, most of us eat foods that lack the vital nutrients we need. The reasons for this are varied and include poor eating habits, the over-processing and refining of food, depleted mineral content in the soil, shoddy packaging and refrigeration, shipping conditions that expose food to excessive heat, over-extended shelf life, numerous food additives, etc. In light of this, it is wise to supplement our diet with nutritional supplements. (Many researchers consider the high rate of chronic and degenerative diseases that afflict many in the Western world as a testament to this lack of proper nutrition.)

Given the staggering array of dietary and nutritional supplements available and the personal preferences many of us have, I have limited the following list to a few items that many people have found helpful in maximizing good health.

Super "Green" Foods. The nutritional use of vegetable-based and nutrient-dense, "super foods" has also become popular of late. And for good reason. The amount of vital nutrients these foods deliver in proportion to the amount used is phenomenal. Super foods come in a variety of forms. They can be a single concentrated plant such as barley, Kamut®, carrots, or beets, or, most often, they may come in a combination form that includes seaweed (extremely high in organic, easily assimilated minerals), alfalfa, wheat grass, spirlina, barley, and other highly nourishing plant-based sources of vitamins, minerals, enzymes, and co-factors.

Nutrients such as seaweed and alfalfa might not sound appetizing to many people. One reason nutritious foods such as super green shakes seem foreign is that many people no longer know what real food tastes like. Most of us have had our taste buds corrupted by overly processed foods and the enormous amount of sweeteners and artificial flavorings that are added to most food products today.

Because these super green foods are so nutritious, people have come up with innovative ways to help consume them, such as making super food shakes. This is done by mixing the super food with some fresh fruit and pure water or juice and pureeing it in a blender. (I like to add some natural-flavored protein powder or brewer's yeast and lecithin. One way I have found to get my children to drink super food shakes is to add a little maple syrup or honey to the shake.) Super green food shakes make a low-fat, high-energy drink that helps maintain energy levels throughout the day.

In general, super foods have a fairly stable shelf life (six months to a year) and given the fact that fresh fruits and vegetables might be in short supply during the Y2K transition, I recommend stocking up on a lot of this vital product.

Y2K TIP

Those who are looking for a high-quality vitamin might consider the whole-food source vitamin and mineral supplement made by *Rainbow Light*. By whole-food source I mean a vitamin and mineral complex that is derived from natural fruit, vegetable, and herbal plant sources, as opposed to fractionated and synthetically created, laboratory-produced vitamins that lack many of the synergistic co-factors found in "live," nutrient-rich food. In addition to their superior nutrition and lack of artificial ingredients, whole-food source nutrients are easier to digest and assimilate. Whole plant-based vitamins are especially important for pregnant and lactating women. *Juice Plus* (available at your local health food store) and *Mannatech's Phyto-Bears* (telephone 207-834-6934, e-mail <maple@mannapages.com>) are quality whole-food vitamins for children.

Enzymes. In the eyes of many natural health practitioners, health begins in a properly functioning digestion and elimination system. Our body cannot function to optimal capacity if we do not digest and assimilate our food properly. That is, if the food we eat is not sufficiently broken down and transported to our cells, we will not experience maximum health. Because our diet might undergo major change and stress during Y2K, it is important that we assist our body in its ability to break down vital nutrients.

Of late, plant-based digestive enzymes have become a popular supplement. Enzymes are naturally occurring chemical catalysts contained in all fresh, "live," or uncooked foods, that aid in the breakdown and assimilation of nutrients. (Heat destroys enzymes; therefore heating foods makes our digestive system work overtime to process the food, whereas enzymes would ordinarily help break down food in our stomach.) A good plant-based enzyme supplement offers a full spectrum of enzymes. That is, it contains protease to assist in digesting protein, lipase to break down fats, amylase and cellulase to digest carbohydrates and fibers, lactase to help in digesting milk products, and sucrase to assist in the breakdown of sugars.

The Healing Network, <http://www.anaturalchoice.com/absorb.shtml>, offers a full-spectrum enzyme supplement called Absorbaid, which comes in a powdered form that allows you to drink the enzymes with your meal. Taking enzymes in this way is especially good for those who use or need antacids and other digestive aids to help with gas, reflux, and bloating. There are a lot of other good enzyme formulas on the market, so I advise you to consult with your health care practitioner or local health food store counselor for the purchase best suited to your needs.

Friendly Flora. A number of health theorists suspect that disruptions in the bowel ecology of the beneficial bacteria that inhabit our GI (gastro-intestinal) tract—whether through improper diet or the overuse of antibi-otics—are a major contributing cause to bowel-related troubles. (See the Health World essay "Intestinal Dysbiosis and the Causes of Disease" by Leo Galland, M.D. and Stephen Barrie, N.D., which explains the scientific data supporting the idea that "gut dysbiosis [such as flora imbalance] plays the major etiologic role in a number of diseases" <http://www.healthy.net/hwlibraryarticles/galland/dybiosis1.htm>.) The beneficial bacteria or "friend-ly microflora" that colonize our intestines play an important role in both the digestion and elimination of the food we eat, and in maintaining a healthy bowel ecology that does not allow harmful bacteria to overdevelop.

In light of these findings, a number of companies offer "pro-biotic" or "friendly flora" supplements that help maintain a vibrant colony of healthy bacteria in the small and large intestines. It is important to look for a formula that includes a wide variety of friendly flora, including Lactobacillus aci-dophilus, which helps, among other things, to reduce cholesterol and reduce vaginal yeast and herpes; Lactobacillus bulgarium, which helps destroy pathogens in the large intestine; Lactobacillus plantarum, which is sturdy and powerful enough to digest organic waste in septic tanks; Bifidobacteria infantis, which manufactures B-vitamins and is useful for children with allergies and infants who have a hard time digesting mother's milk; Bifidobacterium, which helps with colon-related problems such as constipation, diarrhea, irri-table bowel syndrome, etc. In general you want a formula that supports both the small intestine (lactobacillus) and the large intestine (bifidus).

It is also important to get a formula with a total flora count of at least three billion per serving. The higher the flora count, the better the chance that these bowel-friendly microbes will "colonize" in your large intestine.

Those wanting a more "natural" approach to their flora might want to stock up on fermented foods, since they are a rich source of friendly flora. Studies have found that non-digestible oligosaccharides (NDOs) such as fructooligosaccharide (FOS) aid the growth of intestinal microflora and thereby help increase the potential number of beneficial microorganisms in the GI tract. Some pro-biotic formulas have FOS in them. Foods high in FOS include Jerusalem artichoke tubers, and fermented foods such as kimchi, tempeh, and yogurt.

Elimination Assists. Along with eating good, quality food and making sure it gets digested properly, good health also depends upon the evacuation or elimination of waste material from the body. A number of studies support the theory of the Leaky Gut Syndrome (LGS), which holds that an overly permeable colon leads to autointoxication of the body. Put simply, improper digestion and elimination lead to constipation and excessive gas, which overly expands and stretches the colon. As the colon balloons out, its membrane weakens, and partially digested food and unhealthy bacteria leak into the bloodstream and cause a variety of symptoms, including auto-immune diseases, fatigue, Irritable Bowel Syndrome (IBS), unclear thinking, bloatedness, etc. A leaky gut puts enormous stress on the liver and can profoundly affect the body, including the endocrine, immune, metabolic, and neurological systems.

As natural healer Dr. Richard Schulze points out, close study of the *Merck Manual of Diagnosis and Therapy*—a standard physician's reference guide—reveals that bowel-related problems such as constipation, Chron's disease, Irritable Bowel Syndrome (IBS), diverticulosis, and diverticulitis have risen dramatically over the past half-century. Some health advocates attribute this rise to the consumption of too much overly processed food coupled with a diet that lacks sufficient fiber. (In addition, the increase in stress and an increasingly underactive and sedentary lifestyle might also be contributing factors.)

Eating foods with lots of fiber and using herbs to aid the elimination process can help play a big role in maintaining good health during the challenging diet days of Y2K. Most health food stores carry supplements that aid the elimination process.

Anti-Oxidants. A number of media reports have drawn attention to the value of anti-oxidants—the free-radical scavengers that keep renegade hydrogen electrons from doing damage at the cellular level. Free radical damage results from a number of causes, including poor diet, stress, and environmental pollution, as well as from normal metabolic processes in the body. As mentioned earlier, free radicals have been implicated in a number of ailments, including heart disease, cancer, premature aging, and autoimmune disease. It would be wise to have a supply of anti-oxidants available to help mitigate the damage Y2K stress and lifestyle disruptions might cause. In addition to

Vitamins E, C, Beta Carotene, CoQ 10, and selenium, there are a number of high-quality anti-oxidants available at health food stores.

At the same time, it is important to note that too many anti-oxidants can also be damaging to the body by suppressing some of our immune system's responses. As in many things, moderation is a vital principle to keep in mind when taking supplements.

MSM. Many people are touting the beneficial effects of MSM or Methylsulfonylmethane. The name sounds dangerous, but in fact, MSM is an organic form of nutritional sulfur that is found in many foods, including meat, dairy products, fruits, and vegetables. Our body requires large amounts of MSM to function properly. Cruciferous vegetables such as cabbage, cauliflower, and broccoli contain some of the highest amounts of MSM. Unfortunately, many people do not like the taste of these vegetables, and since MSM is very water-soluble and is easily lost or destroyed in the cooking process, many of us are deficient in this crucial nutrient. Because of this, many people find taking MSM as a supplement benefits their body in many ways, including relieving constipation, helping the lungs to function better, limiting the body's response to allergens, reducing excessive stomach acid, repairing damaged tissue and organs, fighting free-radicals, and helping those with arthritis. My wife Judi and I find that MSM-based hand and face lotions make our skin soft and supple. (I also find it helps keep my fingers from cramping up when I write 10 to 12 hours a day on my computer.)

Glyconutritionals. A recent study conducted by researchers at the University of California at Irvine, published in the *Journal of the American Nutraceutical Association* (Winter 1999) and entitled "An In Vitro Screening Study of 196 Natural Products for Toxicity and Efficacy," looked for the most ideal nutritional supplements as determined by their non-toxicity, their enhancement of NK (Natural Killer Cell) function, their antioxidant activity, and their protection against viruses. The study found that garlic, aloe, and several products *(Ambrotose* and *Phyt-Aloe)* from *Mannatech Corporation* lead the list. *Mannatech Corporation* specializes in cutting-edge glyconutritional research and products that enhance cell-to-cell communication and beneficial immune response. In brief, glyconutritionals are dietary supplements that contain specific monosaccharides that the body needs for proper cell growth and development. Scientific studies are confirming that such glyconutritional supplements can play a key health-promoting role for those afflicted with a wide spectrum of conditions caused by poor diet, stress, and environmental toxins. Those interested in the study and in obtaining *Mannatech* products can contact Karen Boutot (telephone 207-834-6934, e-mail <maple@mannapages.com>) for more information.

The list of innovative supplements available today is almost endless. For example, the coenzyme NADH has been shown in scientific studies to greatly aid victims of chronic fatigue, Alzheimer's, and Parkinson's diseases. ENADA, the enteric-coated version of NADH, which helps this fragile nutrient survive passage through the digestive tract, is available from, among other places, *Peggy's Health Center,* <http://www.peggyshealth.com>, e-mail <pegshealth@aol.com>.

Other supplements include lecithin, which is a good source of phosphatidyl choline, an important precursor for neurotransmitters in the brain. Such a supplement might be beneficial for those suffering from depression or certain neurological disorders. Brewer's yeast is a good natural source of a variety of nutrients, such as the entire vitamin B complex. *(Lewis Laboratories*—whose products are available at most health food stores—makes a high-quality, pleasant-tasting variety of both these nutrients. If you don't live near a health food store or can't find a product mentioned, *Vitamin City,* <http://www.vitamincity. com/catalog.htm>, e-mail <staff@vitamincity.com>, one of the largest online vitamin and supplement vendors, might be able to help you.)

In conclusion, I suggest you visit your local health food store to get advice on nutritional supplements, herbs, and foods that could be of direct benefit to your specific needs.

Dental Concerns

The thought of someone in my Preparedness Group having a toothache during Y2K and not being able to get to a dentist, is sobering. Thus I will be sure to have plenty of tincture of clove *(Syzygium aromaticum)*—which helps deaden toothache and gum pain—on hand. *Dr. Christopher's Herb Shop* (telephone 800-453-1406, <http://www.drchristopher.com/>) carries *X-Ceptic* tincture, which they claim is good for a variety of mouth-related problems, including pyorrhea, infection, thrush, toothaches, and bleeding gums. *X-Ceptic* is made from oak bark *(Quercas alba),* golden seal root *(Hydrastis canadensis),* garlic *(Allium sativum),* comfrey *(Symhytum officinale),* myrrh *(Commiphora myrrha),* and capsicum *(Capsicum annuum)*—all potent healing herbs.

Mouthwashes made of Golden Seal and Myrrh and Tea Tree oil are other good items to have on hand for potential mouth, gum, and teeth problems. Sugarless gum can be a good substitute for cleaning teeth if conserving water proves to be an issue. However, be sure the gum does not contain harmful sugar substitutes. I prefer sugarless gum that contains the naturally occurring and more slowly metabolized sugars sorbitol, mannitol, or xylitol, rather than saccharin, aspartame, acesulfame potassium, or other harsh and health-questionable artificial sweeteners. (Studies have shown that xylitol reduces plaque on teeth—See the *European Journal of Oral Sciences,* Vol. 105, Issue 2, pp. 170–177.)

The Cutting Edge, <http://www.cutcat.com/>, e-mail <cutcat@cutcat.com>, a company that focuses on holistic health-care products, carries the *Dyna Dental Ion Toothbrush,* which uses negatively charged ions to break up positively charged plaque on the teeth. The advantage of this unit is that it requires little, if any, water to clean your teeth. *Butler, Braun* and other companies carry battery-operated *plaque removers* that pulsate and/or oscillate at high speeds and break up the plaque that sticks to gums and teeth. However, such devices must be used carefully, especially by children, so that gum tissue is not harmed. Consult with your dentist about these and other ways to help maintain proper dental health.

The *Preserve Enviro-Tooth Brush,* made from recycled plastic, is ergonomically angled and designed to reach the difficult-to-get-to spots in the mouth. (When you finish with this special brush, you can send it back to the company to be recycled.)

Y2K TIP

You can use hydrogen peroxide or antiseptic mouthwash to rinse off toothbrushes to save water during the Y2K transition.

If you anticipate dental emergencies, it might be wise to pick up a copy of *Where There Is No Dentist* by Murray Dickson, as well as the inexpensive *Dental Emergency Kit* (item # C99C-21103, about $10), available from *The Sportsman's Guide,* <http://www.sportsmansguide.com/>. This kit can help repair temporarily a broken tooth or a lost filling, or calm a toothache.

Special Considerations and Conclusion

For those allergic to peanuts and bee and wasp stings, you might ask your doctor for a prescription to get *Epipen* (epinephrine). Diabetics should make sure they have a sufficient supply of the things they need to regulate blood sugar. They should also consider experimenting with a raw-food diet such as that proposed by George Malkmus of *Hallelujah Acres,* <http://www.hacres.com>, e-mail <help@hacres.com>. Malkmus's book *God's Way to Ultimate Health: A Common Sense Guide for Elimination of Sickness Through Nutrition* and his wife Rhonda's *Recipes For Life From God's Garden* are designed for those who want tasty meals based upon raw foods and minimal cooking. According to Malkmus, his raw food and natural lifestyle diet has helped many people find relief from a variety of chronic and debilitating diseases and conditions.

CHAPTER 7

Preparedness Products to Heat Your Home and Keep You Warm

• • • • • • • • • • •

"The prudent see danger and take refuge,
but the simple keep going and suffer for it." —Proverbs 27:12

Y2K will arrive with winter. A number of factors cause people who follow Y2K to be concerned that the infrastructure that supports the heating and electrical industries might be disrupted by Year 2000 computer glitches. Chief among them is the way the transportation industry (which supplies materials for energy production) depends upon accurate, date-sensitive information to run properly—everything from the oil supertankers that deliver heating fuel, to the railroad cars that transport the coal used by many electricity-generating plants. On top of this, many local and regional power supply companies are deeply intertwined, so that a failure in one part of the supply chain could cause "pocket failures" someplace else.

Y2K TIP
Remember to get your heating oil and propane tanks filled prior to January 1, 2000. There is a good chance your local power company will be operating before the heating fuel supply chain gets back to normal.

Coming up with an alternative way to provide heat and warmth for your family will require some effort. Most people have no idea how complex the system is that supplies heat and electricity to our home. What I offer in this chapter is a range of ideas from the inexpensive and simple, to the pricey and sophisticated. What is right for you will depend upon your budget, building structure, climate, and the special needs of your Preparedness Group.

Alternative forms of heating are not cheap. However, we need to look at them as an investment rather than a "purchase." That is, we need to conceive of them as a way to save money and help us live in a more self-empowered manner. For example, if the global economy takes the hit many predict, the price of fuel could soar, and what might seem expensive today could result in huge savings tomorrow. Considering such a scenario, now is the time to make those repairs that we have put off doing, such as adding more insulation to our home, caulking drafty doors and windows, or installing energy-efficient double-paned windows. (If you need inspiration and guidance on how to make your home more energy-efficient, pick up a copy of *The Independent Home: Living Well With Power from the Sun, Wind, and Water* by Michael Potts [available from *Amazon.com*, <http://www.amazon.com>]. This book chronicles the author's journey to turn his home into an independent homestead.)

Types of Heating Energy

Most heating systems and units can be divided into two main types, namely those requiring nonrenewable fossil fuel and those that don't. Nonrenewable fossil fuels include oil, gasoline, diesel fuel, coal, natural gas, propane, kerosene, and other combustible materials that come from ancient organic matter deposits in the earth. Over the last century the use of this type of fuel has been critical in the development of the electrical power system that supports the infrastructure of Western civilization. However, because fossil fuels are not renewable (it takes millions of years to produce coal and oil), because they generate toxic by-products such as ozone, carbon dioxide, and other forms of pollution, and because large amounts of energy are required to produce, transport, and utilize them, they are coming under increasing criticism by environmentalists and governmental agencies. They are also not the type of energy you want to be dependent upon if the power grid and transportation infrastructure collapse during Y2K.

In contrast, non-fossil "fuels," also referred to as renewable or sustainable energy sources, include solar and wind energy, water, wood, fuel pellets made from recycled cardboard, sawdust, corn husks, and other renewable waste products. The advantage of wind and solar energy is that they are endlessly renewable, non-polluting, and, once the system is in place, inexpensive to maintain and operate.

In the remainder of this chapter I will list a variety of ways to help you ensure you are kept warm in case of local Y2K-related power failures. Many people find a combination of sustainable and nonsustainable energy to be a workable compromise. What type of heating fuel you use will depend upon your needs, your budget, and your personal philosophy.

> ## Y2K Tip
> You can consult the *Hearthnet* Web site, <http://www.hearth.com/calc/btucalc.html>, to help you determine the amount of BTUs (British Thermal Units—a standard of heat measurement) you will need to heat a room

or house. This type of calculation—which depends upon climate and room size—is important so that you do not purchase a heating unit or system that is either too big or too small for your needs. The *Hearthnet* Web site also offers a Web page that helps you find a qualified U.S. or Canadian "Hearth Retailer" in your area (<http://www.hearth.com/shops.html>).

Gasoline and Diesel Generators

When it comes to backup power, many people think of a gasoline or diesel generator. For short-term purposes, such units can be helpful. But they require a lot of fuel—often eight to ten gallons a day—and they might not be beneficial if the power grid fails for an extended period of time or fuel becomes hard to get. (Because some fuels might be harder to get than others, you might consider a generator that can run on multiple fuel sources, such as the Kohler multi-fuel propane/natural gas generators available from Yellowstone River Trading Company, <http://www.yellowstonetrading.com/generators.html>, e-mail <info@yellowstonetrading.com>.)

If you do decide to hook a gasoline or diesel generator to your home or business, make sure a licensed electrician who can route and attach it to your circuit breaker in a safe and reliable manner, installs it properly. Also make sure your generator is protected from the weather and is properly ventilated: Diesel and gasoline fumes are deadly. In addition, make sure you get a unit that generates the amount of wattage that you need—some furnaces need 2600 watts of power to run properly. If you get a gasoline generator with an auto-idle control you will not waste precious fuel when you are not drawing power from it. (Unfortunately, diesel generators do not have this fuel saving accessory. However, many people consider diesel generators to be better than gasoline generators because they last a lot longer and use less fuel than gasoline generators, and because diesel fuel is much less flammable and safer to store than gasoline, diesel generators are less likely to explode in the event of a fuel spill.)

You can purchase portable gasoline or diesel generators from a number of places, including Imperial Diesel, <http://michaelhyatt.com/Imperial/order.htm>, e-mail <Imp123@aol.com>, Master Distributors (telephone 800-446-1446), Genex Power (telephone 800-782-5509), and NH Northern (telephone 800-533-5545, <http://www.northern-online.com>). The Imperial diesel generators are efficient, in some cases delivering 10,000 watts of continuous power on as little as a third of a gallon of fuel per hour of operation. (Be forewarned, though, that there is a run on generators, especially diesel ones, and that the back-order time for these products can be quite lengthy.)

In order to cut down on fuel costs, many people use their generator to charge a bank of batteries and then run appliances such as their furnace from this stored energy. If you do this, you will only need to run the generator periodically to charge the batteries. However, you will also need a trace inverter to convert the DC power to AC for domestic use. A number of companies such as RMS Electric Inc., <http://www.rmse.com/>, who specialize in helping homeowners become energy independent, can help you do this. RMS Electric Inc. carries the Gen-Charger system, which has a generator/battery/photovoltaic system that enables you to store large amounts of power and get maximum efficiency from your generator.

Other companies specializing in helping people become less "grid-dependent" include Jade Mountain Inc., <http://www.jademountain.com/>, e-mail <info@jademountain.com>; Mr. Solar <http://www.mrsolar.com/>, e-mail <CharlieCollins@mrsolar.com>; and Real Goods, <http://www.realgoods.com>, e-mail <techs@realgoods.com>. (Those looking for other ecologically friendly home design and heating ideas should consult the Naturalusa home design page, <http://www.naturalusa.com/Homedesign2.html>, and its natural living resource guide, <http://www.naturalusa.com/catalog.html/>, which lists numerous products by environment- and health-conscious vendors.)

Y2K TIP

If you do buy a generator, be sure to get it properly installed by a certified electrician. Especially make sure that you have a dual protection automatic transfer switch installed to prevent your generator from receiving a surge from outside your home or sending electricity that may injure a powerline worker. (Outside power surges can cause your generator to explode.)

If you plan on storing fuel, something that must be done with great caution, check the zoning laws in your area. Also, be sure to label and date your fuel cans and rotate them as you would canned food. *Captain Dave's Survival Shop*, <http://survival-center.com/>, and other vendors offer gasoline and diesel fuel preservers and restorers that protect your fuel for up to ten years.

Fireplaces, Stoves, and Other Heating Alternatives

Those fortunate to have a working fireplace (and a sufficient amount of wood) will feel more secure during Y2K. However, it is important that you have your fireplace inspected, repaired, and cleaned before Y2K arrives, especially if it has not been used for a while. It is also important to stock up on wood as soon as possible. Not only is the price of wood most likely to rise substantially during the fall of 1999 when everyone jumps on board the Y2K preparation wagon, but also you want to be sure the wood is sufficiently seasoned to burn more efficiently. Though kiln-dried wood costs more, it ensures that your firewood will burn better and give off more heat. (You also might want to roll your own "logs" from newspaper—visit your local hardware store for devices to do this.)

Y2K TIP

Because many forms of heating might be employed during the Y2K, the chance of carbon monoxide poisoning grows proportionately. Make sure your smoke, fire, and carbon monoxide detectors are in good working order and that you have plenty of fire extinguishers nearby in case of fire. Lehman's Non-Electric, <http://www.lehmans.com>, carries a radiation-free smoke alarm, and Real Goods, <http://www.realgoods.com>, among other vendors, carries the First Alert Smoke and Carbon Monoxide Alarm (about $70). Remember, you can't smell, taste, or see carbon monoxide, which can leak from any type of fuel-burning unit, including woodstoves, gas heaters, grills, furnaces, coal heaters, fireplaces, etc.

Inserts. Fireplaces are notoriously inefficient sources of heat, since most of the heat shoots up the flue. If you own a fireplace, you might consider an "insert" that can transform your traditional fireplace into an efficient and cost-effective way to heat your home. Inserts come in a variety of forms, including those that burn natural gas, liquid propane, or coal. See your local hearth shop for advice.

Alco-Brite, <http://www.alco-brite.com/>, e-mail <alcoinfo@alco-brite.com>, makes a Fireplace Insert that burns gelled ethanol fuel. The advantage of these self-contained units is that they do not need a chimney or vent. They can fit right inside your fireplace (or almost any other place in your home). The Alco-Brite Fireplace Insert is easy to install and offers an inexpensive backup source of heat. (Three cans of gelled ethanol fuel provide a seven-hour fire that generates approximately 30,000 BTUs at the cost of about $1.25 an hour.)

Soapstone. Soapstone radiant heaters are another efficient heat generating source to consider. Many native cultures relied upon soapstone's unique ability to withstand high temperatures and to hold and radiate heat for a long time, to heat their homes in the days before electricity. Pioneering North Americans quarried soapstone and used it for making bed warmers, as well as foot warmers and cooking instruments. Later soapstone was adapted to woodstoves. Today many companies make and sell soapstone radiant heating systems and stoves. If you can't find one in your area, you can contact Hearthstone, <http://www.hearth.com/hearthstone/hearthstone.html>, e-mail <hearthstone@ hearth.com>, a Northern Vermont manufacturer of soapstone heating products. Consult their Web site (<http://chi.hearth.com/hs/hssearch.html>) to find a distributor near you.

Masonry Heaters. The Masonry Heater Virtual Mall <http://mha-net.org/html/mall.htm>, sponsored by the Masonry Heater Association of North America, lists a number of companies offering various forms of masonry heating units and systems. Masonry heaters work on the principle of storing heat in a thermal mass and releasing it slowly during the day. Because they only need a brief, hot-burning fire to generate the stored heat, masonry heaters are the most efficient and cleanest way to burn cordwood. They can also make a great aesthetic addition to any home or room.

Woodstoves. The number and variety of woodstoves on the market is vast. A visit to any hearth shop is an educational experience. In general, catalytic stoves are more environmentally helpful. Catalytic stoves have a built-in chamber that helps wood burn at a higher temperature and thus prevent creosol build-up and reduce the amount of particulate material and hydrocarbons emitted from the smoke and heat. They also help wood burn more efficiently (so you use less firewood) and thus are more cost-effective than noncatalytic stoves. See the HearthNet Web page, <http://hearth.com/ shops.html>, for a list of U.S. and Canadian hearth, woodstove, and fireplace dealers in your area.

Pellet Stoves. Many people who do not like the work of attending a fire, like the convenience of pellet-burning stoves and inserts, which burn small, condensed chunks of recycled paper and wood material. (Check with your local hearth and fireplace shop or contact places such as Travis Industries, Inc., <http://hearth.com/travis/travis.html>, e-mail <traviscs@earthlink.net>, which carry the Lopi line of "earth-safe and ultra-convenient" pellet stoves that are said to allow up to 50 hours of uninterrupted heating.)

> ## Y2K TIP
> Before purchasing any auxiliary, supplemental, or alternative source of heat, it is important to consider how heat-efficient the unit is. Efficiency is defined as the percentage of

heat available in the fuel that is actually delivered into the room or living space. For more information on heat efficiency and charts of how different fuels and heating systems compare with one another, consult the HearthNet Web page, <http://www.hearth.com/what/specific.html>. This site also contains lots of valuable information on numerous home heating units and systems.

Kerosene. Many people use kerosene heaters as a way to keep their homes warm during the winter. However, take note of the following precautions: Kerosene cook stoves and heaters must be used with great care, they must have proper ventilation, they require only clear 1 K grade kerosene, their wicks must be kept clean and trimmed to the proper length, they must be refueled outdoors—and then only when the unit has cooled down, etc. Because kerosene heaters are such a fire hazard, if you do purchase one, be sure it has an automatic safety switch that will shut the unit off if it's accidentally tipped over. Many people also don't recommend kerosene heaters because they produce low levels of "carbon monoxide and nitrogen dioxide and should not be used by those with chronic respiratory and/or circulatory health problems" (the Delaware City–County Health Department's Web site, <http://www.iwaynet.net/~dcchd1/wren0113.html>).

Vented and Ventless Gas and Propane Heaters. Efficient gas and propane heaters are becoming an increasingly popular and inexpensive way to heat homes. These units operate on natural gas or propane and come in a variety of forms, including space heaters, gas logs, and the above-mentioned fireplace inserts. (See your local hearth shop for more details.)

There are two major types of gas heaters—vented and ventless. Ventless units are becoming increasingly popular because they are inexpensive and easy to install, since they do not require an outside vent or flue to dispel emissions. They also do not require electricity to operate and thus are considered an attractive "off-grid" alternative for keeping warm during Y2K.

The *Valor Classic Vent-Free Infrared Gas Heater* is a popular heating unit that uses either propane or natural gas. These units burn with 99% efficiency, can generate from 5,000 to 25,000 BTUs, have thermostat control, and do not require electricity to operate. They also have a built-in sensor to let you know if there is not enough oxygen in the room. They range in price from $230 to $550 and can be purchased from *Sierra Solar Systems,* <http://www.sierrasolar.com/>, e-mail <solarjon@sierrasolar.com>.

Empire Comfort Systems, <http://www.empirecomfort.com/ventfree.html>, e-mail <info@empirecomfort.com>, also offers an array of ventless gas heaters. You can contact them to obtain the name of a dealer near you.

However, because ventless heaters do not vent their exhaust combustion, some people have raised health and safety concerns about them. According to the *HearthNet* database, "ventless stoves can have problems if they are used too heavily. They should be considered only as an attended and supplemental heat source . . . like a kerosene heater" (<http://chi.hearth.com—on this page search for the article title that equals "Ventless gas safety concerns"; when the search results page is displayed, click on the article title to read the full article). There is also a concern about the effect of ventless heaters on those who suffer from asthma, respiratory problems, and multiple chemical sensitivities.

According to *Jade Mountain Inc.,* unvented heaters generating "less than 10,000 BTUs (are) approved for sleeping rooms. . . . Larger sizes (are) not recommended for sleeping rooms" (<http://nationalguild.com/master/jade/jadetransfer/spacht.html>). For safety reasons, many experts recommend that ventless heaters be used for only a few hours a day, rather than as a primary source of heat.

Fortunately, many of the safer and more heat-efficient vented gas heaters are easy to install and do not require a major vent pipe or hole in your roof. *Jade Mountain Inc.*'s *Cozy Direct Vent Wall Furnace* is easy to install, and is designed for heating large spaces. *Jade Mountain Inc.* also offers the innovative *Hydronic Space Heating* systems that heat from the floor or ground up. Those who can afford it might look into this type of system, given that it produces a comfortable form of heat as it warms the lower body and keeps the upper body "relatively cool and alert" (<http://nationalguild.com/master/jade/jadetransfer/hydronic.html>).

Jade Mountain Inc. and *Sierra Solar Systems* carry the *Platinum Cat* room heater, which they describe as an "ultra-efficient radiant-type catalytic wall heater." Like the sun, this heater "warms people and objects directly—even if the room's air is cool." In essence, this unit generates radiant heat that "penetrates the skin to provide more effective, truly pleasant comfort" (<http://www.sierrasolar.com/products/propane/platinum.htm>). These units are controlled by a thermostat, run on either propane or natural gas, and have an exhaust fan that can be powered by either 12VDC or 110VAC. They can generate about 5,000 BTUs and use one gallon (3.78 liters) of propane to heat a room for 17 hours. They currently range in price from $380 to $420.

Y2K TIP

Having your own propane tank makes you less dependent upon others to provide for your needs. (In some areas of the U.S. you can rent a 250-gallon [946 liters] propane tank and a heater that will heat your whole house. Such a unit can be a valuable short-term investment during Y2K.) Your local propane and natural gas dealer can offer suggestions on other heating products. If you purchase a propane or natural gas heater, make sure it does not have an electric starter or need electricity to operate. Many of the companies that specialize in alternative heating can help you design a solar/gas combination system for maximum off-grid comfort and security.

Gelled Fuels. As mentioned previously, gelled fuels offer a relatively safe and inexpensive way to generate temporary forms of heat. *Ecofuel,* available from *Embassy Imports* (toll-free telephone 877-y2kfuel [925-3835]), *Alco-Brite*'s gelled ethanol, <http://www.alco-brite.com>, e-mail <alcoinfo@alco-brite.com>; and *Heat It,* available from *Insight Discounts,* <http://www.insightdiscounts.com/y2k.htm>, e-mail <sales@insightdiscounts.com>, can help maintain warmth and comfort if you lose power during Y2K. (See the section on gelled fuels in Chapter Five for more details.)

> ### Y2K TIP
>
> *Ecofuel, Alco-Brite*'s gelled ethanol, and *Heat It* could be an economical way to keep pipes from freezing, if you lose power during a cold snap. (You should also consider purchasing a *4-in-1* tool that fit most water and gas turn valves, available at your local hardware shop.) You also might consider purchasing an inexpensive small wood stove to warm up the cellar, garage, or wherever your pipes are the most vulnerable. *Lehman's Non-Electric* offers a "bare bones" unit for under $200. It is also important to make sure heating appliances are UL approved for indoor use.

Solar Power and Wind Power. The sophistication and popularity of solar and wind power generating equipment have grown immensely over the past decade. No longer confined to the ghetto of idealistic dreamers, rural homesteaders, and counter-culture types, solar and wind power have become an energy source of choice for those who desire a safe, quiet, and continually renewable source of energy.

In essence, solar-generated power is based upon the concept that light-sensitive panels, called photovoltaic modules, transform the radiant energy of the sun into electricity, which then is stored in batteries. (Most solar units have a built-in regulating device that automatically turns off the electrical flow once the batteries are fully charged.) This DC (direct current) battery-stored energy can be used to run any battery-operated appliance or accessory, or can be converted through an inverter to AC (alternating current) for operating normal home appliances and heating systems. (For about $180 to $370,

---

you can even get a portable solar-powered generator to run your laptop computer; one source of supply is Jade Mountain Inc., <http://www. jademountain. com/>.)

A good consultant can determine if your home is sufficiently south-facing and if your geographical and climatic area receives the necessary Equivalent Sun Hours (ESH) to operate solar power. The consultant can also determine what type of rooftop solar panels are suited to your needs, and whether special shade-tolerant solar units are required.

Wind-generated power is becoming popular in many parts of the country. Just as with solar systems, you need to be sure your geographical climate receives the necessary equivalent wind hours suited for wind turbo generators. (Wind-energy machines are most efficient when winds average about 28 to 30 mph [45 to 48 kph].) In general, wind generators are less expensive than solar-powered systems (generally around $1000). The experts at Real Goods, <http://www.realgoods.com>, e-mail <techs@realgoods.com>, recommend three-blade wind power units for quieter, more reliable service. (For information on how wind energy machines can be an inexpensive form of backup power, or to help you get completely off-grid, you can read Paul Gipe's *Wind Power for Home and Business*. Gipe's comprehensive book focuses on the new turbine units that allow for total energy autonomy. It is available from Amazon.com, <http://www.amazon.com/>.)

However, because of the enormous amounts of energy required to heat (and cool) a home, many experts recommend a hybrid solar/wind system. Such a system can be cost effective, especially if the local power company has a utility "intertie" system agreement that requires them to buy back power from those customers who generate a surplus of their own power—something a well designed solar and wind power system can do. (Those interested in using this method to subsidize their conversion to solar and wind power should check with their local power company to see what its policy entails. They should also consult articles such as the one by Jonathan Hill on the *Sierra Solar Systems* Web site, <http://www.sierrasolar.com/pv_systems.htm>, that gives a good overview of the types of solar photovoltaic systems available to consumers today.

Wind and Solar Power Vendors. There are a number of consultants and vendors who specialize in helping consumers and businesses set up a solar/wind power system or find the right source of alternative power for their needs. If you can't find a solar/wind power expert and supplier in your area, you can contact Real Goods, <http://www.realgoods.com>, an industry leader in solar, wind, and other forms of sustainable and renewable power generation for homes, small businesses, and industry. (Their innovations include solar shingles for those who do not like the sight of large, shiny photovoltaic reflectors mounted on their housetop. Call for their free educational catalog, or you can save paper and view their catalog online at the address given above.)

Jade Mountain Inc. is another excellent source of alternative power equipment and products. (Jade Mountain Inc. even offers battery-powered bicycles; see <http://www.jademountain.com/alttrans.html>.) Their staff is dedicated to a "green" business ethic that helps you find the solutions appropriate to your needs, rather than just telling you what they want you to buy.

Gridfree.com (telephone 888-440-8025) offers sophisticated "tri-power" systems for energy independence. The units work with solar, wind, and fuel generators to ensure sufficient power in any type of weather.

Alternative Energy Engineering, <http://www.alt-energy.com>, e-mail <energy@alt-energy.com>, is another major supplier of solar power information and products.

Mr. Solar, <http://www.mrsolar.com/>, e-mail <CharlieCollins@ mrsolar. com>, has years of experience helping people find the best way to get "off-grid." Charlie Collins *(Mr. Solar)* designed and built his own self-sufficient homestead and enjoys helping others do the same. *Mr. Solar* offers top-quality power windmills and related field-proven products, and will help you determine what is best for your situation. They also carry a sophisticated solar-powered *Radiant Floor Heating System* that can generate warmth for your entire home at no cost once it is installed. These units are pricey (about $19,000 per 1,000-square-foot [93 square meters] home in cold northern climates) but they can reduce your heating bills.

Wakeman Porter at *Twisted Oak Alternative Energy,* <http://www. twistedoak.com/>, e-mail <jwporter@twistedoak.com>, is another knowledgeable alternative power expert. For the mechanically inclined, *Twisted Oak Alternative Energy* offers a dual-purpose steam engine that generates and supplies both heat and power. For under $1000 you can buy a one-horsepower steam engine that generates 80 amps at 24 volts, which, when coupled to the right type of DC batteries, can supply and hold an eight to ten kilowatt reserve of power. Along this same line, *Eco-Tech,* <http://www. njefferson.com>, e-mail <eco-tech@cvn.net>, carries the *Conestoga Boiler* (about $3,500)—a backyard wood-burning unit that will generate enough heat to keep your house, barn, place of business, or swimming pool toasty warm during the winter months.

Steve and Elizabeth Willey own and operate *Backwoods Solar Electric Systems,* <http://backwoodssolar.com/>, e-mail <info@backwoodssolar.com>, a company that offers solid advice for those interested in upgrading or converting their home to more independent power sources.

> ## Y2K TIP
> Wind power generators are good at pumping water from wells—something to consider if you are dependent upon publicly generated electricity to retrieve your water. *Soiltech* (telephone 800-296-6026) makes a geared well *Hand Pump* that will pump water from wells as deep as 150 feet. It can also be adapted to windmills. Readers who live in small towns that generate or distribute their own energy—especially those in remote, cold areas—might want to have local authorities look into backup wind turbines such as *The Atlantic Orient 15/50 Turbine*, which for about $60,000 can generate enough power for a small town. Contact *Mr. Solar* for more information, or search sites on the Large Wind Energy Electric Generators Businesses in the World Wide Web site <http://www.sourceguides.com/energy/businesses/byP/wRP/lWG/lWG.html>, which lists companies specializing in large-capacity wind energy generation.

The Old-Fashioned Way. Given that Y2K might require us to sleep in colder than normal room temperatures—inside a warm sleeping bag and wearing a woolen hat, sweaters and socks can make this adventure much more pleasant. If you don't already have warm goose down comforters, woolen blankets, fleece bedding items, and a quality sleeping bag, now is the time to invest in them.

Depending on your geographical area, you'll need a sleeping bag good for either above- or below-freezing temperatures. This choice is important: too warm a bag and you sweat, too cool a bag and you shiver all night. Get advice from your local camping store expert for the best type of winter bag for your area, as well as the best type of lightweight thermal underwear and socks that have a high "wicking" capacity—the ability to throw off perspiration. "Layering" items such as these enables you to adjust your bodily comfort by wearing thermal clothes if you are too cold, or by taking them off if you become too warm.

Vendors of Cold Weather Clothing and Gear. Most areas have vendors that carry quality outdoor and winter weather gear. If you prefer to shop on the Web, *Action Gear,* <http://www.actionshop.

com/_vti_bin/shtml.exe/manuf.htm/map>, is a good place to find manufacturers and distributors of a wide variety of outdoor clothing and camping gear. The *Equipped to Survive* Web site, <http://www.equipped.org/>, offers a host of highly informative product sites and information pages on emergency preparedness and survival.

Northern Mountain Supply, <http://northernmountain.com/tocs/filters.html>, e-mail <mtn@northernmountain.com>, carries a wide range of sleeping bags at "killer prices."

The Sportsman's Guide, <http://www.sportsmansguide.com/>, is a good source of inexpensive, good-quality "military" surplus goods, as well as new blankets, sleeping bags, boots, and other cold weather and winter gear.

Eagle Enterprises, <http://www.alaskamall.com/eagle/>, e-mail <eagleent@alaska.net>, is a good company for hard-core winter survival gear. *Moosejaw Mountaineering,* <http://www.moosejawonline.com/catalog/accessories.html>, e-mail <moose@voyager.net> or <wigod@voyager.net>, carries a wide variety of quality outdoor camping gear.

In Canada, *Mountain Equipment Co-Op* (telephone 800-663-2667) is the premier place to purchase quality equipment for wilderness-oriented activities. *Mountain Equipment Co-Op* has stores located in several major Canadian cities, including Calgary, Edmonton, Ottawa, Toronto, and Vancouver. A good resource for outdoor survival advice, they also have a mail-order catalog.

Y2K TIP

Reading outdoor, survival, and preparedness catalogs (such as the *Survival Civilian Catalog* by *Pernith Survival Equipment,* e-mail <Survival@cumbria.com>) will both stimulate your thinking and help you tailor your specific Preparedness Plan in terms of your geography, climate, and other relevant factors.

B&A Products, <http://www.baproducts.com/catalog.htm>, and a number of other preparedness and outdoor gear vendors, carry "hi-tech blankets" such as the *Polarshield Emergency Blanket* (about $13), built to retain body heat. Although they do not offer the "snuggle" weight that many people like to cuddle up to when they sleep, these blankets are lightweight and easily stored. Therefore, combining "hi-tech" blankets with a hefty 100% wool blanket might be a good option for some people.

Survival Enhanced, <http://www.survivalenhanced.com/welcome.html>, e-mail <katadyn@kktv.com>, carries the *Survival Cocoon,* "a thermal protective aid—an emergency survival bag for use on land or sea." This cold weather survival "cocoon" weighs only 18 ounces (510 grams), is waterproof, and is easily stored in a small bag. An item such as this might be good to carry in your car while traveling during the early stages of the Y2K transition.

For those who don't like being confined to a sleeping bag, *On-Line Health Products,* <http://www.dhi.com/>, among other places, carries a line of *Snugfleece* woolen mattress covers that offer superlative warmth in the winter and coolness in the summer. These plush, soft, high-wicking mattress covers can absorb up to 35% of their weight in moisture and still remain dry. They are especially good for nursing mothers, so they can keep their baby warm and relaxed. The swaddling and snuggling quality of soft wool is soothing for both babies and adults. The plush wool also helps to distribute body weight evenly and to reduce pressure on parts of the body without losing support for the spine as happens in waterbeds.

Y2K TIP

Waterbeds are a great way to keep warm on cold winter nights. Solar power panels can be an inexpensive way to ensure the water remains comfortable if the power grid fails. Along this line, if you have an aquarium you should also consider some type of solar-based backup power system to oxygenate the water and keep your fish tank warm.

Children Concerns. Those with infants and young children need to take special precautions to ensure their safety and comfort during Y2K. *Molehill Mountain Equipment, Inc,* <http://www.molehillmtn.com/>, e-mail <Info@MolehillMtn.com>, specializes in outdoor and cold-weather apparel for infants and children, including outfits that allow for changing diapers easily. A husband-and-wife team who could not find quality winter clothing for their young daughter, started their own company, *Molehill Mountain Equipment, Inc.,* to fill their need. *Molehill Mountain Equipment, Inc.* carries an extensive line of "waterproof, breathable, all-weather gear" for infants, toddlers, and juniors. Their high-wicking multiple-layering approach to clothing is especially child-friendly.

Outdoor Kids' Source, <http://www.kidssource.com/>, e-mail <oks@ mt-mansfield.com>, carries the *Windbreaker Fleece Baby Blanket,* specially designed for infant comfort. They also carry child-sized sleeping bags as well as child-sized backpacks, first-aid kits and other outdoor gear. *Outdoor Kids'*

Source has a Web page, <http://www.kidssource.com/info.htm>, dedicated to helping families with children find appropriate cold weather gear, as well as information on child-related outdoor survival and safety issues.

Chuck Roast, <http://www.chuckroast.com/>, e-mail <custserv@ chuckroast.com>, is another company specializing in outdoor gear for children. *Chuck Roast* also has a lifetime warranty on their products.

Hot Water Bottles. It would also be wise to acquire hot water bottles to be used as bed and foot warmers. (Hot water bottles are expensive. To cut down on expenses you can also use two-liter plastic soda pop or soft drink bottles.) It would also be a good idea to practice heating the water for these items, using your backup cooking system, and to log the best heating (and cooling) times in your Y2K Preparedness Journal so that you don't melt the bottles.

Hand warmers. Many preparedness and winter gear vendors such as *Captain Dave's Survival Center,* <http://survival-center.com/>, sell small, chemically generated heat packs that might be worth stocking up on. They are inexpensive, come in packages of four, and normally last about six hours each. They can be placed inside a sleeping bag or coat to help keep you warm or take away a nasty chill. (However, some of these units get very hot—about 160°F [71°C]—and should not be placed next to the skin.) *Epicenter,* <http://www.theepicenter.com>, carries the inexpensive (under $2) *Sports Heat Body Warming Pads* that generate warmth for up to 20 hours. *Emergency Essentials,* <http://www.beprepared.com/home.html>, offers the *18-Hour Hand and Body Warmer* that comes in a ten-pack (about $10) and uses "natural ingredients" to warm hands, feet, legs, etc.

Just as keeping warm is a vital consideration during Y2K, so is the ability to see at night—a topic taken up in the next chapter.

CHAPTER 8

Lighting Up Your Life

• •|• • • • • • • •

"Will the lights stay on 1/1/2000? That is the $64,000 question!"
—Jim Ashkar, Boston Edison Managing

The issue of safe, alternative lighting in the event we lose electrical power during Y2K is of paramount concern. I stress "safe" lighting because if the power fails we might be spending a lot of time indoors with the windows and doors tightly sealed to keep out the cold. Accordingly, kerosene and other types of fossil-fuel lanterns could pose health problems.

Alternative Flashlights. Given that flashlight batteries might be in short supply during Y2K, you might consider getting a flashlight that is not dependent upon batteries. *Epicenter, Jade Mountain Inc., Real Goods, Xtreme Needs, A&B,* and a number of other vendors, carry the *Baygen Freeplay Wind-Up or Self-Powered Lantern*—a hand-wound flashlight that also has a built-in three-volt DC generator and jack so that you can power small electronics (such as a radio) with it. 30 seconds of winding gives more than three minutes of light.

Epicenter, <http://www.theepicenter.com>, *and Jade Mountain Inc.,* <http://www.jademountain.com/>, carry the Russian-made *Dynamo* flashlight that uses pump action to keep it powered. *Real Goods,* <http://www.realgoods.com>, carries the *SolarVeter* flashlight (about $30), which runs on both solar and battery power. An eight-hour charge by the sun will give about 2.5 hours of continuous light. (Similar versions of this solar-powered flashlight are also offered on *eBay,* a popular Internet auction firm, found at <http://www.ebay.com/>.)

Solar Battery Charger. Given the amount of light we might need, those using conventional battery-operated flashlights, radios, etc., might consider obtaining an inexpensive solar-operated battery charger. (Battery chargers save money and help reduce toxic waste.) *Epicenter* offers two types—one for charging AAA, AA, C, and D *NiCad* battery sizes, and a charger for AA batteries that also has a 1/8-inch [32.75 millimeters], 3.5-volt power output jack for running your radio directly from the power of the sun. *Jade*

Mountain Inc. carries a *Solar NiCad Charger* that can recharge over ten batteries a day. *Jade Mountain Inc.* also carries *Powersonic NiCad* batteries, which hold their charge much longer than most commercial batteries. *A&B Products* offers an inexpensive solar-powered battery charger ($23) that can charge two batteries at a time.

> ## Y2K TIP
> The amount of Equivalent Sun Hours (ESH) needed to fully charge solar photovoltaic cells might not be available during winter in some parts of the country, so it's important to have either several solar units or a variety of lighting systems on hand.

Other Lighting Sources. *Insight Discounts* <http://www.insightdiscounts.com/y2k.htm>, e-mail <sales@insightdiscounts.com>, carries the *Sun Trakker Compact Solar-Lighting System*, which is a carefree and convenient way to generate power to light two 50-watt light bulbs for up to six hours a night. (Systems such as this enable you to conserve precious generator fuel during an extended loss of power.) They also carry the inexpensive *Sun-Mate® Solar Multi-Purpose/Survival Flashlight* (about $20) that runs on both solar power and AA batteries.

The Survival Center, <http://www.zyz.com/survivalcenter/>, sells a *Solar Powered Rechargeable Lantern* (about $70) which, according to their literature, generates "three types of Solar Lighting: Continuous Fluorescent, Torch Incandescent (Searchlight) and Blinking Red Light."

Maglites®, which come in a variety of sizes and are available at most hardware and department stores, are extremely bright for their size. Since they are also very light, rugged and portable, you might consider having everyone in your Preparedness Group wear one strung around the neck at night. (You should also carry one with you when you enter public buildings, given that there might be periodic electrical failures at any time during the Year 2000.)

Petzl makes a hands-free halogen focusable headlamp (like the ones coal miners wear) that makes working in the dark a lot easier. This is a great device to have in the kitchen or when working outdoors. It can be purchased from number of places such as *Jade Mountain; Karst Sports,* <http://svis.org/MSC/karst.htm>, e-mail <karst.sports@svis.org>, which specializes in caving, climbing, and rescue equipment; or *Adventure Gear,*

<http://www.ewalker.com/adgear/adgear.htm>, e-mail <adventure@ ewalker.com>, which offers a vast array of camping and outdoor products. (See the *Petzl* Web site, <http://www.petzl.com/>, for a list of both products and local dealers.)

The *Survival Center* carries an inexpensive *Deluxe Waterproof Headlamp* with a krypton bulb (about $14), and *Epicenter* carries the popular "Light Sticks" that come in a variety of colors. "Light Sticks" (also called "Glow Sticks") are based upon chemiluminescence, the natural phenomenon seen in fireflies. These flexible, colorful lighting units don't give off a lot of light, but they can help you find your way in the dark, and children enjoy using them.

In addition to their famous camping lanterns, *Coleman,* <http://www.colemanoutdoor.com/>, makes a rechargeable *Nightsight* lamp with an adjustable stand. It will give 60 minutes of light when fully charged. Nonelectric lamps such as this one might be very helpful.

Jade Mountain Inc., <http://www.jademountain.com/sollantflsh.html>, stocks a portable *LED Mini-Reading Lamp* that can be run or charged by plugging into a 12-volt DC outlet or a power supply from an optional AC 12-volt "Mini-Transformer," as well as a "Power Glow" pen that lets you write in the dark (a fun way to keep your Y2K Preparedness Journal). They also offer the *Lighthawk* (about $55) rechargeable lantern that has a built-in dimmer. This nifty unit supplies lots of light and can be recharged from AC power or from your car or boat battery. *Jade Mountain Inc.* also offers a *Spector Solar Lantern* (about $225) that can run up to five hours from a day's charge in the sun.

The *Survival Center,* <http://www.zyz.com/survivalcenter/>, carries a *Solar and Dynamo* (wind-up) *Powered Flashlight and AM/FM Radio* combination unit with an optional AC/DC adapter (about $50).

Tilley Endurables, <http://www.tilley.com/index2.html>, and *Epicenter* offer the *Flashcard,* a credit card-sized flashlight that easily fits in a shirt pocket. The paper-thin, card-like flashlights are waterproof and cast a bright beam for up to one hour. These super small lights will be ideal to carry around during Y2K in the event of intermittent power failures in buildings and dark places.

Special Candles. Besides being a warm and romantic source of light, if candles are big enough they can also add extra warmth and serve as a source of heat to boil water or cook food. Given that conventional candles are short-lasting and messy, you might want to consider purchasing long-burning candles. (If you prefer the more traditional candlesticks I suggest you search local flea markets, where you can often find good deals.)

Votive candles are an inexpensive long-term type of candle. However, for serious emergency preparedness you should consider super long-lasting "survival candles" such as those made by *Nuwick*. The *Nuwick* candles can be bought in the 44- or 120-hour size and not only provide exceptionally long-lasting light, but they also allow you to add wicks to increase the amount of heat they give off. (The heat from these candles can help warm a small living space, heat up soup or chili, fry an egg, or boil water in 20 minutes or less.) *Nuwick* candles are non-toxic—they are made from food-grade paraffin wax—the type used on fruit and vegetables in conventional supermarkets. The 120-hour candles cost about $10 each and are much cheaper when bought by the case. They can be purchased from *B&A Products, Nitro-Pak, Bruce Hopkins, Xtreme Needs,* and *Campmor,* which offers some of the cheapest prices.

Insight Discounts carries the *Adjustable Wick Emergency Heating Fuel* unit. With wicks that can be adjusted to obtain high, low, or medium output, these units are very inexpensive ($15.95 per six-pack, or $54.95 per 24-pack).

Emergency Essentials, <http://www.beprepared.com/home.html>, carries the inexpensive *100 Hour Emergency Candle* (about $4.50). This an odorless and smokeless product that also burns liquid paraffin. *Captain Dave's Survival Shop* has 50-hour emergency candles, packed in a can, that can be used for both heating and light. *Epicenter* stocks *Liquid Candle*—an inexpensive emergency lighting source that last for 50 hours. *The Survival Center* carries the "6½ day" candle that burns for almost a whole week. At twelve candles per case (about $35), five cases will generate a year's supply of light. *South Summit,* <http://www.southsummit.com/>, stocks an adjustable-wick 100-hour candle at a bargain price (about $3.95).

Y 2 K   T I P

Although many open-flame products are billed as safe, they must be used with caution—that is, you need to be careful about fire hazards, proper ventilation, children and pets burning themselves, etc. Always have a pot of water nearby and plenty of multipurpose fire extinguishers on hand. Remember also to acquire lots of matches and butane lighters. (Flea markets are a good place to buy butane lighters cheaply and in bulk.) Be sure to keep them in a safe, dry place.

Those concerned about security and safety if the power grid fails, should look into long-lasting solar-powered lights such as the White *LED Outdoor Spotlight* (about $49) carried by *Jade Mountain Inc.* These extremely power-efficient units burn less than 3/5 of a watt and are great for lighting important safety areas such as front and back porches, entryways, carports, garages, walkways, etc. A single charge of these solar units enables them to burn for more than 65 nights. They come with an optional *mini-Sunrise/Sunset* switch that automatically turns on the unit when it gets dark and turns it off when it gets light. *Jade Mountain Inc.* carries a variety of LED lights—some of which last 100,000 hours or 12 years of continuous use, 24 hours a day. Their online catalog is quite informative.

As important as light is, the next chapter highlights something we absolutely cannot live without.

CHAPTER 9
Water-Related
Preparedness Issues
• • | • • • • • • • •

"'Y2K, the Year 2000, or the Millennium Bug' computer problem
could adversely affect the operation of the nation's drinking water
and wastewater treatment systems if it is not corrected."
—The US Environmental Protection Agency, 30 December 1998

Most survival and preparedness experts claim potable water is the most important element to have on hand in the event of a long-term emergency. They estimate we need a minimum of two gallons of water per person per day for drinking, cooking, cleaning, etc. (This does not include water for bathing or washing clothes.) Therefore, given the chance that the computers and embedded microchips used in many water processing and distribution plants might malfunction during Y2K, it would be wise to have a supply of good water on hand.

In this chapter I will outline ways to help you obtain the highest quality drinking water as you plan and prepare for Y2K. Unfortunately, many in the preparedness field look at drinkable water solely in terms of whether or not it is free from harmful microbes such as Giardia, parasites, bacteria, and viruses, while often overlooking the health hazards of volatile organic compounds (VOCs), chlorine by-products such as trihalomethanes (THMs) and heavy metals such as lead, arsenic, mercury, radionuclides, etc., found in many local water supplies. (For more information on the staggering number of harmful contaminants found in household and local water sources consult *The Water Quality Association*'s home page <http://www.wqa.org/>.)

Y2K TIP
It is important to note that boiling water will destroy harmful microorganisms but it will not remove heavy metals, chlorine by-products, and numerous other contaminants. In addition, if you lose your local water supply during Y2K, be sure to turn off the in-flow valve before water pressure drops so low that you will not be able to use the water stored in your pipes. Doing this will also help prevent contaminated water from the public mains from flowing back into your domestic water pipes.

Water Purification. In their zest for safe drinking water, many pre-paredness writers recommend adding a disinfectant such as chlorine bleach to keep microorganisms from growing in the water. The normal recommen-dation for emergency water purification is adding two drops of four to six percent sodium hypochlorite solution (*Clorox, Purex,* or a similar liquid chlorine bleach) per quart (940 milliliters) of clear water (or four drops if the water is cloudy) and allowing the mixture to stand for 30 minutes before using. (See the Water Storage and Purification Web site, <http://members.amaonline.com/jeri/Water.htm>.)

However, an important health concern is often overlooked by this pro-cedure. Many local sources of drinking water, such as those used by munici-pal facilities, contain a number of organic solvents that react with chlorine and form deadly compounds such as trihalomethanes (THMs.) According to the *American Water Works Association,* THMs and other disinfecting by-products are formed when chlorine reacts "with naturally occurring organic matter in the source water" (<http://www.virginia-beach.va.us/services/putility/wq/awwa-thm.htm>). THMs have been implicated in a number of health-related problems such as cancer and miscarriages.

Survival experts also recommend adding iodine tablets or solution to water to help kill pathogens. (If you use iodine solution to purify water it takes a minimum of 30 minutes of contact time to kill off the microbes.) However, like chlorine, iodine is a poison and must be used with caution. People with thyroid problems, pregnant women, and those who are chemi-cally sensitive should avoid this popular water treatment method. (Iodine can cause fetal deformities and should not be used by pregnant women or those who might get pregnant.)

Both the use of chlorine bleach and iodine for water purification might be necessary in an absolute emergency when no other option is available. However, since we know the exact moment when Y2K will arrive, we can plan more carefully. Therefore, if you plan to use bleach or iodine it is impor-tant that you run the finished water through an activated charcoal filter before you drink it. Activated charcoal helps remove chlorine, iodine, THMs, and other organic volatile compounds from water. *IPC Future Foods,* <http://www.ipcfuturefoods.com/y2k.htm>, carries the *Tri-Pure Filtration System*, which, according to their literature, will remove "chlorine, lead, mer-cury, radon decay products, E. Coli, trihalomethenes, pesticides, PCBs," as well as removing "odors and aftertastes" (<http://www.ipcfuturefoods.com/waterb.htm>). This unit can be attached to your sink faucet, or it has the option of a hand-operated pump that enables you to purify water from any source—including your storage containers.

Multipure makes a small carbon-block filter that hooks up to a hand-operated siphon pump that lets you run your stored water through a medium that screens out most organic contaminants, including chlorine. There a number of independent *Multipure* distributors who can help you devise this system, including Royal Field (telephone 303-425-5664) or Don Adams (telephone 970-353-7172).

Alternative Water Purification. Thankfully, a number of companies offer a new generation of products worth investigating as a safer alternative to adding chlorine and/or iodine solutions to water.

The American Freedom Network, <http://www.amerifree.com/>, e-mail <comments@amerifree.com>, among other places, carries the *Alive Water Survival Systems Straw* with water treatment drops (about $25). This device, recently approved by the EPA, allows you to drink nonpotable water from a straw. The unit is good for about 5000 gallons (19,000 liters); many people carry one in their car or travel bag so they will always have a way to obtain potable drinking water.

Sam Andy®, <http://www.karinya.com/sandy.htm>, carries the *Arloxy-100 Universal Disinfectant,* which is made up of "safe," "tasteless and odorless" "ion-oxygen." According to their literature, "just a few drops kills Giardia and infectious bacteria, (and) removes chlorine." A two-fluid-ounce (about 60 milliliters) bottle with dropper will treat "hundreds of quarts (liters) of water" as well as "neutralize insect stings, reduce risk of infection on cuts and scrapes. (It is) a first-aid kit in a bottle" (<http://www.karinya.com/wtrstor.htm>).

Watertanks.com carries *Aerobic Oxygen,* which "consists of stabilized oxygen molecules" used for "treating potable drinking water for long-term storage." According to their Web site, *Aerobic Oxygen* kills "all anaerobic (infectious) bacteria" as well as adding beneficial "oxygen to your blood and body, rejuvenating tired muscles" (<http://www.watertanks.com/aerob.html>).

Walton Feed, <http://waltonfeed.com>, and *Bruce Hopkins,* <http://web2.airmail.net/foodstr2>, also offer *ion-stabilized oxygen* in two-ounce (about 60 milliliters) bottles.

Making Your Own Water. Another way to ensure quality drinking water is to make it yourself. There are a number of filters that provide good water. However, many experts prefer either reverse osmosis (RO) water filters, which force water through a permeable membrane to screen out contaminants, or distillers, which convert water to steam and allow it condense back to water, as the best ways to ensure high-quality drinking water. However, both systems must have a sufficiently large carbon post-filter to eliminate the problem of THMs and other volatile hydrocarbons. This is especially true of distillers since the heating process contributes to chlorine by-product build-up.

The advantage to making your own water is that assuming the water-related problems associated with Y2K will not last too long (hopefully no longer than a few weeks), and assuming you store your water in clean, well sealed, sterile containers that are kept away from sunlight, you should not have to add chlorine, iodine, or any other chemical purifiers to prevent microbial build-up.

Wild Water. If you plan on moving to a small cabin in the woods during Y2K, or using a local river, lake, or nearby pond as a backup for your drinking water, or if you want to make sure the water you have stored away is good, a high-quality hand-operated water filter/purifier is a wise investment.

Given the importance of water, it is prudent to buy the best filter you can afford. (See the *Gear Addict* Web page <http://www.web-dzine.com/gearaddict/rvfilters.html> for reviews on a number of the leading portable water purifiers.) Many Y2Kers recommend the *Katadyn Combi Filter,* available from a number of vendors, including *Homestead Products,* <http://elaine.teleport.com/~dany/mill/>, *New Millennium Products,* <http://www.newmillenniumproducts.com/>, *USA Marketing Associates,* <http://www.y2ksupplies.com/>, as well as your local camping store. The *Katadyn Combi Filter* is a great device for filtering out all known harmful microorganisms as well as many toxic chemicals and by-products in most water sources. However, the parts for this filter need lots of maintenance and frequent replacement, and many distributors of the *Katadyn* filters cannot fulfill their orders.

Many people consider the *PureFlow 2000* to be a much better quality filter. This filter offers a three-step process that removes dirt, heavy metals, chemicals, viruses, and bacteria. Although it is not as portable as the *Katadyn Combi Filter*, it does contain a much larger carbon block filter and a larger ceramic filter that does not have to be cleaned as often. The versatile *PureFlow 2000* (about $350) can be hooked up to your faucet or taken out to the local mud puddle. It is also much easier to obtain than the *Katadyn Combi Filter* and is available from *Supplies4Y2K.com,* <http://www.supplies4y2k.com/catalog2.htm>, e-mail <sales@supplies4y2k.com>.

Ozark Water Service carries the *Pro-Flo Emergency Response 3* water purification unit (about $500). This sophisticated, self-contained, hand-operated system is designed for remote, emergency, and disaster relief water treatment. The unit requires no electricity and has three filters to remove microbial, chemical (lead, mercury, cadmium, organic compounds, etc.) and aesthetic (taste) contaminants. The advantage of this system is that it does not require periodic cartridge brushing and back washing as do other systems such as the ceramic-based units listed above.

Pur makes a number of quality portable water purifiers, such as the *Explorer* and the *Voyager,* designed to remove microbial contaminants. *Pur* filters have a built-in self-cleaner that makes them easy to operate when using nonclear water. *Pur* filters are available from many local camping stores as well as *InfiNet Communications, Inc.* (telephone 406-585-9324).

Sweetwater Guardian and *MSR Waterworks* also make reliable portable water purifiers that are available from many local camping stores.

Ozark Water Service carries the *Bottoms-Up Mobile Water Purifier,* a portable water filter designed for everyday use. This inexpensive squeeze-bottle type unit (under $25) contains a small ceramic/carbon filter that can treat up to 200 gallons (750 liters) of water. Surprisingly, this small unit has been tested to remove bacteria; dissolved solids such as lead, mercury, aluminum, and asbestos; industrial volatile compounds—PCBs, THMs, etc.; as well as radon 222. Those concerned about viruses in their water might consider the *Travel Water Mate* (about $45) that contains iodinated resin and media to kill bacteria and viruses, as well as special filters to remove residual iodine and other foul tastes and chemicals from the water.

Captain Dave's Survival Center, <http://survival-center.com/>, offers a number of combination ceramic/activated charcoal micro-filter systems, as well as a *Pro Portable Water Filter* that uses ion-exchanged resins for purifying water sources that have a high sediment content.

For those who live near the ocean, *Safe-Trek Outfitters—Essentials Inc.,* <http://www.safetrek.com>, carries the *Pur Survivor-35* (about $1,475) that can make up to 1.2 gallons (4.5 liters) per hour of fresh water from sea water.

If you plan on procuring water from a local lake or stream, the collapsible *Dromedary Bags* offer a handy way to transport water over a distance. They come in two-, four-, six-, or ten-liter sizes. (The *Platypus,* another version of a collapsible water container, can be purchased from *Cascade Designs,*

<http://survival-center.com/>, e-mail <webmaster@survival-center.com>.) *Dromedary Bags* also have special threaded openings that attach directly to the bottom of many of the popular filters on the market. Be sure to test this feature on your specific filter. The three-in-one cap of the *Dromedary Bag* also lets you drink from, pour from, or fill the unit with ease. If you can't find this product locally, you can order it from *Moosejaw Mountaineering,* <http://www.moose-jawonline.com/catalog/accessories.html>, e-mail <moose@voyager.net> or <wigod@voyager.net>.

Y2K TIP

It is important to remember that cloudy or dirty water will clog a filter. Therefore, it is important to use only clear water, or to let murky water settle before filtering it. You can also strain cloudy water through a coffee filter (preferably the unbleached kind available at health food stores) or a fine-textured cloth to remove the large particles before you filter it. See the *Explore Magazine* archive page, <http://www.explore-mag.com/geararc/water.html>, for good information on portable water filtration and purification systems.

Water Storage. The proper storage of water is another major preparedness concern. Currently a number of vendors offer large 55-gallon (208 liters) plastic drums and barrels for water storage. If you do purchase large 55-gallon water drums you will need a *bung nut wrench* to remove the special lid, as well as a hand-operated *siphon pump* to get water from these super-heavy containers. Both the large containers, and the extra equipment needed to operate them, can be purchased from a variety of places, including *The American Freedom Network, A&B, Bruce Hopkins, Walton Feed, Captain Dave's Survival Shop,* and *Epicenter. USA Marketing Associates Inc.,* <http://www.y2ksupplies.com/>, has some of the best prices for 55-gallon (208 liters) containers ($34 to $38).

Emergency Essentials, <http://www.beprepared.com/home.html>, offers a less expensive (and more practical) alternative to the monstrously heavy— about 450 pounds (204 kilograms) when full—55-gallon (208 liters) containers that many preparedness experts recommend. Their *Basic 25 Gallon Boxed Water Kit* (about $30.00) comes with five Mylar bags and matching boxes that will hold up to 25 gallons (95 liters) of water each. This kit allows you to conveniently store up to 125 gallons (473 liters) of water and, unlike the 55-gallon drums, the kit can be stacked and moved about with ease. According to *Emergency Essentials* the super strong, opaque, metalized Mylar bags are "spore-free direct from the factory to inhibit the growth of most algae and bacteria" and should allow you to store water "straight from your faucet for a year or more" (<http://www.beprepared.com/product/h2oprod.html>; click on "25 gallon water storage kit").

Emergency Essentials also offers the ingenious *Deluxe Water/Sanitation Kit* (about $7.00) that allows you store five gallons (18.9 liters) of water in a metalized plastic bag that fits within a sturdy cardboard box, and when you have finished drinking the water, you can cut along the dotted lines and have a ready-made disposable toilet.

Wayne J Carroll & Associates, <http://www.y2kdehydratedfoods.com/>, carries a three-gallon (11.3 liters) collapsible plastic water container that has a spigot. Some people are buying containers such as these to fill with water to freeze and bury in their root cellar to keep vegetables from spoiling.

Y2K TIP

Do not store water in plastic milk bottles: they are made of a thin plastic that will decompose and develop leaks. Remember also that many types of plastic containers such as trash bags and the vinyl used in waterbeds are not approved for food contact. It is also important not to store water near contaminants such as gasoline, diesel fuel, paint, pesticides, etc.: Hydrocarbon vapors can penetrate plastic containers and contaminate the water. (You can contact water chemist Warren Clough at *Ozark Water Service* [telephone 800-835-8908] for other suggestions on how best to safely purify and store your drinking water.)

For mass water storage (for churches, synagogues, community centers, etc.) and for containers that hold hundreds or thousands of gallons of water, you can contact *Watertanks.com,* <http://www.watertanks.com>, e-mail <info@watertanks.com> or <sales@watertanks.com>, a company that specializes in large-scale barrels, drums, and tanks. One item, *"The Bag"* (48 x 40 x 24 inches [122 x 102 x 61 centimeters]), holds up to 200 gallons [757 liters] of water and is an inexpensive way (about $89) to store large amounts of water. It has a built-in spout, or you can attach a *Dispensing Pump* (about $22) that "dispenses 16 ounces (470 milliliters) per stroke."

Aquaflex makes the *Softank*, a "foldable, durable, flexible, and re-useable" water storage system that is made of a "tough food-grade co-extruded low density polyethylene that has outstanding tensile, tear, impact, and abrasion resistance," and has an "excellent water vapor barrier with strong chemical resistance" (<http://www.baproducts.com/softank.htm>). These water storage units come in a variety of sizes from 30 gallons [113.5 liters] (about $40) to 350 gallons [1325 liters] (about $140) and are available from *B & A Products*, <http://www.baproducts.com/catalog.htm>, and *Brian Golden* (telephone 303-440-4893).

Note: Many water storage containers that are promoted as "food grade" are made of polyethylene and other plasticizers that might leach toxins into your water supply. According to research, many polyvinyl chloride containers contain DEPH, a known toxin, which the EPA lists as a probable cause of liver cancer. It is important to check with the manufacturer to make sure that the plastic containers you buy do not contain polyvinyl chloride or other harmful chemicals.

Ideally, your emergency source of water should be stored in tightly sealed glass containers. However, glass is expensive, heavy, and fragile. The next-best way to store water is in hard plastic polycarbonate containers, not polyethelyene or other forms of "soft" plastic. Hard plastics such as polycarbonate help prevent plasticizers and other chlorine by-products used in plastic containers from leaching into the water. *(Ozark Water Service* [telephone 800-835-8908] carries a line of health-friendly polycarbonate storage bottles.)

The important point is that no matter what you add to water to make or keep it pure, and no matter how you store it, for maximum safety you should filter the water through an activated carbon medium or filtering device before you drink it. I realize this means a lot of extra effort, but the health benefits can be substantial. Remember, an ounce of prevention is worth a ton of cure.

Well Concerns. If you have the right geography, drilling a well might be a viable alternative for having a good supply of potable drinking water. The *Life Canada* well drilling Web site, <http://www.lifewater.ca/ndexman.htm>, offers a wealth of information on well-making and low-cost drilling methods. Of course, such well water needs to be tested for microbes, heavy metals, pesticides, and other toxic contaminants before it is consumed. (Ultra-violet light can be an effective way to ensure microbe-free drinking water. *Ozark Water Service* [telephone 800-835-8908] can help advise you on the best ways to obtain pure drinking water from your well.)

Those readers who already have a well should consider having it inspected during the fall of 1999 to ensure it has no harmful contaminants. You should also consider a manual or solar backup system if an electrical pump runs your well, in the event the power grid in your area takes a hit during Y2K. *Insight Discounts*, <http://www.insightdiscounts.com/y2k.htm>, supplies a *Solar Pump–Solar Water-Distribution System* that hooks up to your hose and allows you to use a sun-powered pump to draw water from a well, pond, or lake. The built-in solar-charged batteries can pump up to 390 gallons [1,544 liters] on a full charge. This maintenance-free item is pricey (about $690), but it could be a life-saving unit for your family, neighborhood, church group, or community. It also comes with a "Deep Well" option that pumps water from as deep as 230 feet (70 meters).

Showers. Those living in Florida, southern California, Hawaii, and other warm places, might want to invest in a portable shower that can be heated by the sun. The *Packshower*, which can be hung anywhere, is a 20-liter bag with a shower hose, which will deliver a gentle ten-minute shower. It is available from *Cascade Designs, Inc.*, <http://www.cascadedesigns.com/cascade.htm>. *Alternative Energy Engineering, The Survival Center,* and *Major Surplus* carry the *Solar Shower* (about $15), made of black polyethylene that attracts the radiant energy from the sun and generates warm water for a shower in the event your water heater does not work. Those concerned about dressing for Y2K success might consider purchasing a DC-powered 12-volt hair dryer that can be run from the cigarette lighter in a car (about $12 and available from *Alternative Energy Engineering*, <http://www.alt-energy.com>, e-mail <energy@alt-energy.com>).

Water is the most common and least inexpensive of all preparedness items. However, its simplicity can be deceiving. Obtaining good quality water takes effort, but because it is so essential, going this extra mile should be a vital part of our preparedness program.

Just as pure drinking water helps to ensure good health, so too does another related issue, namely personal hygiene—an important topic treated in the next chapter.

CHAPTER 10

Waste Disposal

• •│• • • • • • • •

"The Public Staff has observed that most of our water and sewer companies are not sufficiently familiar with the Year 2000 compliance problem to know whether or not they may have potential problems."
—James D. Little, Chairman, North Carolina Public Staff Water & Sewer Y2K Committee

Although this chapter is short and deals with an unpleasant topic, its topic is vitally important if we are to maintain maximum health and well-being during Y2K. Having an alternative human waste disposal system could come in handy during the Y2K transition, especially if the municipal water supply does not function properly. Those who are serious about their Y2K preparation plans need to take into consideration how they will deal with the problem of urine and fecal waste—including diaper disposal.

Simple Backup Toilets. A number of companies offer portable and backup toilets ranging from the utterly simple to the very elaborate. *B&A Products,* <http://www.baproducts.com/catalog.htm>, carries a fold-up unit (about $16.50) that comes with a "durable white plastic molded seat" and "heavy duty tubular steel legs" that uses plastic garbage bags held in place by a removable plastic ring. *Major Surplus,* <http://www.MajorSurplusNSurvival.com>, and *Epicenter,* <http://www.theepicenter.com>, offer the *Lugable Loo Portable Chemical Toilet* (about $30). This unit includes a toilet seat mounted above a rugged, lightweight plastic body with handles to make waste disposal and transportation easier. *Epicenter's* unit comes with a packet of *Bio-Blue Sol-U-Pak,* which breaks down toilet paper and human waste and lessens foul odors.

Deer Park Emergency Preparedness Center Total Survival.com, <http://www.totalsurvival.com/>, e-mail <sales@totalsurvival.com>, carries an extensive line of light-use portable toilets and related storage and cleaning products.

Those desiring a more serious conventional—fresh water-based—toilet alternative, should explore the *Thetford Portable Toilets* Web site, <http://www.thetford.com/index.pl>. *Thetford* makes a variety of human waste systems that have no-spill features, built-in deodorant storage, and low-water tank evacuation. *Thetford's* products are available at Wal-Mart and recreational vehicle (RV) dealerships, as well as at selected camping goods and hardware stores. You can also contact *Thetford Portable Toilets,* e-mail <info@thetford.com>, for information on where to find units in your area.

Major Surplus, <http://www.MajorSurplusNSurvival.com>, e-mail <info@MajorSurplusNSurvival.com>, carries the *Porta Potti 135* (about $109), which has a 2.6-gallon (9.8 liters) holding tank and a seat and cover designed for easy cleaning.

Important Waste Supplies. To better control and handle waste problems, you will need a number of items such as a large quantity of disposable trash bags. (The *Renew* brand is environmentally friendly, meaning that their trash bags are made of 100% recycled domestic and industrial recovered materials.) Plastic bags help making the transporting, storage, and disposal of garbage and waste a lot easier.

If you purchase a portable-type toilet, you need to stock up on biodegradable toilet waste-eaters and deodorants that control human waste odors. *Epicenter* offers the *Bio-Blue Sol-U-Pak* that helps break down the toilet paper and waste. *Major Surplus* carries *Biodegradable Toilet Tissue, Bio-Green Digester,* and *Bio Blue Toilet Deodorant* to break down human waste and keep water-based toilets from smelling foul. Many local pharmacies carry *Nilodor's Tap A Drop,* which the manufacturer advertises as a nontoxic (no formaldehyde or hexachlorame) odor neutralizer. As with most things in this book, you should test it beforehand to see if it works for you.

MicrobiaLogic, <http://www.microbialogic.com/>, e-mail <info@microbialogic.com>, goes one step further by offering "bacterial bioaugmentation products" that contain naturally occurring bacteria that deodorize and break down human waste. This is an effective, nontoxic way to "control odor and speed up the digestion of waste solids." These products come in easy-to-use packets of a dry, concentrated, self-dissolving material that you use by dumping it into your toilet unit, adding a little water, and letting nature take its course. The packets have a two-year shelf life, and most important, this product will not eat through garbage disposal bags. This means that these microbial agents can be used with many of the small portable toilets listed above. If you double- or triple-line your plastic unit you should, depending on how many people use it, get a week's worth of use out of one packet.

> **Y 2 K   T I P**
> It is important to note that all of the above toilets require some way to dispose of the waste that accumulates—whether by flushing it down the toilet, burying it in the ground, creating a "compost" heap, storing it in large 55-gallon (208 liters) drums to be dealt with later, etc.

Compost and Alternative Toilets. For those looking for both an environmentally friendly and efficient, long-term toilet alternative that does not need a septic tank or a way of disposing of the waste, a number of vendors carry the innovative "composting" toilets. *BioLet,* <http://www.biolet. com/products.htm>, e-mail <info@biolet.com>, *Lehman's Non-Electric, Real Goods, Jade Mountain Inc., Alternative Energy Engineering,* and *Sun-Mar,* <http://www.sun-mar.com/>, e-mail <compost@sun-mar.com>, and in Canada *Clivus Multrum,* <http://clivusmultrum.com/>, e-mail <forinfo@clivusmultrum.com>, offer an extensive line of "composting" no-waste toilets that require no septic tank, water, or chemicals or pollutants to safely and non-toxically dispose of human waste.

These international award-winning composting units use aerobic bacteria and carbon–nitrogen interaction to decompose and "recycle" human waste into a harmless, odorless, dry, soil-like, nutrient-rich material that can be used as fertilizer or placed on the ground. Unlike water-based toilet systems, there is almost no possibility of the bacteria contamination risks associated with conventional leach bed and septic systems. Composting toilets also save an enormous amount of water—which could be a precious commodity during the Y2K transition. Many composting toilets require a thermostatically controlled heater that a backup solar-powered panel and a DC battery system could accommodate. Both *Jade Mountain Inc.* and *Real Goods,* who carry these toilets and who also specialize in solar power, can help you in this regard.

Note: Composting toilets do not treat "gray" water—the refuse water from showers, washing machines, sinks, and bathtubs. This gray water needs a septic tank, a conventional municipal sewage system, or special gray water treatment units.

The Canadian government and the American *National Sanitation Foundation (NSF)*—an independent testing laboratory—have approved composting toilets. *NSF* certification means that these units meet the requirements of both sanitary engineers and building inspectors. Composting toilets start at about $1000, are odorless in operation, and produce great fertilizer. You can buy low- to medium-capacity single units or high-capacity "whole-house" systems that let you use multiple toilets at once. Composting toilets require about a cup of peat moss per person using the unit per day. Many composting toilets, such as the *BioLet Non-Electric,* available from *Insight Discounts,* <http://www.insightdiscounts.com/y2k.htm>, and *Y2K Prep,* <http://michaelhyatt.com/biolet/prod.htm>, e-mail <feedback@michaelhyatt. com>, do not require electricity to operate, making them perfect for either off-grid or grid-malfunction living. (For more information on composting toilets you should consult the "Urban Agriculture Notes" home page, <http://www.cityfarmer.org/comptoilet64.html>, published by *City Farmer*, Canada's Office of Urban Agriculture. This site shows how even big business and corporations can use composting waste disposal systems, and lists numerous companies around the world that specialize in composting toilets and urinals.)

Lehman's Non-Electric, <http://www.lehmans.com>, also carries the *Storburn Wilderness Comfort Station,* an alternative toilet that uses propane or natural gas to safely burn human waste into an odorless and non-toxic ash.

CHAPTER 11

General and Personal Concerns

• • • • • • • • • •

"The proof will be in the pudding,
and the pudding date will be the January 1 weekend."
—Bob Cohen, Analyst with the Information Technology Association of America

No book can cover every situation important to every reader. Therefore it is vital that you and your Preparedness Group anticipate needs that have not been addressed. In this chapter, I will cover a variety of general topics to help better ensure overall Y2K preparedness.

Radio and Communication Issues. Knowing what is happening in your city, in your nation, and in other countries around the world during the Y2K challenge will be extremely important. A portable battery- or solar-powered AM/FM/Shortwave radio will be a vital item to have on hand. (Shortwave is particularly important if the local and regional television and radio broadcasting systems are not functioning. Shortwave radio is also highly educational for the children in your Preparedness Group as you hear music, news, and commentary from around the world.) You should also make sure you have one or more headsets so that you will not disturb others if you listen to the radio at night. *Bruce Hopkins,* <http://web2.airmail.net/foodstr2>; *The American Freedom Network,* <http://www.amerifree.com/>, e-mail <comments@amerifree.com>; *Insight Discounts,* <http://www.insightdiscounts. com/y2k.htm>; and *Epicenter,* <http://www.theepicenter.com>, e-mail <bjnelson@ TheEpicenter.com>, as well as a number of other vendors, offer the *Baygen Freeplay Radio,* an AM/FM/Shortwave unit (under $100) that operates by a self-powered dynamo, meaning that it can run without batteries, electricity, or solar power. You simply wind it up—60 cranks—and it will play for 30 minutes. An item such as this can be a major asset during a time when batteries might be scarce.

The *American Freedom Network,* <http://www.amerifree.com/>, e-mail <comments@amerifree.com>, and *Bruce Hopkins,* <http://web2. airmail.net/foodstr2>, offer solar-powered radios. These units are also ecologically friendly, given that you do not have to dispose of toxic battery waste (or use electricity to charge them). *Captain Dave's Survival*

Shop, <http://survival-center.com/>, e-mail <webmaster@survival-center.com>, carries a combination solar-powered–hand-cranked AM/FM radio, as well as an inexpensive shortwave radio that runs on two AA batteries. *Epicenter,* <http://www.theepicenter.com>, e-mail <bjnelson@TheEpicenter.com>, stocks an *AM/FM Survival Radio* that uses solar power to charge its NiCad batteries.

Insight Discounts, <http://www.insightdiscounts.com/y2k.htm>, also offers the inexpensive *Multiband World Solar and Generator Power Radio* (about $59.95). This radio can also be run by four AA NiCad Rechargeable Batteries or a built-in self-cranked *Dynamo Power Generator* that will generate up to one hour of playing time from "five minutes of turning." This is a great backup system to have for any extended emergency.

The Preparedness Centers, <http://www.healthyharvest.com>, e-mail <n.russell@worldnet.att.net>, carry the *Solar Dynamo Radio with Flashlight* (about $35), an AM/FM unit that works from four different power sources: solar, dynamo wind-up crank, batteries, and AC power.

CB Radios. Michael Hyatt has an informative article on how to use and set up a CB radio communication system (<http://www.y2kprep.com/askmichael/007.htm>). Using these inexpensive units could be a good way to communicate with nearby friends and neighbors if the telephone and cellular phone systems malfunction.

Solar Battery Chargers. There is a good chance many of us will need to rely on a lot of battery power during the Y2K transition. You can save money and protect the environment by investing in a solar-powered battery charger. *Major Surplus,* <http://www.MajorSurplusNSurvival.com>, e-mail <info@MajorSurplusNSurvival.com>, offers the *Deluxe Solar Battery Charger* with a built-in meter (about $18). This handy unit uses sunlight to charge eleven different types of batteries and has a meter to tell you how much power your batteries contain. *B&A Products,* <http://www.baproducts.com/catalog.htm>, e-mail <byron@baproducts.com>, carries a *Combination Solar Panel/Charger* (about $22) that can both charge AA batteries and power radios and small DC devices.

Household Concerns. In case the power fails if you are away during Y2K you might consider purchasing a battery-operated answering machine. *Alternative Energy Engineering,* <http://www.alt-energy.com>, e-mail <energy@alt-energy.com>, carries a *12 Volt Telephone Answering Machine* (about $78) that runs on solar power or batteries and is completely digital, with no moving parts to wear out.

If you expect power failures in your area, you might want to stock up on clothes and related items that do not need a lot of washing or drying. The *Packtowel* (available from *Cascade Designs,* <http://www. cascadedesigns.com/cascade.htm>) is a good example of such a product. Made of 100% viscose, these towels are highly absorbent and are fast drying (by hand-wringing). They also become softer and more "flannel-like" with each use. *Real Goods,* <http://www.realgoods.com>, e-mail <techs@ realgoods.com>, carries a wind-powered *Solar Rotary Clothes Dryer* for drying clothes outdoors if the power fails.

For wrinkle-free, easy-to-clean apparel that you can let hang out in the rain to wash and put in the sun to dry, you should order *Travel Smith's Outfitting Guide and Catalog. Travel Smith* specializes in classy, durable, easy-care clothing.

Business and Money Considerations. As with any impending economic emergency, it is important to prepare your financial affairs. Talk to your financial planner about safe havens during the impending national and global recession that many predict Y2K to foment.

If you own a small- to medium-sized business, look into contingency plans (such as stockpiling essential items) in case your vendors cannot supply the goods you need to run your business. (Make sure your computer[s], software and databases are Y2K "compliant." In the Appendix I have included books and Web sites that cover these concerns.)

I also suggest you begin "socking away" small change and paper money in small denominations. Some are predicting a "run" on banks as people panic when Y2K closes in. We do not have enough cash reserves in either the local or national vaults to cover such a demand. You might also want to obtain some gold and silver coins—(pre-1965 silver U.S. dimes, quarters, and half dollars are over 90 percent pure silver, unlike the later "clad" coins that use a mixture of cheaper metals)—which some Y2K experts predict will be one of the more viable currencies should there be a major economic "downturn," or if Y2K brings hyperinflation in its wake. For more information on silver and gold coins, contact your local coin dealer or national coin distributors such as *Brooks Grace International Rarity Group* (telephone 800-947-2646) or *F. J. Vollmer & Co.* (telephone 888-309-8189).

Many people are also recommending putting 20 percent to 25 percent of your "liquid" assets into precious metals such as gold bullion, rare precious coins, and platinum. *Swiss America,* <http://www.buycoin.com>, e-mail <coindude@buycoin.com>, is a leader in the rare and precious coins market and can offer investing advice for those looking for a hedge against a potential downturn in the conventional stock market.

A Special Note For Apartment Dwellers and Those Who Might Lose Power in Their Home. Those who live in high-rise apartments have special concerns. Because of rental and condo agreements, it is likely that you will not be able to make structural changes to your dwelling. If you purchase a generator, make sure you can place it outdoors, for example on a balcony. (However, be aware that generators cause noise pollution, and that there may be regulations against their use.) Storage of fuel will present another problem, namely that of safety, legality, and space. Therefore, I suggest you acquire plenty of "arctic" quality thermal underwear and an excellent cold weather sleeping bag for each member of your group.

The *Ecofuel* and *Nuwick* candles and other emergency sources of heat and light listed in Chapters Seven and Eight would be good items to have on hand to keep one of the smaller rooms in your apartment warm. It is also important to remember that the walls of poorly insulated buildings will draw heat from your body even if the room feels warm. (This is why you never really feel warm in a drafty house.) It is therefore important that you place a barrier between yourself and the cold wall or drafty cracks in the room(s) where you will be spending the bulk of your time. Hanging thick curtains or tacking a layer of space blankets and woolen blankets to the walls will help retain heat in both your body and in the room.

If your area is vulnerable to power loss, it would be wise to purchase high density plastic sheets to cover the windows in the room(s) where you will do most of your living and sleeping, to cut down on drafts and hold heat in if the power fails. You might also consider using woolen blankets to pitch a small cold-weather tent in the best-insulated room where you live. Remember to use caution if you use candles or open flames in, or near, blankets and tents, and to make sure your living and sleeping space is sufficiently ventilated so that your heating systems do not generate deadly carbon monoxide.

Keeping a flashlight nearby, preferably around your neck, at night will be important given the increased chance of fire as people cook and heat their homes with unfamiliar and "alternative" fuels.

Water is a special concern for those who live in high-rise apartments. If the electricity goes out, the pumps that supply water will not work. Thus, having a backup supply of water will become important.

If You Live in a Hot Climate. Those people with respiratory and heart problems who live or plan to be in an area that requires air conditioning, might want to contact *Real Goods,* <http://www.realgoods.com>, e-mail <techs@realgoods.com>, or *Jade Mountain Inc.,* <http://www.jademountain. com/>, e-mail <info@jademountain.com>, for suggestions on nonelectric-based forms of cooling systems. You also might consider purchasing a *Solar Cool Cap* from *Alternative Energy Engineering,* <http://www.alt-energy. com>, e-mail <energy@alt-energy.com>. These hats have a solar panel on top to power a small fan that keeps your head cool.

Special Kits. Emergency "bug out," or quick-flight "reach and go" packs, are popular with a number of hard-core emergency preparedness people. These packs contain most of what you need to survive in a variety of climate and weather conditions—food, water packets, important paperwork, a first-aid kit, a flashlight, a thermal blanket, hand-warmers, etc. Having a "bug-out" kit packed and ready to go might be a good idea during the Y2K transition, especially if you have to leave on a moment's notice—for example if approaching civil unrest or a massive fire is sweeping your way. "Bug-Out" kits can be purchased from a variety of places, including *Captain Dave's Survival Center,* <http://survival-center.com/>, e-mail <webmaster@survival-center.com>. (You should also include a copy of all your important documents in your kit, as well as a *Multi-Purpose Camp Tool* that functions as a hatchet, a saw, a shovel, a hammer, and a bottle opener, and a *Magnesium Fire Starter Tool* that has a built-in flint to ignite a fire from the thin magnesium shavings. The latter could come in handy if you run out of matches or encounter wet conditions. Both are available from *Epicenter,* <http://www.theepicenter.com>, e-mail <bjnelson@TheEpicenter.com>.

Some Final Considerations. Those who think that Y2K will cause cataclysmic damage to the public infrastructure, and who want to "get out of Dodge" in case of large-scale violence and civil unrest, might consider purchasing or renting a place away from the city. Such a place would ideally be very well insulated, have sufficient space to store food, have a well or a flowing stream of water nearby, have a woodstove and plenty of wood, have fertile soil to plant food, and have a road with limited access. For those remaining in urban and suburban areas, it will be wise to forge strong, protective bonds with your neighbors and to generate (and practice) a community Preparedness Plan.

Conclusion

• •|• • • • • • • •

"God is our refuge and our strength, a tested help in times of trouble.
And so we need not fear even if the world blows up,
and the mountains crumble into the sea." —Psalm 46:1–2 (Living Bible)

The coming Y2K challenge is unique among potential disasters. Unlike the case of earthquakes and tornadoes, we know the exact moment when it will arrive. Although no one knows how big or small the consequences and disruptions will be, given the way the entire infrastructure of modern civilization, including manufacturing, shipping and transportation, public utilities, telecommunications, and the business and financial markets dependent upon computers in general and mainframes and "embedded systems" in particular, common sense indicates that some preparation is in order.

A recent USA TODAY/Gallup Poll for the National Science Foundation, <http://www.usatoday.com/news/ndstue07.htm>, conducted in March of 1999, revealed that the more people learn about Y2K the less worried they become and the more likely they are to take action to "protect themselves." In response to the polling data, the U.S. government Y2K czar John Koskinen found the results reassuring, but stressed "there's some real concern" and that "we need to focus on what's happening in 'my neighborhood.'"

In light of this advice, it is vital that individuals, families, and communities begin as soon as possible to prepare for major challenges that might affect our lives in the months ahead. This book has sought to assist this endeavor by offering a positive, proactive approach to Y2K preparation by helping you apply principles that will be beneficial for your health and well-being. My intent is to help you not only survive but to thrive during the uncertain times ahead.

My hope is that you will, like Bill in the opening story of this book, develop your unique and personally tailored Preparedness Plan, procure the necessary items you will need, and practice the preparedness skills necessary to make the best of Y2K. I also hope you will see the importance of organizing and working with others around you to make the coming transition and potential turmoil as smooth and as stress-free as possible.

I have also stressed some of the benefits Y2K might offer, such as renewing family bonds, discovering the beauty of simplicity, and rediscovering some of the important values that we often overlook in our overly busy lives.

Ironically, just as many of the comforts computers have brought to our lives have spoiled us, their loss during Y2K can also help us mature. It is important to keep this thought in mind as we begin to lose the technological conveniences upon which we have come to depend so much.

Although this manual has primarily stressed "physical," "emotional," and "relational" preparedness, I urge you not to forget another important component of a truly "holistic" approach to Y2K preparation: It is also important to look at Y2K as a time that will enable us to reevaluate our lives and reflect on what is long lasting and essential to our existence. Y2K will also be a time that will make us dependent upon others—including God. My final hope is that we can experience the impact of a loving Creator who can be with us during our time of need, and upon Whom we can call for strength and support. Do not discount this possibility. There is a strong probability that Y2K will generate widespread fear and panic. We can avoid the immense harm that panic and desperate self-interest engender if we have a deeper perspective and context within which to ground our lives. Faith has served people, great and small, throughout human history. The trying times ahead might help us realize how fragile our self-sufficiency truly is and what a gift to humanity faith and trust in Someone greater than ourselves can be.

A Y2K Essential "To-Do" List

Many readers might feel overwhelmed and even paralyzed by the enormous number of items to purchase, strategies to conduct, and action steps to undertake for Y2K preparation. Others may be reading this book when there is little time left to prepare. In light of this, I offer the following short list that narrows the essential things that should be done to help ensure adequate preparation for Y2K.

However, this short list is not meant to be a substitute for carefully reading this whole manual and discussing what might be best for your Y2K Preparedness Group. This list covers the "essentials," not the optimal items for Y2K preparedness.

1. Focus on essential food items. Purchase at least a three-month supply of grains, beans, cereals, soymilk, canned goods, etc.
2. Have a backup method to prepare your food items in the event you lose electrical power.
3. Have backup lighting sources: candles, flashlights, extra batteries.
4. Focus on ways to keep warm: backup heating, sleeping bags, extra thermal gloves, underwear, etc.
5. Have a good backup supply of pure water.
6. Have an alternative human waste and garbage disposal system.
7. Make hard copies (and a duplicate packet stored in another place) of all essential paperwork such as wills, passports, birth certificates, bank accounts, mortgage payments, trusts, school records, pension plans, government benefits, etc.
8. Have at least a three-month supply of all special-need items, i.e., medicines, diapers, baby formulas, personal hygiene supplies, etc.
9. Create a neighborhood Y2K Vigilance Group to help protect and watch out for one another.
10. Stock up on as many of the items as you can from the list in Appendix B.

An Important Y2K Checklist

• • | • • • • • • • •

"Happiness belongs to the self-sufficient." —Aristotle

The following is a "minimal" list intended to stimulate your thinking. Other items need to be added according to your specific situation and the special needs of those in your Preparedness Group such as young children, the elderly, the handicapped, the infirm, etc. Remember to check off items as you get them and to mark the quantity you purchase so that you will be able to estimate more accurately how long your Y2K supplies will last.

Food Items	Shelter/Warmth Items	Water Items
grains	extra woolen blankets	water storage containers
legumes	hand warmers	water container spouts
dried green foods	sleeping bag(s)	water filtration system
alternative protein	matches	extra filters for the system
core-food package	long underwear	water purifying solution
Essential Fatty Acids	lighters	hose
cooking oil	propane	charcoal filter
baby food	boots	siphon pump
yeast for making bread	raincoats	
seeds (sprouting and garden)	hats/gloves	
spices	matches	
salt/pepper (if you use them)		
alternative cooking stove (solar/propane)		
sweeteners		
can opener		
canned goods		

Lighting Needs

candles

matches

various screwdrivers

assorted flashlights

assorted batteries

solar battery charger

extra light bulbs

full-spectrum lights
(e.g., *Chromalux*)

Medicine and Health Needs

extra eye glasses

herbal first-aid kit

conventional first-aid kit

first-aid manual(s)

moisturizer

supplements

ice pack(s)

extra medications

hot water bottle

smoke detectors

CO_2 detector

special health-related items
(bedpans, catheter tubes, etc.)

Well-Being Needs

good books

writing paper

pens/pencils

games

soothing music

aromatherapy oils

crayons for children

books for children

sunglasses

Hygiene Needs

backup (alternative) toilet

biodegradable toilet paper

toilet waste eaters

toilet disinfectant/cleaner

(eco-friendly) garbage bags

biodegradable paper towels

combs/hair brushes

toothbrushes

toothpaste/dental floss

feminine hygiene products

mouth wash

antiseptic wash
(to cleanse toothbrush
when water is low)

antibacterial dry hand soap
(to conserve water)

diapers

baby wipes

nail clippers

Kleenex

Tools

Grain, seed, spice grinder(s)

hoe

seed sprouter

shovel

rake

jeweler's screwdriver kit

storage containers
(a variety of cans, jars, etc.)

paper plates, cups,
plastic utensils,
scouring sponges, etc.

clothesline rope
(to dry hand-washed
items in the sun)

needles/thread

hammer, nails, pliers,
screwdrivers, crow bar, etc.

Miscellaneous

AM/FM/Shortwave radio

batteries

lots of small change

lots of cash (1's, 5's, 10's)
[#1 and #2 coins in
Canada]

silver and gold coins

Important Reminders

Get your quality core-food supply first

Do it NOW

Have a dental check-up

Get a complete physical

Get your car inspected and tuned up

Photocopy (or print out) important documents

APPENDIX C
Long-Term Storage Tips

In general, many preparedness experts recommend the following principles and procedures to ensure the maximum shelf life and nutritional value of your stored food items.

Guidelines for Storing Foods Safely:

- Remember that the quality of the food you store is only as good as the quality of the food you buy. As one vendor says, "If you don't like it, don't store it." If you want to survive well, buy the best tasting and most nutritionally and healthy food you can afford. Five factors determine the quality of food: How it was grown, processed, preserved, shipped, and stored. Ask about these factors before you make a purchase.

- If you plan on packing and sealing your food items for long-term storage (more than six months), be sure to vacuum seal your products and/or to use nitrogen and other oxygen-absorbing gases and products. This will help keep the products from spoiling and will stop insect larvae from hatching and destroying your grains and legumes.

- Remember that seeds (for sprouting and growing) need to breathe and that they should be moved periodically from one container to another so that they will be oxygenated. (See the section on Seeds and Sprouting in the next chapter.)

- Be sure to clearly label and date all cans, boxes, and other stored items, and make sure labels can be easily read. This will save time identifying both the content and storage date of each item, making utilization and rotation a lot easier. Keep your labels away from moisture so that they will not peel off and get lost.

- Remember that "rotation" is the key to successful food storage. The first food in should be the first food out. Violate this principle and you risk your food turning into tasteless and nutritionally worthless "slop." Store the items you will use the most, closest to the front. Make sure there is easy access to the items stored so that you can rotate them easily. The harder things are to get to, the less likely you are to either use them or rotate them properly. Place professionally packed, extremely long-term shelf-stable food items that do not have to be rotated, at the back of your storage space. Near the front, place things such as cereal, canned soups and beans, soymilk, etc., that need periodic rotation.

- Assign someone to be the food "rotator" to make sure this job gets done.
- For those who expect to store a lot of canned food items, it is important to know the production date of the food, given that most canned food items have a shelf live of 12 months or less. Often this date is written in code and is therefore difficult to determine. *Glitchproof.com,* <http://www.glitchproof.com/glitchproof/ storlifofgro.html>, has a Web page entitled "Food Shelf Life Recommendations" that includes a helpful chart listing the packaging date codes and shelf life of many popular foods.
- To save space, use banana boxes from your local health food store or grocer to store things. Banana boxes stack evenly and allow you to pack a lot of items in a small amount of space. Be sure to clearly date and label each box.
- Be careful to handle and stack your stored items carefully. You do not want to drop, crack, or break items, since oxygen is one of the main enemies of long-term storage.
- Avoid temperature extremes. Overall, 55°F (13°C) offers the best temperature to ensure lasting quality (viability, taste, and nutritional value) of your stored food items. Every 18 degrees F (10 degrees C) above this temperature cuts the shelf life of a food product in half. This means you should not store food items in hot attics, barns, garages, trailers, or the trunks of cars and trucks, or in non-temperature-controlled warehouses and self-storage sheds.
- Oxygen is an enemy of food. It oxidizes and spoils food, especially oils. This is why long-term food storage providers like to keep food in cans or buckets that have less than two percent oxygen content. There are three main ways to achieve this goal—vacuum sealing, flushing with inert gas such as nitrogen or carbon dioxide, and using oxygen-absorbing packs.
- Avoid moist places. Damp floors, garages, sheds, and porches are also not good places to store your grains, legumes, and dehydrated foods. Don't store your long-term goods on concrete floors. Condensation and osmosis are powerful forces, and moisture can eventually seep through any container. Depending on where you live, you might also install a dehumidifier to keep humidity in your storage unit under control.
- Avoid light. Transparent containers transfer light energy to food,

speeding up its deterioration. Keep food in opaque containers or in dark places.

- Beware of insects, rodents, and other animals and pests that can bore through, penetrate, and feast on your food supplies. Using tightly sealed containers, diatomaceous earth, or crushed bay leaves can be very helpful in repelling pests. You might also try the pest repellers that emit ultrasonic sound wave frequencies, to keep bugs, rodents, snakes, and other pests away from food storage areas. For example, *Harmony Seventh Generation* (tel. 800-869-3446, fax 800-456-1139), a company that specializes in environmentally and health-friendly products, carries an extensive line of nontoxic and cruelty-free *pest repellers. Heartland America,* <http://www.heartlandamerica.com/dprod325.html>, carries the *2-In-1 Pest Repeller* that gives off both sound and magnetic pulsations designed to rid a 900-square-foot (84 square meters) area from a variety of pests and to keep food-spoiling intruders from destroying your food items. A number of other companies offer sophisticated insect and rodent pest repellers, such as *A1 Solutions, L.L.C.,* <http://www.a1solutions.com/order.htm>. *Real Goods,* <http://www.realgoods.com>, offers a battery-operated *Insect, Mice, Bat, Spider and Other Pests Repeller* in case you have a power failure. Spreading hot cayenne pepper powder around your containers can also help keep away sniffing animals and insects. However, you must be careful of using cayenne around children and pets. Though not deadly, it will give a painful burn that lasts a short while.
- Keep a flashlight handy at the entrance of the storage place in case the electricity fails during one of the anticipated Y2K brown- or blackouts.
- Keep a multi-purpose fire extinguisher and fire alarm near your food supply . . . just in case!
- Consult food storage resources such as those listed above or Douglas E. Renz's cogent short essay on the "Basics of Food Shelf Lives," <http://www.y2kdehydratedfoods.com/shelflif.htm>. The *Y2KFoods* Web site, <http://y2kfoods.com>, offers valuable information on a popular type of oxygen absorber used by many in the long-term food storage industry: "*FreshPax*™ is a patented oxygen absorber pioneered by *Multisorb Technologies* to protect packaged foods and other products. *FreshPax* protects against spoilage, mold growth, color change, rancidity, loss of nutritive values, insect damage, and losses of quality. Produced in packet form using food grade ingredients, *FreshPax* irreversibly absorbs oxygen inside sealed packaging to less than 0.01% and maintains this level indefinitely" <http://y2kfoods.com/s39p679.htm>. If you plan on using oxygen

absorbers when you pack your "super pails," see this Web page for more information on the comparative advantages of various oxygen absorbers. *Lumen Foods* also has a Web site, <http://soybean.com/zpttoc.htm>, offering detailed information on how to use oxygen absorbers for long-term food storage. *Walton Feed* has a Web page that focuses on how to use dry ice to remove oxygen from your food containers (<http://waltonfeed.com/grain/faqs/ivb1.html>).

- Those readers living near an agricultural area might consider purchasing grains and legumes directly from the field. However, this can be a risky bulk-food source. Examine the grain closely for mold, and get a signed statement from the farmer or grain dealer stating that the grain is safe for human consumption, i.e., that it has no mold, fungus, or harmful chemicals, such as pesticides, that are unfit for human consumption. Store-bought grain has already been tested for these two potential health-compromising problems. Molds produce toxic substances known as mycotoxins that are not destroyed by cooking and that can be deadly. Even if the grain is certified organic it can still have harmful molds in it. The best way to prevent mold is to keep your grains and other perishable food items dry. Mold cannot grow in any food item that has less than ten percent moisture content. (See Alan Hagan's article for a simple way to test moisture content (<http://www.efn.org/~kathyy/foodfaq.300>.)

Sources of Bulk Food Storage Equipment

Many of the food companies listed in this book, such as *Walton Feed, Bruce Hopkins,* and *Captain Dave's Survival Shop,* offer "super pails"—the approximately six-gallon (23 liters) metal buckets can be lined with mylar bags and be vacuum sealed and packed with nitrogen and/or oxygen absorbers to retard spoilage. "Super pails" are a popular way to keep your grains and vegetables fresh and nutritious during long-term storage by protecting them from insects, light, moisture, and oxygen.

Some long-term storage advocates claim that adding nitrogen and taking out all the oxygen from containers holding "live" grains and legumes contributes to the breakdown of vital nutrients and effectively destroys the seed so that it cannot be used for sprouting or growing later. Though there is debate about this issue, it will only be a concern if you plan on true "long"-term storage, for example, five to 15 years. If you plan to use up your supply of "super pail" grains, legumes, and seeds within a year or two, or rotate them on a regular basis, this potential problem should not affect you.

Many companies such as *The Survival Center,* <http://www.zyz.com/survivalcenter/)>, e-mail <sales@survivalcenter.com>, carry the reusable

Gamma Seal Lid—a snap-on adapter—that "transforms" your "super pails" and grain buckets into reusable and "airtight and leak-proof heavy-duty storage containers." This handy item allows you continued easy access to your storage pails and should be placed on the buckets you will use on a daily basis. The *Gamma Seal Lid* (about $8.00) fits most 3.5- to 7-gallon (13.25 to 26.5 liters) buckets and pails.

Your local health food store will also be able to supply you with various bulk food products that you can store yourself, although it will be more expensive to go this route. You can also purchase "bagged" bulk foods available from many of the suppliers listed above. Many of these bags weigh between 25 and 50 pounds (11.3 to 22.7 kilograms). However, these bagged goods need to be stored and sealed properly in containers such as "super pails" to prevent spoilage and nutritional loss.

Regardless of how you buy your bulk grains, they must be stored properly to prevent insect larvae from growing and destroying your grain. Many people mix diatomaceous earth with their bulk grains and beans to kill larvae as they hatch. Diatomaceous earth is comprised of microscopic fossil shells, which quickly kill invading insects by cutting up their stomachs when they come in contact with it. The recommended dose is one cup per six-gallon (22 liters) bucket of your grains. Most diatomaceous earth (which can be ordered from *Countryside Granary*, <http://www.countrysidegranary.8m.com>, e-mail <csgranary@aol.com>—about $35 per 50-pound (22.7 kilograms) bag—is generally considered safe for human consumption. However, be sure to confirm that the type you are purchasing is food-grade quality. Be cautious also not to inhale it. As with any fine powder, including herbs, it is always wise to wear a fine particle-filtering mask and either mix the substance outdoors, or have air purifiers operating in the indoor space where you work.

If the thought of mixing diatomaceous earth with your food supply does not appeal to you, many people have found adding two or three ground-up bay leaves to stored grains keeps bugs from hatching.

Y2K-Related Companies

The following list represents the major vendors mentioned in this text. Many of the vendors in this Appendix B offer both online as well as traditional paper mail order catalogs. Many of these catalogs (such as those by *Jade Mountain*, *Lehman's Non-Electric*, and *Real Goods*) are highly educational and are filled with helpful advice and suggestions. Be sure to ask for a catalog when you make contact with a company.

- *A1 Solutions, L.L.C.* tel. 509-738-6574, 888-327-6868, P.O. Box 1017, Kettle Falls, WA 99141, Web site <http://www.a1solutions.com/order.htm>, e-mail <info@a1solutions.com>

- *Abraham Solar Equipment.* tel. 970-731-4675, 124 Creekside Place, Pagosa Springs, CO 81147

- *Action Gear.* Web site <http://www.actionshop.com/_vti_bin/shtml.exe/manuf.htm/map>

- *Adventure Gear.* tel. 888-241-1864, 770-577-7722, fax 770-577-7744, 6861 Fairways Drive, Douglasville, GA 30134, Web site <http://www.ewalker.com/adgear/adgear.htm>, e-mail <adventure@ewalker.com>

- *Alco-Brite.* tel. 800-473-0717, 435-874-1025, fax 435-874-1026, P.O. Box 840926, 685 N. Hildale Rd., Hildale, UT 84784, Web site <http://www.alco-brite.com/>, e-mail <alcoinfo@alco-brite.com>

- *AlpineAire.* tel. 800-322-6325, 530-272-1971, fax 530-272-2624, P.O. Box 926, Nevada City, CA 95959, Web site <http://www.Alpineairefoods.com/>

- *Alternative Energy Engineering.* tel. 800-777-6609 or 707-923-3982, fax 800-777-6648, P.O. Box 339, Redway, CA 95560, Web site <http://www.alt-energy.com>, e-mail <energy@alt-energy.com>

- *Amazon.com.* Web site <http://www.amazon.com>

- *American Academy of Husband-Coached Childbirth®.* tel. 800-4-A-BIRTH (422-4784), Box 5224, Sherman Oaks, CA 91413-5224,

Web site <http://www.bradleybirth.com/>, e-mail
<marjiehathaway@bradleybirth.com>

- *American Botanical Pharmacy.* tel. 310-453-1987, P.O. Box 3027, Santa Monica, CA 90408

- *The American Freedom Network.* tel. 800-205-6245, P.O. Box 1750, Johnstown, CO 80534, Web site <http://www.amerifree.com/>, e-mail <comments@amerifree.com>

- *Annie's Homegrown Inc.* tel. 415-331-4363, P.O. Box 128, Hampton, CT 06247, Web site <http://www.annies.com>, e-mail <bernie@annies.com>

- *Arizona Brand Nutritionals, Inc.* tel. 602-968-5935, 115 South River Drive, Tempe, AZ 85281-3010

- *The Ark Institute.* tel. 800-255-1912 or 513-726-5935, P.O. Box 142, Oxford, OH 45056, <http://www.arkinstitute.com/>, e-mail <arkinst@concentric.net>

- *ASONTV.COM* Tel. 800-368-3763, Web site <http://www.asontv.com/>

- *B&A Products.* tel. 918-696-5998, fax 918-696-5999, Rte 1, Box 100, Bunch, OK 74931-9705, Web site <http://www.baproducts.com/catalog.htm>, e-mail <byron@baproducts.com>

- *Back to Basics.* tel. 800-688-1989 or 801-571-7349, fax 801-571-6061, 11660 South State Street, Draper, UT 84020, Web site <http://www.backtobasicsproducts.com/>

- *Back To Eden.* tel. 970-527-3375, fax 970-527-6221, c/o TLC Greenhouse, Inc., 3976 M-50 Lane, Paonia, CO 81428, Web site <http://www.farmboys.com/seeds/>, e-mail <seeds@tlchub.com>

- *Backwoods Home Magazine.* tel. 800-835-2415 or 541-247-8900, P.O. Box 712, Gold Beach, OR 97444, Web site <http://backwoodshome.com/>, e-mail <editor@backwoodshome.com>

- *Backwoods Solar Electric Systems.* tel. 208-263-4290, fax 208-265-4788, 1395 Rolling Thunder Ridge, Sandpoint, ID 83864, Web site <http://backwoodssolar.com/>, e-mail <info@backwoodssolar.com>

- *Big-Web Marketing, Inc.* tel. 954-747-3830, 4960 NW 72 Terrace, Lauderhill, FL 33319, Web site <http://www.coolandunusual.com/y2k/y2kstore/y5twok/orderfrm.html>

- *BioLet.* tel. 800-5Biolet (524-6538), fax 617-578-0465, 45 Newbury Street, Boston, MA 02116, <http://www.biolet.com/products.htm>, e-mail <info@biolet.com>

- *Bio-Tech USA.* tel. 800-228-4MLO (228-4656) or 707-399-2500, 2351 N. Watney Way, Suite C, Fairfield, CA 94533, Web site <www.mlo-products.com>. In Canada, distributor information can be obtained from Dave Mehat at *Nutrition Zone,* tel. 800-667-6645 for the West Coast, or from *Maxion Nutrition,* Canadian toll-free 888-302-9996, or 416-524-5870, for East Coast dealers.

- *Bragg Live Foods.* tel. 800-446-1990, Box 7, Santa Barbara, CA 93102, Web site <http://www.bragg.com/>, e-mail <info@bragg.com>

- *Brain Garden.* tel. 800-481-9987, fax 602-874-0494, 741 N SR 198, Salem, UT 84653.

- *Brian Golden.* tel. 303-440-4893, P.O. Box 4331, Boulder, CO 80306

- *The Brick Oven Page,* Web site <http://mha-net.org/msb/html/bakeov.htm>, or Alan Scott, tel. 415-663-9010, *Ovencrafters,* 5600 Marshall-Petaluma Road, Petaluma, CA 94952, Web site <http://www.nbn.com/~ovncraft/>, e-mail <ovencrft@nbn.com>

- *Brooks Grace International Rarity Group.* tel. 800-947-2646

- *Bruce Hopkins.* tel. 972-226-9945, fax 972-226-9927, 2611 N. Beltline Road, Suite 127, Sunnyvale (Dallas), TX 75182, Web site <http://web2.airmail.net/foodstr2>

- *Buckskin Mountain Trading,* LLC. tel. 800-873-5522, Web site <http://www.buckskintrading.com/>, e-mail <buckskin2@aol.com>

- *Campmor.* tel. 800-230-2151 or 201-825-8300, 29 Parkway, Upper Saddle, NJ 07458, Web site <http://www.campmor.com/>, e-mail <webmaster@campmor.com>

- *Captain Dave's Survival Center.* tel. 412-886-0667, P.O. Box 14743, Pittsburgh, PA 15234, Web site <http://survival-center.com/>, e-mail <webmaster@survival-center.com>

- *Cascade Designs.* tel. 800-531-9531, fax 206-505-9525, 4000 First Ave., South Seattle, WA 98134, Web site <http://www.cascadedesigns.com/cascade.htm>

- *Christian Family Resources.* tel. 719-962-3228, fax 719-962-3232, P.O. Box 405, Kit Carson, CO 80825

- *Dr. Christopher Enterprises.* Web site <http://www.drchristopher.com/>

- *Chuck Roast.* tel. 603-447-5492, fax 603-447-2277, P.O. Box 2080, Conway, NH 03818, Web site <http://www.chuckroast.com/>, e-mail <custserv@chuckroast.com>

- *Clivus Multrum.* tel. 800-425-4887 or 978-725-5591, P.O. Box 3212, Winnipeg, Manitoba R3C 4E7, Canada, Web site <http://clivusmultrum.com/>, e-mail <forinfo@clivusmultrum.com>

- *Coleman.* tel. 800-835-3278, Web site <http://www.colemanoutdoor.com/>

- *Countryside Granary.* tel. 888-236-8780, fax 712-938-2355, P.O. Box 23, Rock Valley, IA 51247, Web site <http://www.countrysidegranary.8m.com>, e-mail <csgranary@aol.com>

- *Countryside & Small Stock Journal.* tel. 800-551-5691 or 715-785-7979, fax 715-785-7414, W11564 Hwy 64, Withee, WI 54498, Web site <http://www.countrysidemag.com/>, e-mail <csymag@midway.tds.net>

- *Cris Enterprises.* Web site <http://www.grainmills.com/auth_retail.html>, e-mail <sales@cris-enterprises.com>

- *CSIN.* tel. 512-428-9200, fax 512-428-9250, 4202 Santiago Bldg. #3, Austin, TX 78745, Web site <http://www.csin.com/>, e-mail <csin@csin.com>

- *The Cutting Edge.* tel. 800-497-9516 or 516-287-3813, fax 516-287-3112, P.O. Box 5034, Southampton, NY 11969, Web site <http://www.cutcat.com/>, e-mail <cutcat@cutcat.com>

- *Deer Park Emergency Preparedness Center Total Survival.com.* tel. 888-276-2119 or 509-276-1119, fax 509-276-1347, N.23 Weber Rd., Suite # C-4, Deer Park, WA 99006, Web site <http://www.totalsurvival.com/>, e-mail <sales@totalsurvival.com>

- *Desert Mountain Provisions.* tel. 307-279-3595, Cokeville, WY 83114

- *Dragon Herbarium.* tel. 800-TWO-DRAG (896-3724) or 503-244-7049, 4638 SW Beaverton Hillsdale Hwy., Portland, OR 97221, Web site <http://www.seahorse.com/dragon/orderinf.htm>

- *The Dry Store.* tel. 608-231-1524, 3810 Odana Road, Madison, WI 53711, Web site <http://services.polaristel.net/~drystore>, e-mail <marytbell@aol.com>

- *Eagle Enterprises.* tel. 800-478-2331 or 907-562-2331, fax 907-562-6955, 700 W. International Airport Rd., Anchorage, AL 99518, Web site <http://www.alaskamall.com/eagle/>, e-mail <eagleent@alaska.net>

- *Earthen Scents.* tel. 740-767-2885, RR 3 Box 450, Glouster, Ohio 45732, Web site <http://well-being.com/earthen-scents/>, e-mail <DrFrog@frognet.net>

- *Earth's Best Baby Foods.* tel. 800-442-4221, Web site <http://www.earthsbest.com>

- *Earthshirtz.* tel. 800-845-3469, Box 827, Shady Cove, OR 97530, Web site <http://www.earthshirtz.com/>

- *EAS.* tel. 800-297-9776, 555 Corporate Circle, Golden, CO 80401

- *Eco-Tech.* tel. 717-337-9325, fax 717-337-9486. One Hanover St., Gettysburg, PA 17325, Web site <http://www.njefferson.com/>, e-mail <eco-tech@cvn.net>

- *Eden Foods Inc.* tel. 800-248-0320, 701 Tecumseh, Clinton, MI 49236, Web site <http://www.healthyreferral.com/sponsors/eden/>

- *Elixa.* tel. 800-766-4544 or 505-293-4648, fax 505-293-7569, 1805 Kriss NE, Albuquerque, NM 87112-4730, Web site <http://www.elixa.com/nutrient/travel.htm>, e-mail <psafier@elixa.com>

- *Embassy Imports.* tel. toll-free 877-y2kfuel (925-3835)

- *Emergency Essentials.* tel. 800-999-1863 or 801-467-1297, 165 South Mountain Way Drive, Orem, UT 84058. Or, tel. 801-467-1297, 3272 South West Temple, Salt Lake City, UT. Web site <http://www.beprepared.com/home.html>, e-mail <webmaster@beprepared.com>

- *Empire Comfort Systems.* tel. 800-851-3153, 918 Freeburg Avenue, Belleville, IL 62222, Web site <http://www.empirecomfort.com/ventfree.html>, e-mail <info@empirecomfort.com>

- *Epicenter.* tel. 206-937-5658, 6523 California Ave., Suite #161, Seattle, WA 98136, Web site <http://www.theepicenter.com>, e-mail <bjnelson@TheEpicenter.com >

- *Euresia Co.* tel. 0041-091-605-20-74, fax 0041-091-967-33-38, CH-6936 Cademario, Switzerland, Web site <http://www.euresia.com>, e-mail <Info@euresia.com>

- *Family Food Storage*. tel. 801-531-8996 or 801-556-1966, fax 801-484-4886, 255 East 400 South #150, Salt Lake City, UT 84111, Web site <http://downtown-web.com/psi/famfood.htm>, e-mail <psiusa@aros.net>

- *Fitness Industries Inc*. tel. 888-215-9217, fax 517-552-1371, 118 Main Centre, Suite 213, Northville, MI 48167, Web site <http://www.y2k-foods.com/>, e-mail <order@y2k-foods.com>

- *Food Reserves Inc*. P.O. Box 36, Ivujivik, Quebec J0M 1H0, Canada, Web site <http://www.osiem.org/Ospre/foodreserves.htm>

- *Food Storage On-Line*. tel. 877-914-1218 or 801-492-0850, Web site <http://users.itsnet.com/~foodnow/>, e-mail <info@foodstorageonline.com>

- *Food Storage Solutions*. tel. 801-756-2488 or 801-756-8853, cellular tel. 801-358-8590 or 801-225-0845, 160 North 800 East, American Fork, UT 84003, Web site <http://users.itsnet.com/~skelling/>, e-mail <permapak@iname.com>

- *Franklin Sanders*. tel. 901-853-6136

- *Fresh Cleanse*™. tel. 800-767-2208 or 916-491-5088, Lake Forest Plaza, 2222 Francisco Drive, 510-174, El Dorado Hills, CA 95762, Web site <http://www.freshcleanse.com/>, e-mail <info@freshcleanse.com>

- *FSI Culvert Inc*. tel. 403-489-7733, fax 403-489-1821, Web site <http://www.fsiculvert.com/>, e-mail <admin@fsiculvert.com>

- *Future Foods Inc*. tel. 612-504-2930, fax 612-504-2943, 5401 Boone Ave. North, New Hope, MN 55428

- *Genex Power*. tel. 800-782-5509 or 909-782-8188, fax 909-782-8612, 3339 First Street, Riverside, CA 92501

- *GB Food Supply*. District Road #3, Huntsville, Ontario P0A 1K0, Canada

- *Glenn Foods, Inc*. tel. 800-211-9796, 181 South Franklin Ave., Valley Stream, NY 11581

- *Glitchproof.com*. Web site <http://www.glitchproof.com/glitchproof/>

- *Gold Mine Natural Food Co*. tel. 800-475-FOOD (475-3663), fax 619-296-9756, Customer Service 619-296-8536, 3419 Hancock Street, San Diego, CA 92110-4307, Web site <http://www.natural-connection.com/mall/catalogs/gold_mine_natural_foods/>

- *Green Kamut Corporation.* tel. 888-743-4600, Web site <http://www.galaxymall.com/retail/phyto/index.html>

- *Gridfree.com.* tel. 888-440-8025, P.O. Box 454, Gilbert, AZ 85299-0454

- *H & W Distributors, Inc.* tel. 888-301-8307 or 888-611-4879 or 505-267-1274, fax 505-267-4699, P.O. Box 813, 316 E. Hall, Hatch, NM 87937, Web site <http://www.zianet.com/hwd/food.htm>, e-mail <hwd@zianet.com>

- *Hallelujah Acres.* tel. 704-481-1700, P.O. Box 2388, Shelby, NC 28151 <http://www.hacres.com>, e-mail <help@hacres.com>

- *Happy Hovel Storable Foods.* tel. 800-637-7772 or 360-458-4445, fax 360-458-7977, Yelm, WA, Web site <http://www.wwmagic.com/haphov/>, e-mail <haphov@seanet.com>

- *Harmony Seventh Generation.* tel. 800-869-3446, fax 800-456-1139, 360 Interlocken Boulevard, Suite 300, Broomfield, CO 80021

- *Harvest Direct.* tel. 800-835-2867 or 423-523-2304, fax 423-523-3372, P.O. Box 988 Knoxville, TN 37901-0988, Web site <http://www.harvestdirect.com/>, e-mail <maryellen@harvestdirect.com>

- *Harvest Foodworks.* tel. 800-268-4268 or 613-275-1359, fax 613-275-1359, Toledo, Ontario, Canada, Web site <http://www.harvest.on.ca/new.htm>, e-mail <thefolks@harvest.on.ca>

- *Haugh's Products, Ltd.* 10 Atlas Court, Brampton, Ontario L6T 5C1, Canada

- *The Healing Network.* tel. 800-583-7238, fax 305-361-6072, Web site <http://www.anaturalchoice.com/absorb.shtml>, e-mail <info@thehealingnetwork.com>

- *Health Food Heaven.* tel. 409-892-5911, 3515 Fannin, Suite 104, Beaumont, TX 777701

- *Health Valley.* tel. 800-423-4846, 16100 Foothill Blvd., Irwindale, CA 91706

- *Hearthstone.* tel. 800-827-8603, ext. 400, Web site <http://www.hearth.com/hearthstone/hearthstone.html>, e-mail <hearthstone@hearth.com>

- *Heartland America.* tel. 800-229-2901, 8085 Century Blvd., Chaska, MN 55318-3056, Web site <http://www.heartlandamerica.com/dprod325.html>

- *Herbs First.* fax 801-818-4155, 501 West 965 North, Suite 3, Orem, UT 84057, Web site <http://www.herbsfirst.com/pricelist.html>, e-mail <herbs@herbsfirst.com>

- *Hi-Country Snack Foods Inc.* tel. 800-752-2158 or 406-362-4203, fax 406-362-4275, P.O. Box 159, Lincoln, MT 59639, Web site <http://www.hicountry.com>, e-mail <mt@hicountry.com>

- *Home-Health Resource.* tel. 870-598-1000 or 870-598-3384, 2242 CR 341, Piggott, AR 72454, Web site <http://www.homehealthresource.net/catalog.html>, e-mail <hhr@piggott.net>

- *Homestead Products.* tel. 541-688-9263, fax 541-688-9775, Web site <http://elaine.teleport.com/~dany/mill/index.htm>, e-mail <dany@teleport.com>

- *Imperial Diesel.* tel. 888-Y2K-NETT (925-6388) or 615-790-2265, 1900 Lewisburg Pike, Franklin, TN 37064, Web site <http://michaelhyatt.com/Imperial/order.htm>, e-mail <Imp123@aol.com>

- *InfiNet Communications, Inc.* tel. 406-585-9324, fax 406-585-0671, 8551 Cottonwood Road, Bozeman, MT 59718, e-mail <pur@mtmarketplace.com>

- *Insight Discounts.* tel. 877-299-5421, Web site <http://www.insightdiscounts.com/y2k.htm>, e-mail <sales@insightdiscounts.com>

- *IPC Future Foods.* tel. 800-77-FOODS (773-6637) or 801-343-0866, fax 801-343-0867, 709 N. 1890 W. Suite 39A, Provo, UT 94601, Web site <http://www.ipcfuturefoods.com/y2k.htm>, e-mail <T10319@aol.com>

- *Jade Mountain Inc.* tel. 800-442-1972, fax 303-449-8266, 717 Poplar Ave., Boulder, CO 80304, Web site <http://www.jademountain.com/>, e-mail <info@jademountain.com>

- *J&K Enterprises.* 519 Griffith Ave., Terrell, TX 75160, Web site <http://www.charactercounts.com/foods.htm>, e-mail <jseitz@hischaracter.com>

- *Joseph's Storehouse.* tel. 800-664-4808, 1341 North Cedar Blvd., Cedar City, UT 84720, Web site <http://www.josephs-storehouse.com/y2k.htm>, e-mail <brandon@josephs-storehouse.com>

- *The Kamut Association of North America.* tel. 800-644-6450 or 406-622-5439, P.O. Box 691, Fort Benton, MT 59442, Web site <http://www.kamut.com/>, e-mail <7kana@3rivers.net>

- *Karst Sports.* tel. 304-592-2600, fax 304-592-1608, P.O. Box 555, Shinnston, WV 26431-0555, Web site <http://svis.org/MSC/karst.htm>, e-mail <karst.sports@svis.org>

- *Lakeridge Food Storage.* tel. 800-336-7127, fax 801-221-8207, 896 E 640 N, Orem, UT, Web site <http://www.shopsite.com/dehydrate/index.html>, e-mail <http://www.shopsite.com/lfs/>

- *Lehman's Non-Electric.* tel. 330-857-5757, fax 330-857-5785, P.O. Box 41, Kidron, OH 44636, Web site <http://www.lehmans.com>

- *Life Sprouts.* tel. 800-241-1516 or 435-245-3891, P. O. Box 150, Hyrum, UT 84328

- *LiteSource.* tel. 905-427-8381, fax 905-420-8421, 55 Ontoro Blvd., Ajax, Ontario L1S 4S7, Canada

- *The Living and Raw Foods Marketplace.* Web site <http://www.living-foods.com/marketplace/>, e-mail <help@discountjuicers.com>

- *LMG Holding Company.* tel. 406-585-9324, 8551 Cottonwood Road, Bozeman, MT 59718, Web site <http://www.webcom.com/infinet/organic_foods.html>, e-mail <og@mtmarketplace.com>

- *Lumen Foods.* tel. 800-256-2253 or 318-436-6748, fax 318-436-1769, 409 Scott Street, Lake Charles, LA 70601, Web site <http://soybean.com/index2.htm>, e-mail <LumenFoods@aol.com>

- *Magic Mill–Linda's Home Products.* tel. 801-943-8860, 7246 South 1600 East, Salt Lake City, UT 84121

- *Maine Coast Sea Vegetables.* RR1 Box 78, Franklin, ME 04634, Web site <http://www.seaveg.com/Intro.html>, e-mail <info@seaveg.com>

- *Major Surplus.* tel. 800-441-8855 or 310-324-8855, fax 310-324-6909, 435 W. Alondra Blvd., Gardena, CA 90248, Web site <http://www.MajorSurplusNSurvival.com>, e-mail <info@MajorSurplusNSurvival.com>

- *Master Distributors.* tel. 800-446-1446, 1251 Mound Ave. N.W., Grand Rapids, MI 49504

- *Mendocino Sea Vegetables.* tel. 707-937-2050, P.O. Box 1265, Mendocino, CA 95460, Web site <http://www.seaweed.net/>, e-mail <info@seaweed.net>

- *MicrobiaLogic.* tel. 888-535-PACKETS or 602-375-3596, fax 602-375-0699, P.O. Box 47700-395, Phoenix, AZ 85068-7700, Web site <http://www.microbialogic.com/>, e-mail <info@microbialogic.com>

- *Millennium Gourmet Food Reserves.* tel. 800-500-9893, P.O. Box 50597, Provo, UT 84605, e-mail <food@itsnet.com>

- *Millennium III Foods.* tel. 888-883-1603, P.O. Box 10010, Bozeman, MT 59719, Web site <http://www.millennium3foods.com/>, e-mail <corporate@millennium3foods.com>

- *Molehill Mountain Equipment, Inc.* tel. 800-804-0820 or 303-271-1106, fax 303-271-1106, Web site <http://www.molehillmtn.com/>, e-mail <Info@MolehillMtn.com>

- *The Montana Marketplace,* which is "brought to you by" *Infinet Communications, Inc.* tel. 406-585-9324, fax 406-585-0671, 8551 Cottonwood Rd., Bozeman MT 59718, Web site <http://www.webcom.com>, e-mail <webmaster@mtmarketplace.com>

- *Moosejaw Mountaineering.* tel. 888-208-2258, East Lansing, MI, Web site <http://www.moosejawonline.com/catalog/accessories.html>, e-mail <moose@voyager.net>, <wigod@voyager.net>

- *Morning Dew Farms.* tel. and fax 314-561-GROW (561-4769), P.O. Box 3022, Lake St. Louis, MO 63367 Web site <http://ascc.artsci.wustl.edu/~jjharlan/contact.htm> e-mail <jjharlan@artsci.wustl.edu>

- *Mountain Equipment Co-Op.* tel. 800-663-2667 or 604-876-6221, fax 800-722-1960, 130 West Broadway, Vancouver, B.C. V5Y 1P3, Canada

- *Mr. Solar* (Charlie Collins). tel. 435-877-1061, *DO IT HOMESTEAD* Inc., P.O. Box 852, La Verkin, UT 84745, Web site <http://www.mrsolar.com/>, e-mail <CharlieCollins@mrsolar.com>

- *Multipure.* Royal Field, tel. 303-425-5664, or Don Adams, tel. 970-353-7172

- *Naturade Products Inc.* tel. 800-367-2880 or 562-531-8120 or 562-531-3417, fax 562-531-8170 or 562-531-7760, 7110 Jackson Street, Paramount, CA 90723, Web site <http://www.naturade.com/>, e-mail <mzreik@naturade.com>

- *New Millennium Products.* tel. 800-208-9044 or 910-791-3398, fax 910-791-7535, 3609 Bohicket Way, Wilmington, NC 28408, Web site <http://www.newmillenniumproducts.com/>, e-mail <TPB51@aol.com>

- *NH Northern.* tel. 800-533-5545, fax 612-894-0083, P.O. Box 1499, Burnsville, MN 55337-0499, Web site <http://www.northern-online.com>

- *Nitro-Pak Preparedness Center.* tel. 800-866-4876, fax 801-654-3860, Center 151 N. Main St., Heber, UT 84032, Web site <http://www.nitro-pak.com/index.html>

- *Noah's Pantry.* tel. 888-925-6624 or 918-343-9500, fax 918-342-4675, 902 W. First Street, Claremore, OK 74017, Web site <http://www.noahspantry.com/>, e-mail <mail@noahspantry.com>

- *Northern Mountain Supply.* tel. 800-878-3583 or 707-445-1711, fax 707-445-0781, 125 West Fifth Street, Eureka, CA 95501, Web site <http://northernmountain.com/tocs/filters.html>, e-mail <mtn@northernmountain.com>

- *On-Line Health Products.* tel. 800-789-1577 or 208-234-9352, 387 Yellowstone Ave., Pocatello, ID 83201, Web site <http://www.dhi.com/index.htm>, e-mail <zaccardi@juno.com>

- *Organic Gardening.* tel. 610-967-5171, fax 610-967-8963, Rodale Press, Inc., 33 East Minor Street, Emmaus, PA 18098-0099, Web site <https://www.enews.com/network/nnorders/>

- *Outdoor Kids' Source.* tel. 888-672-7657 or 802-253-6784, 449 Beach Hill Rd., Stowe, VT 05672, Web site <http://www.kidssource.com/>, e-mail <oks@mt-mansfield.com>

- *Ozark Water Service.* tel. 800-835-8908 or 501-298-3483, 114 Spring Street, Sulphur Springs, AK 72768

- *Paramount Farms.* tel. 785-754-2151, fax 785-754-3656, Quinter, KS 67752, e-mail <paramnt@ruraltel.net>

- *Peggy's Health Center.* tel. 800-862-9191 or 650-948-9191, fax 650-941-9512, 151 First Street, Los Altos, CA 94022, Web site <http://www.peggyshealth.com>, e-mail <pegshealth@aol.com>

- *Perfect Health.* tel. 800-444-4584 or 805-382-2021, fax 805-984-2780, 5423 Driftwood St., Oxnard, CA 93035, Web site <http://www.juicing.com>, e-mail <perhlt@juicing.com>

- *(Access) Perma Pak Food Storage.* tel. 435-673-6224, 473 East 165 South Ivins, UT 84738, Web site <http://www.acomputing.com/food/order.html>, e-mail <access@infowest.com>

- *Pernith Survival Equipment.* tel. 01931-714444, Cumbria, England CA10 3AZ, e-mail <Survival@cumbria.com>

- *Pilgrim's Products.* tel. 785-966-2900, fax 785-935-2475, e-mail <pilgrimsproducts@iname.com>

- *Planet Natural.* tel. 800-289-6656 (for orders only), 406-587-5891 (for information), fax 406-587-0223, Web site <http://www.planetnatural.com/>, e-mail <ecostore@mcn.net>

- *The Preparedness Centers.* tel. 888-311-8940 or 360-256-9131, fax 360-687-0939, 11013 A NE 39th Street, Vancouver, WA 98662, Web site <http://www.healthyharvest.com>, e-mail <n.russell@worldnet.att.net>

- *Prolab Nutrition.* tel. 800-Prolab-1 (776-5521), 11 Briton Drive, Bloomfield, CT 06002, Web site <http://www.prolabnutrition.com>

- *Puritan's Pride.* tel. 800-645-1030, fax 516-471-5693, 1233 Montauk Highway, P.O. Box 9001, Oakdale, NY 11769-9001, Web site <http://puritan.com>, e-mail <info@puritan.com>

- *Purity Foods.* tel. 517-351-9231, fax 517-351-9391, 2871 W. Jolly Road, Okemos, MI 48864, Web site <http://www.purityfoods.com/>, e-mail <purityfoods@vixa.voyager.net>

- *Ready Reserve.* Web site <http://www.readyreservefoods.com>, e-mail <sales@readyreservefoods.com>

- *Real Goods.* tel. 800-919-2400 or 707-468-9292, ext. 2210, fax 707-462-4807, Web site <http://www.realgoods.com>, e-mail <techs@realgoods.com>

- *REI (Recreational Equipment Incorporation).* tel. 800-426-4840 or 253-891-2500, Sumner, WA 98352, Web site <http://www.rei.com/>

- *Rescue Northwest.* tel. 800-580-0363, 201 Scott Dr., Cle Elum, WA 98922-9458, Web site <http://www.rescuenorthwest.com/>

- *Rich's.* tel. 800-354-3633, fax 425-742-2310, 16504 Highway 99, Lynnwood, WA or 17750 West Valley Highway, Southcenter, WA

- *Rident Enterprises.* tel. 604-467-3340, 22015 126th Ave., Maple Ridge, British Columbia, Canada

- *Rivard International Corporation.* tel. 513-984-8821, 10979 Reed Hartman Highway, Suite 200, Cincinnati, OH 45242, Web site <http://www.rivard-usa.com/>, e-mail <help@rivard-usa.com>

- *RMS Electric, Inc.* tel. 800-767-5909 or 303-444-5909, fax 303-444-1615, 2560 28th Street, Boulder, CO 80301, Web site <http://www.rmse.com/>

- *Rocky Mountain Food Storage Products.* tel. 303-368-7900, fax 303-368-9806, 2045 S. Valentia #17, Denver, CO 80231

- *Rocky Mountain Institute.* tel. 970-927-3851, fax 970-927-3420, 1739 Snowmass Creek Road, Snowmass, CO 81654-9199, Web site <http://rmi.org/about.html>, e-mail <emalia@rmi.org>

- *Roland's Sea Vegetables.* tel. 506-662-3468, fax 506-662-3468, P.O. Box 26, Castalia, Grand Manan Island, New Brunswick EOG 1L0, Canada

- *Safe-Trek Outfitters—Essentials, Inc.* tel. 800-424-7870 or 406-587-5571, fax 406-586-4842, 90 Safetrek Pl., Bozeman, MT 59718, Web site <http://www.safetrek.com>, e-mail <sales@safetrek.com>

- *Sam Andy®.* tel. 800-331-0358, fax 214-717-1332, P.O. Box 14171, Irving, TX 75014, Web site <http://www.karinya.com/sandy.htm>

- *Sayfer Botanicals.* tel. 519-472-0011, fax 519-686-0804, 530 Oxford Street, West London, Ontario N6H 1T6, Canada, Web site <http://www.herbmeds.com/>, e-mail <wizard@herbmeds.com>

- *Seeds Blum.* tel. 800-528-3658, fax 208-338-5658, HC 33, Box 2057, Boise, ID 83706, Web site <http://www.seedsblum.com/>, e-mail <webmaster@seedsblum.com>

- *Seeds of Change.* tel. 888-762-4240 or 800-95-SEEDS (957-3337) or 888-762-7333, P.O. Box 1570, Santa Fe, NM 87506, Web site <http://seedsofchange.com/catalog/index_cat.html>, e-mail <gardener@seedsofchange.com>

- *Seeds of Diversity Canada.* tel. 905-623-0353, Box 36 Stn Q, Toronto, Ontario M4T 2L7, Canada, Web site <http://www.interlog.com/~sodc/home.html>, e-mail <sodc@interlog.com>

- *Seedtime and Harvest.* tel. 712-439-2809, fax 712-439-1861, Box 511, Hull, IA, e-mail <maverick@rconnect.com>

- *Sierra Solar Systems.* tel. (technical information) 530-265-8441, (orders) 800-51-SOLAR (517-6527), fax 530-265-6151, 109 Argall Way, Nevada City, CA 95959, Web site <http://www.sierrasolar.com/index>, e-mail <solarjon@sierrasolar.com>

- *Soiltech.* tel. 800-296-6026, fax 740-498-5929, 607 E. Canal St., Newcomerstown, OH 43832-1207

- *South Summit.* tel. 800-364-3270, fax 972-495-9579, P.O. Box 851293, Richardson, TX 75085, Web site <http://www.southsummit.com/>

- *Special Foods Home Page.* tel. 703-644-0991, 9207 Shotgun Court, Springfield, VA 22153, Web site <http://www.specialfoods.com>, e-mail <kslimak@ix.netcom.com>

- *Spectrum Naturals.* 133 Copeland St. Petaluma, CA 94952, e-mail <spectrumnaturals@netdex.com>

- *The Sportsman's Guide.* tel. 800-888-3006, fax 800-333-6933, 411 Farwell Ave. So., St. Paul, MN 55075-0239, Web site <http://www.sportsmansguide.com/>

- *The Sprout House.* tel. 800-S-P-R-O-U-T-S (777-6887) or 760-788-4800, fax 760-788-7979, 17267 Sundance Drive, Ramona, CA 92065, Web site <http://www.sprouthouse.com/>, e-mail <info@SproutHouse.com>

- *Sprout Master.* tel. 705-322-2222, fax 705-322-8386, R.R. #3, Box 43, Site 'W' Elmvale, Ontario LOL 1P0, Canada, Web site <http://www.mid.igs.net/~sproutm/sproutm/index.htm>, e-mail <sproutm@mid.igs.net>

- *Store-Well Foods.* tel. 509-522-4799, fax 509-522-4810, P.O. Box 665, College Place, WA 99324, e-mail <s-wfoods@valint.net>

- *Sun-Mar.* tel. 800-461-2461 or 905-332-1314, Web site <http://www.sun-mar.com/>, e-mail <compost@sun-mar.com>

- *SunOrganic Farm.* tel. 888-269-9888, fax 760-751-1141, P.O. Box 2429, Valley Center, CA 92082, Web site <http://www.sunorganic.com>, e-mail <sales@sunorganic.com>

- *Sun Ovens International.* tel. 800-408-7019, fax 630-208-7386, 39 W835 Midan Drive, Elburn, IL 60119, e-mail <sunovens@execpc.com>

- *Supplies4Y2K.com.* tel. 406-375-9282, fax 888-624-5706, 610 N. 1st Street, Suite #5-150, Hamilton, MT, Web site <http://www.supplies4y2k.com/catalog2.htm>, e-mail <sales@supplies4y2k.com>

- *The Survival Center.* tel. 800-321-2900 or 360-458-6778, fax 360-458-6868, P.O. Box 234, McKenna, WA 98558, Web site <http://www.zyz.com/survivalcenter/>, e-mail <sales@survivalcenter.com>

- *Survival Enhanced.* tel. 719-495-8533, fax 719-495-8533, 7935 Forest Heights, Colorado Springs, CO 80908, Web site <http://www.survivalenhanced.com/welcome.html>, e-mail <katadyn@kktv.com>

- *Swiss America.* tel. 800-289-2646 ext. 1018, or tel. 602-443-3050, 14455 N. Hayden Rd. #226, Scottsdale, AZ 85260, Web site <http://www.buycoin.com>, e-mail <coindude@buycoin.com>

- *Thetford Portable Toilets.* tel. 800-521-3032, Web site <http://www.thetford.com/index.pl>, e-mail <info@thetford.com>

- *Thompson Culvert Company.* tel. 800-325-2150, Web site <http://www.thompsonculvert.com/menu.html>, e-mail <tcc-sales@thompsonculvert.com>

- *Tilley Endurables.* tel. 800-363-8737, 300 Langer Road West, Seneca, NY 14224, Web site <http://www.tilley.com/index2.html>

- *Travel Smith's Outfitting Guide and Catalog.* tel. 800-950-1600 or 415-884-1350, fax 800-950-1656, P.O. Box 5729, Novato, CA 94948-5729, Web site <http://st7.yahoo.com/cc8006/>, e-mail <YahooOrders@catalogcity.com>

- *Travis Industries, Inc.* tel. 425-827-9505, 10850 117th Place NE, Kirkland, WA 98033, Web site <http://hearth.com/travis/travis.html>, e-mail <traviscs@earthlink.net>

- *Twisted Oak Alternative Energy.* tel. 877-252-8754 or 870-453-7248, HCR 64, Box 534G, Flippin, AR 72634-0381, Web site <http://www.twistedoak.com/>, e-mail <jwporter@twistedoak.com>

- *USA Marketing Associates Inc.* tel. 877-580-7844 or 407-773-8778, fax 407-777-7507, P.O. Box 33536, Indialantic, FL 32903, Web site <http://www.y2ksupplies.com/>, e-mail <sales@y2ksupplies.com> or <info@y2ksupplies.com>

- *Veggies Unite.* P.O. Box 5312, Fort Wayne, IN 46895-5312, Web site <http://www.vegweb.com/food/>, e-mail <veggie@vegweb.com>
- *Vitamin City.* P.O. Box 699 Silver Lake, WI 53170-0699, Web site <http://www.vitamincity.com/catalog.htm>, e-mail <staff@vitamincity.com>
- *Volcano.* tel. 801-566-5496, fax 801-566-1993, 3450 West South, West Jordan, UT 84088.
- *F. J. Vollmer & Co.* tel. 888-309-8189, #3 Towanda Access Road, Bloomington, IL 61701
- *Walton Feed, Inc.* Montpelier, ID, tel. 800-847-0465 or 208-847-0465, Web site <http://waltonfeed.com>, e-mail <mark@waltonfeed.com>
- *Watertanks.com.* tel. 888-742-6275 or 760-727-3266, fax 760-727-8233, 770 Sycamore Avenue, Suite J, Vista, CA 92083, Web site <http://www.watertanks.com>, e-mail (information) <info@watertanks.com>, sales <sales@watertanks.com>
- *Wayne J Carroll & Associates.* tel. 800-505 2246, Big Fork Harbor, MT, Web site <http://www.y2kdehydratedfoods.com/>, e-mail <y2kfoods@2000biz.com>
- *Western Botanicals.* tel. 800-651-HERB (651-4372) or 916-989-4700, 7122 Almond Avenue, Orangevale, CA 95662, Web site <http://www.westernbotanical.com/>
- *Wisdom of the Ancients.* tel. 800-899-9908, Web site <http://www.wisdomherbs.com/>, e-mail <info@wisdomherbs.com>
- *Wolfsong Herbs.* tel. 804-963-6635, Rt. 1 Box 357, Wingina, VA 24599, e-mail <wolfsongherbs@mindspring.com>
- *Worldwide Sport Nutritional Supplements.* tel. 800-854-5019, fax 727-541-3182, 10540 72nd Street, Largo FL 33777
- *The Wornick Company.* tel. 210-687-9401, 200 North First Street, McAllen, TX 78501
- *Xtreme Needs.* tel. 208-377-2520, fax 208-375-4256, P.O. Box 4023, Boise, ID 83711, Web site <http://www.xtreme-needs.com/survival/>, e-mail <xtreme@rmci.net>
- *Y2K Food Store.* tel. 888-Y2K-0333 (925-0333), 321 Independence Square, Franklin, TN 37064, Web site <http://www.Y2KFoodStore.com/>, e-mail <nathan@y2k2000.org>

- *Y2KFoods.* tel. 888-889-6373 or 800-519-6502, Web site <http://y2kfood.com/s39p145.htm>, e-mail <Will@y2kfood.com>

- *Y2K Grub.* tel. 800-742-7219, P.O. Box 270942, Fort Collins, CO 80527, Web site <http://www.y2kgrub.com/>

- *Y2K Prep.* tel. 888-925-2844, 251 Second Avenue South, Franklin, TN 37064, Web site <http://www.y2kprep.com/>, e-mail <feedback@michaelhyatt.com>

- *Y2K Survival Supply Co.* tel. 888-Y2K-Y2K8 (925-9258), Web site <http://www.y2ksupplyco.com/Ultimate-Pak-II.html>

- *Yellowstone River Trading Company.* tel. 800-585-5077, 2010 West Koch Street, Bozeman, MT 59718, Web site <http://www.yellowstonetrading.com/>, e-mail <info@yellowstonetrading.com>

APPENDIX E
Books Related to Y2K Preparedness

• •|• • • • • • • • • •

The following books are cited in this manual. By no means is this list meant to be comprehensive.

Most of the following titles are available from *Amazon.com* at least until midnight December 31, 1999. In addition to the books, there is a magazine dedicated exclusively to the Y2K situation; published every two weeks by Tim Wilson's company *The Trades,* it is called *Y2K News Magazine.* Ask your local news dealer for information.

Y2K-Related Books
- Fletcher, W. Michael. *Computer Crisis 2000.* A good book "to help small and medium-sized businesses prepare for the worst."

- Hyatt, Michael S. *The Millennium Bug: How to Survive the Coming Chaos.* Full of good insights on the way the Y2K challenge will disrupt business as usual.

- Keyes, Tony. *The Year 2000 Computer Crisis: An Investor's Survival Guide.* For those wanting some guidance on investments during what could be a major global financial "correction."

- Laddon, Judy, Ed. *Awakening: The Upside of Y2K.* This book emphasizes the positive emotional and spiritual aspects of Y2K. A good book to help offset doom and gloom scenarios and maintain a larger perspective on Y2K.

- McKeever, James. *Self-Reliant Living.* Omega Publications and Videos, tel. 541-773-5123, P.O. Box 4130, Medford, OR 97501. A detailed book offering lots of practical tips on emergency preparedness and homesteading, including gardening, energy independence, self-protection, etc.

- Morris, J. R. *Year 2000: Personal Protection Guide—How to Protect your Assets, Identity and Credit from the upcoming "Millenium Bug" computer crisis.* Written to help you keep a paper trail of your important assets, bank accounts, annuities, etc., so that they will not get lost in cyberspace if and when the computers fail.

- Wright, Ted. *Wright's Complete Disaster Survival Manual.* Available from Epicenter, tel. 206-937-5658. Billed as the "most complete emergency preparedness-related book known to man," this manual covers all the basics and then some.

- Yourdon, Edward, and Jennifer Yourdon. *Time Bomb 2000: What the Year 2000 Computer Crisis Means.* Details various scenarios of how Y2K could affect/devastate the consumer.

Health And Well-Being Related Books

- Andreola, Karen. *Charlotte Mason Companion: Personal Reflections on the Gentle Art of Learning.* Charlotte Mason Research & Supply Company, 1998. An inspiring work on the true art of learning.

- Batmanghelidg, F. *Your Body's Many Cries for Water.* Global Health Solutions, 1997. tel. 800-759-3999 or 703-848-2333. A contemporary medical masterpiece, with a cure so simple, yet profoundly effective. A must read!

- Bell, Mary. *Mary Bell's Complete Dehydrator Cookbook.* This book can help you save a lot of money and help you design a nutritious shelf-stable food package.

- Boily, Lise. *Bread Ovens of Quebec.* University of Washington Press, 1979. This book chronicles an old tradition that might need to be revived if Y2K proves as bad as pessimists predict.

- Bradley, Robert. *The Bradley Method of Natural Childbirth.* Bantam, 1996. One of the best approaches to natural childbirth.

- Bridwell, Raymond. *Hydroponic Gardening: The "Magic" of Modern Hydroponics for the Home Gardener.* This hydroponic "bestseller" shows you how to automate hydroponic growing so that you do not have to spend much time tending your year-round crop.

- Brill, "Wildman" Steve. *Identifying and Harvesting Edible and Medicinal Plants in Wild (And Not So Wild) Places.* Hearst Books, 1994. This guy knows his stuff and can help you find food almost anywhere.

- Carter, Jill. *The Elimination Diet Cookbook: A 28-Day Plan for Detecting Allergies.* Element, 1997. A book more people should read.

- Castle, Coralie and Robert Kourik. *Cooking from the Gourmet's Garden: Edible Ornamentals, Herbs, and Flowers.* Cole, 1988. How to make common herbs and flowers a delicious delight.

- Cooper, Jane, and Sherry Streeter. *Woodstove Cookery: At Home on the Range.* Storey Books, 1983. A must for those who plan on lots of wood-stove cooking.

- Craighead George, Jean. *Acorn Pancakes, Dandelion Salad and Other Wild Dishes.* Harpercollins, 1995.

- Denckla, Tanya. *The Organic Gardener's Home Reference: A Plant-By-Plant Guide to Growing Fresh, Healthy Food.* Storey Books, 1994. Simple, effective ways to maximize the nutritional power of home-grown vegetables and fruit.

- Dickson, Murray. *Where There Is No Dentist.* Hesperian Foundation, 1983. One book no community should be without during Y2K.

- Dumke, Nicolette M. *Allergy Cooking With Ease: The No Wheat, Milk, Eggs, Corn, Soy, Yeast, Sugar, Grain, and Gluten Cookbook.* Starburst Element, 1992. Important recipes for an often-overlooked health problem.

- Ellis, Sandra K. Livingston. *Dr. Mom.* A great home-remedy and herbal-based first-aid book.

- Erasmus, Udo. *Fats That Heal, Fats That Kill: The Complete Guide to Fats, Oils, Cholesterol and Human Health.* Alive Books, 1993. The classic on EFAs and other beneficial fats.

- Evangelista, Anita. *How to Develop a Low-Cost Family Food-Storage System.* Loompanics Unlimited, 1995. A good primer to a lost art.

- ———. *How to Live Without Electricity—And Like It.* Loompanics Unlimited, 1997.

- Geil, Patti Bazel. *Magic Beans: 150 Delicious Recipes Featuring Nature's Low-Fat, Nutrient-Rich, Disease-Fighting Powerhouse.* This book offers numerous suggestions on how to turn your storehouse of beans into taste-titillating delights.

- Gipes, Paul. *Wind Power for Home & Business: Renewable Energy for the 1990s and Beyond.* Chelsea Green, 1993. Gipe's comprehensive book focuses on the new turbine units that allow for total energy autonomy.

- Halacy, Beth, and Dan Halacy. *Cooking with the Sun.* Morning Sun Press, 1992. A book full of practical "how to" solar cooking ideas, plans, recipes, etc.

- Hoffmann, David. *The Complete Illustrated Holistic Herbal: A Safe and Practical Guide to Making and Using Herbal Remedies.* Element, 1996. Hoffmann is a master herbalist who offers lots of practical health advice.

- King, Kurt. *Herbs to the Rescue: An Herbal First-Aid Handbook.*

- Kofalk, Harriet, and Warren Jefferson. *Solar Cooking: A Primer/Cookbook.* Book Publishers, 1997. A must for people who want to bake with the sun.

- Laddon, Judy, Tom Atlee, and Larry Shook. *Awakening; The Upside of Y2K.* Printed Word, 1999. This book focuses on the positive lifestyle changes and relationships that Y2K can generate, especially how faith and spirituality can overcome any infrastructure disruptions we might face.

- Lewallen, Eleanor and John. *Sea Vegetable Gourmet Cook Book and WildCrafter's Guide.* Mendocino Sea Vegetable Company, 1996.

- Malkmus, George, and Michael Dye. *God's Way to Ultimate Health: A Common Sense Guide for Elimination of Sickness Through Nutrition.* Hallelujah Acres, 1996. tel. 704-481-1700. A radical approach to eating that has revolutionized the health of thousands of people.

- Malkmus, Rhonda. *Recipes For Life From God's Garden.* Hallelujah Acres, 1998. tel. 704-481-1700. Chock full of raw-food and minimal-cooking recipes that can save your life.

- McNair, James K. *James McNair's Beans & Grains.* Thought beans and grains would be boring? Read this and think again.

- McNicol, Jane. *Your Child's Food Allergies: Detecting and Treating Hyperactivity, Congestion, Irritability and Other Symptoms Caused by Common Food Allergies.* John Wiley & Sons, 1992. Keys in on the hidden causes of some common ailments.

- Meyerowitz, Steve. *Kitchen Garden.* Sprout House, 1997.

- ———. *Sprouts, The Miracle Food.* These two books offer lots of good sprouting information by a master sprouter.

- Moore, Raymond S. and Dorothy N. *The Successful Homeschool Family Handbook: A Creative and Stress-Free Approach to Homeschooling.* Thomas Nelson, 1994. Abundant wisdom and advice from a couple dedicated to effective home-based education.

- Potts, Michael. *Independent Home: Living Well With Power from the Sun, Wind, and Water.* Chelsea Green, 1993. Books such as this one are a must-read for those who want to be energy self-sufficient during Y2K.

- Resh, Howard M. *Hydroponic Food Production: A Definitive Guidebook of Soilless Food-Growing Methods.* Resh offers a plethora of techniques for both the commercial and serious home hydroponic grower.

- Roulac, John. *Backyard Composting: Your Complete Guide to Recycling Yard Clippings.* John Roulac Harmonious Technologies, 1995. This is a great book for those interested in trying composting as a way to recycle yard clippings, paper products, and table garbage as a way of having a good supply of people-friendly plant fertilizer.

- Saltzman, Joanne. *Amazing Grains: Creating Vegetarian Main Dishes With Whole Grains.* H. J. Kramer, 1990. This book offers over 100 recipes on how to turn hearty grains such as buckwheat, millet, oats, quinoa, and teff into gourmet delights.

- Saunders, Charles Francis. *Edible and Useful Wild Plants of the United States and Canada.* Dover, 1976. A guide such as this one might mean the difference between life and death for some people during Y2K.

- Sherman, Ed. *How to Build a Bigger and Better Hydroponic Garden for Under 20 Dollars.* Simple techniques for producing hydroponically grown, nutritious foods.

- Talmage, Steven James. *Making the Best of Basics: Family Preparedness Handbook.* Gold Leaf, 1977. This and the companion book below offer loads of practical advice and an abundance of vendors to help procure the items you need.

- ———. *Don't Get Caught With Your Pantry Down!: When the Unexpected Happens!* Historical, 1998.

- Thomas, Noreen Jo. *Dehydrator Delights.* An informative guide to getting the best from your dehydrator.

- *UTNE Reader Y2K Citizen's Action Guide.* Minneapolis, Lens Publishing, 1998. A vital guidebook offering lots of practical advice to help communities and neighborhoods prepare for potential Y2K problems. tel. 612-338-5040.

- Werner, David, Carol Thuman, and Jane Maxwell. *Where There Is No Doctor: A Village Health Care Handbook.* Hesperian Foundation, 1992.

- White, Joanna. *The Dehydrator Cookbook.* Bristol, 1998. An important book for those who want to maximize their use of a dehydrator and create tasty and nutritious dried-food cuisine.

Web Sites Related to Y2K Understanding and Preparedness

• • • • • • • • • • • •

"To be self-sufficing is the greatest of all wealth." —Porphyry

I have found the following Web sites and their links to be helpful in writing this book. For the most part I have used *AltaVista,* <http://www.altavista.com/>, and *Metacrawler,* <http://www.go2net.com/search.html>, as my primary search engines.

- *American Water Works Association* <http://www.awwa.org/> offers information on lots of water products, vendors, and health information for professionals in the water industry.

- *Senator Bob Bennett's* Web site, <http://www.senate.gov/%7Ebennett/y2k.html>, contains a wealth of Y2K information, including key speeches dedicated to Year 2000 issues.

- The *Cassandra Project* is a "grassroots nonprofit organization offering valuable information on a wide variety of topics dedicated to the looming Y2K challenge." This is a good source of information for community action groups. It can be located at <http://millennia-bcs.com/nfcass.htm#top>.

- The CNET Web site, <http://www.y2khour.com/html/news.htm>, offers daily updates on Y2K stories from major newspapers and news networks. This is a great source for keeping up on latest developments.

- Cornell/Oxford University "China Project" study—The China–Cornell–Oxford Project, Division of Nutritional Sciences, Cornell University, Savage Hall, Ithaca, NY 14853-6301, Web site <http://www.human.cornell.edu/dns/chinaproject/chinaproject.html>, e-mail <lc26@cornell.edu>. This is a good site for explaining the health advantages of a plant-based diet—something many of us might be forced to adopt during Y2K.

- *Citizens for Y2K Recovery,* <http://www.cy2kr.com/AdvisoryCouncil.html>, 370 Southwest Cutoff RT 20, Northborough, MA 01532, tel. 508-842-1739, fax 508-393-0026, e-mail <Info@CY2KR.com>, provides information from some of the leading Y2K authorities and experts.

- *Comlinks.com,* <http://www.comlinks.com/mag/faq.htm>, hosted by Alan Simpson, offers a good basic introduction to the Y2K problem. This Web page is a good site to recommend to those who know little about Y2K. Simpson's "Global Food Chain" article, <http://www.comlinks.com/briefings/fchain.htm>, is a sobering wake-up call for those who are skeptical about Y2K or overly optimistic that everything will turn out all right.

- *eBay,* <http://cgi.ebay.com>, the largest Internet auction house, offers a way to pick up Y2K preparedness items and to sell things to get money to prepare for Y2K.

- The *Electric Utilities and the Year 2000* Web site bookstore page, <http://www.euy2k.com/bookstor.htm>, offers an extensive list of Y2K-related books.

- The *Equipped to Survive* Web site, <http://www.equipped.org/>, offers a host of highly informative and educational vendor sites, product sites, and information pages on emergency preparedness and survival.

- The *Food Additive* Web site, <http://www.allergy.pair.com/additives/foodad.htm>, offers valuable information on the potentially harmful side effects caused by food additives.

- The *Food for Self-Reliance* Web site, <http://www.geocities.com/ResearchTriangle/Lab/7731/food.html>, contains a wealth of vital information for those interested taking control of their Y2K destiny. This site also lists a number of wholesale and retail companies dedicated to Y2K emergency preparedness.

- *Glitchproof.com,* <http://www.glitchproof.com/glitchproof/storlifofgro.html>, has a helpful Web page entitled "Food Shelf Life Recommendations" that includes a helpful chart listing the packaging date codes and shelf life of many popular foods.

- Alan T. Hagan's "Prudent Food Storage FAQ" on Web page <http://www.efn.org/~kathyy/foodfaq.300> offers a wealth of information for those interested in long-term storage, as well as a host of companies and vendors dedicated to Y2K-related products.

- The *HearthNet* Web site, <http://www.hearth.com/what/specific.html>, contains lots of valuable information on numerous home heating units and systems.

- *Michael Hyatt's Y2K Prep* Web site, <http://www.y2kprep.com/>, offers a wide range of Y2K-related preparedness information—everything from "Y2K Prep tips" to the latest Y2K news updates. A definite site to explore, especially the "Y2K Prep tips Archive."

- *The Internet Business Directory,* <http://www.okdirect.com/Biz/5/5499A.html>, is a good source for finding your local vendors of herbs, vitamins, supplements, and numerous other products.

- The *JBA Year 2000 Tour* Web site offers a concise explanation of the scope of the Y2K problem. It can be found at <http://www.jbaintl.com/tours/y2k_tour/>.

- *The Joseph Project,* tel. 806-234-2167, Web site, <http://www. josephproject2000.org/default.html>, e-mail <info@josephproject2000.org>, is a "Christian-led" non-profit organization designed to help local churches help their neighbors and community.

- *LaLeche League International,* U.S. tel. 800-LALECHE, Canada tel. 800-665-4324, or 847-519-7730, fax 847-519-0035, 1400 N. Meacham Rd., Schaumburg, IL 60173-4048, Web site <http://www.lalecheleague.org>: This valuable organization can answer questions you may have about breast feeding. Contact them for representatives in your area. See their Web page for how to send them an e-mail, <http://www.lalecheleague.org/contactinfo.html>.

- The *Life Canada* well drilling Web site, <http://www.lifewater.ca/ndexman.htm>, offers a wealth of information on low-cost drills and methods of well making and well water purification.

- The *Masonry Heater Virtual Mall,* <http://mha-net.org/html/mall.htm>, sponsored by the *Masonry Heater Association of North America,* lists a number of companies offering energy-efficient masonry heating units and systems.

- *Millennium Salons,* Web site <http://www.angelfire.com/mn/inforest/grassroots.html>, has a number of excellent articles on the scope of the Y2K problem, and offers practical tools for individuals and communities to cope with the problem.

- The *Naturalusa* home design page, <http://www.naturalusa.com/Homedesign2.html>, and its natural living resource guide, <http://www.naturalusa.com/>, list numerous products by earth- and health-sensitive vendors.

- *Gary North's Y2K Links and Forums,*
  <http://www.garynorth.com/y2k/index.cfm>, offers a detailed array of
  articles and information on the Y2K situation. North was one of the
  early prophets calling people's attention to the massive personal and
  infrastructure implications of the Y2K challenge. Many consider him
  an alarmist, but his is definitely a voice worth listening to.

- The U.S. Government's *Office of Information Technology* has a Web
  site, <http://www.itpolicy.gsa.gov/mks/yr2000/y2khome.htm>, offering
  a variety of facts related to the Federal Government's Y2K preparedness and perspective, including information on the *President's Council
  on Year 2000 Conversion* and 70 position papers written by international Y2K experts.

- *Scott Olmsted's Preparing for the Year 2000/1999 Crash* Web site,
  <http://prepare4y2k.com/>, offers a number of interesting Y2K-related
  links that cut across a wide spectrum of political and ideological views.

- *The Online Homesteading and Small Farming Resource,*
  <http://www.homestead.org/>, is a valuable Web site providing
  practical information on self-reliant living.

- *The Preparedness Insights Archive,*
  <http://www.beprepared.com/Insight/informa.htm>, offers a wealth of
  information for emergency preparedness in general and Y2K in particular. This is a site definitely worth visiting.

- The *President's Council on Year 2000 Conversion* Web site,
  <http://y2k.gov/text/index.htm>, offers the government's take on the
  situation. Unfortunately, as of winter 1998 the focus has been on business, with very little emphasis on Y2K's effects on the average citizen.

- *Rocky Mountain Institute,* a non-profit organization dedicated to the
  "efficient and sustainable use of natural resources," offers lots of
  practical advice and items helpful for Y2K preparation. It can be
  reached at tel. 970-927-3851, fax 970-927-3420, 1739 Snowmass
  Creek Road, Snowmass, CO 81654-9199, Web site
  <http://www.rmi.org/> or <http://rmi.org/about.html>,
  e-mail <emalia@rmi.org>.

- *Larry Sanger's* Web page, <http://www.cruxnet.com/~sanger/y2k/>,
  offers insight into news reports about Y2K-related problems.

- *Alan Scott,* tel. 415-663-9010, of *Ovencrafters,* 5600 Marshall-
  Petaluma Road, Petaluma, CA 94952, Web site
  <http://www.nbn.com/~ovncraft/>, e-mail <ovencrft@nbn.com>, is a

master oven crafter who consults and offers detailed building specs and plans for communities, businesses, and organizations interested in large-scale stone and brick baking ovens.

- *Sharefin's Gold Nuggets,* Web site <http://www.cairns.net.au/~sharefin/ Markets/Alternative.htm >, is a valuable "Web ring" that offers a "monster collation of links to Alternative Information Survival sites where you can find out anything that is of interest in protecting yourself and your family from the potential ravages of the Year 2000 bug."

- *Solar Cooking Archive,* Web page <http://www.accessone.com/~sbcn/ Default.htm>, is an organization dedicated to helping developing nations use solar cooking as a viable alternative for the poor and needy—something "industrialized" and "developed" nations might also consider.

- *Solar Freedom International,* tel. 306-652-1442, P.O. Box 7103, Saskatoon, Saskatchewan S7K 4S1, Canada, is an organization dedicated to furthering the art and understanding of solar cooking.

- *The SurvivalRing,* Web site <http://members.aol.com/rafleet/ survivalring.htm>, contains information about hundreds of Web sites and companies dedicated to helping families and communities find products and information related to Y2K survival.

- The *Utah State University Extension Program* offers an informative Web site, <http://ext.usu.edu/publica/foodpubs.htm>, e-mail <donnaf@ext.usu.edu>, dedicated to food storage issues and nutrition and cooking information.

- The *Veggies Unite* Web page, <http://www.vegweb.com/food/>, e-mail <veggie@vegweb.com>, P.O. Box 5312, Fort Wayne, IN 46895-5312, offers an extensive array of over 2,700 vegan recipes for beans, *TVP*®, pasta, pizza, desserts, snacks, etc. A worthwhile Web site to visit in preparation for Y2K.

- *Village Bakery on the Web*, Web site <http://countrylife.net/bread/>, is dedicated to the art of making nutritious and tasty homemade breads.

- *The Washington D.C. Year 2000 Group* Web site, <http://www. monumental.com/bwebster/y2k/survey/>, offers a sobering assessment of the global, regional, and local infrastructure implications of Y2K. On a scale of "0" (no impact) to "10" (complete collapse), the government and business leaders who were surveyed averaged between 5 and 7 in their predictions.

- *The Water Quality Association*'s Web page, <http://www.wqa.org/>, offers loads of information related to water quality and related health and environmental concerns.

- The *Westergaard Year 2000* Search Engine, <http://www.y2ktimebomb. com/Excite/AT-TimebombCollectionquery.html>, offers a storehouse of Y2K-related information.

- Though it advocates what some would take to be controversial politics, the *Y2K Self-Reliance Libertarian* Web ring, <http://www.geocities.com/ResearchTriangle/Lab/7731/new.html>, has links to lots of sites with practical Y2K information.

- The *Y2KChaos* Web site, <http://y2kchaos.com/>, is not as pessimistic as it sounds; it offers a wide array of information on Y2K.

- *The Y2K Living Journal,* <http://www.jvprofit.com/y2k/signup.htm>, is another good resource on the Web. Their journal issues contain lots of practical and comfort-oriented advice on how to prepare and deal with the Y2K challenge.

- *Y2Knews,* <http://www.y2knews.com/>, tracks up-to-the-minute developments in the news concerning Year 2000 issues.

- *Dr. Ed Yardeni's Economic's Network Y2K Center* Web site, <http://www.yardeni.com/cyber.html>, offers lots of keen insight into the business and economic implications of Y2K. Yardeni is one of the leading authorities on the global and economic impact of Y2K.

- The *Year 2000 National Educational Taskforce,* Web site <http://www.y2knet.com/>, offers lots of information to keep the public up to date about Y2K and the potential problems it might cause.

- *Ed Yourdon's Web site,* <http://www.yourdon.com/index.htm>, offers key insights into the Y2K challenge from one of the leading computer gurus who designed and operated many of the older systems that are now at the center of the Y2K problem. His *Yourdon Report* Web site, <http://www.cutter.com/ads/tyr0697.htm>, offers lots of technical data for IT professionals and those who want technically in-depth Y2K analyses, solutions, and recommendations.

If you are interested in having Ned Vankevich speak to your company, organization, church or synagogue, please contact:

Y2K MADE SIMPLE
Phone: (617) 770-4588

NOTES

NOTES

NOTES

NOTES

NOTES